The influence of Greek ideas and usages upon the Christian Church

By
Edwin Hatch

This work is in the public domain.

ISBN: 9798374840247

THE HIBBERT LECTURES, 1888
READER IN ECCLESIASTICAL HISTORY IN THE
UNIVERSITY OF OXFORD.
EDITED BY A. M. FAIEBAIRN, D.D.
PRINCIPAL OF MANSFIELD COLLEGE, OXFORD.
SIXTH EDITION.
Originally printed:
WILLIAMS AND NORGATE,
14, HENRIETTA STREET, COVENT GARDEN,
LONDON;
20, SOUTH FREDERICK STREET, EDINBURGH;
AND 7, BROAD STREET, OXFORD. 1897.

TABLE OF CONTENTS

2023 Update Notes

This work has been updated to fit modern formats, wording, and style. Liberties have been taken with archaic and English forms of words. Greek words have been transliterated into English and foreign language words have been italicized. Footnotes have been truncated and parts removed due to extensive use of Greek lettering which substantially increases the difficulty of editing. Punctuation, capitalization, and italicized emphasis have been left as true to the original as possible. The goal of this update is to build an accessible work that will endure.

-Christopher Fisher

Original Notes

The Hibbert Trustees cannot add this volume to their series without a few lines of grateful acknowledgment. It is impossible to forget either the courteous readiness with which the accomplished author undertook the task originally, or the admirable qualities he brought to it. "When he died without completing the MS. for the press, the anxiety of the Trustees was at once relieved by the kind effort of his family to obtain adequate assistance. The public will learn from the Preface how much had to be done, and will join the Trustees in grateful appreciation of the services of the gentlemen who responded to the occasion. That Dr. Hatch's friend, Dr. Fairbairn, consented to edit the volume, with the valuable aid of Mr. Bartlet and Professor Sanday, was an ample pledge that the want would be most efficiently met. To those gentlemen the Trustees are greatly indebted for the learned and earnest care with which the laborious revision was made.

PREFACE.

The fittest introduction to these Lectures will be a few words of explanation.

Before his death, Dr. Hatch had written out and sent to press the first eight Lectures. Of these he had corrected six, while the proofs of the seventh and eighth, with some corrections in his own hand, were found among his papers. As regards these two, the duties of the editor were simple: he had only to correct them for the press. But as regards the remaining four Lectures, the work was much more arduous and responsible. A continuous MS., or even a connected outline of any one of the Lectures, could not be said to exist. The Lectures had indeed been delivered a year and a half before, but the delivery had been as it were of selected passages, with the connections orally supplied, while the Lecturer did not always follow the order of his notes, or, as we know from the Lectures he himself prepared for the press, the one into which he meant to work his finished material. What came into the editor's hands was a series of notebooks, which seemed at first sight but an amorphous mass or collection of hurried and disconnected jottings, now in ink, now in pencil; with a multitude of cross references made by symbols and abbreviations whose very significance had to be laboriously learned; with abrupt beginnings and still more abrupt endings; with pages crowded with successive strata, as it were, of reflections and references, followed by pages almost or entirely blank, speaking of sections or fields meant to be further explored; with an equal multitude of erasures, now complete, now incomplete, now cancelled; with passages marked as transposed or as to be transposed, or with a sign of interrogation which indicated, now a suspicion as to the validity or accuracy of a statement, now a simple suspense of judgment, now a doubt as to position or relevance, now a simple query as of one asking. Have I not said this, or something like this, before? In a word, what we had were the notebooks of the scholar and the literary workman, well ordered, perhaps, as a garden to him who made it and had the clue to it, but at once a wilderness and a labyrinth to him who had no hand in its making, and who had to discover the way through it and out of it by research and experiment. But patient, and, I will add, loving and sympathetic work, rewarded the editor and his kind helpers. The clue was found, the work proved more connected and continuous than under the conditions could have been thought to be possible, and the result is now presented to the world.

A considerable proportion of the material for the ninth Lecture had been carefully elaborated; but some of it, and the whole of the material for the other three, was in the state just described. This of course added even more to the responsibilities than to the labors of the editor. In the body of the Lectures most scrupulous care has been taken to preserve the author's *ipsissima verba*, and, wherever possible, the structure and form of his sentences. But from the very necessities of the case, the hand had now and then to be allowed a little more freedom; connecting words, headings, and even here and there a transitional sentence or explanatory clause, had to be added; but in no single instance has a word, phrase or sentence been inserted in the text without warrant from some one part or another of these crowded notebooks. With the footnotes it has been different. One of our earliest and most serious difficulties was to find whence many of the quotations, especially in the ninth Lecture, came. The author's name was given, but often no clue to the book or chapter. We have been, I think, in every case successful in tracing the quotation to its source. Another difficulty was to connect the various references with the paragraph, sentence or statement, each was meant to prove. This involved a new labor; the sources had to be consulted alike for the purposes of verification and determination of relevance and place. The references, too, in the notebooks were often of the briefest, given, as it were, in algebraics, and they had frequently to be expanded and corrected; while the search into the originals led now to the making of excerpts, and now to the discovery of new authorities which it seemed a pity not to use. As a result, the notes to Lecture IX. are mainly the author's, though all as verified by other hands; but the notes to Lecture X., and in part also XI, are largely the editor's. This is stated in order that all responsibility for errors and inaccuracies may be laid at the proper door. It seemed to the editor that, while he could do little to make the text what the author would have made it if it had been by his own hand prepared for the press, he was bound, in the region where the state of the MSS. made a discreet use of freedom not only possible but compulsory, to make the book as little unworthy of the scholarship and scrupulous accuracy of the author as it was in his power to do.

The pleasant duty remains of thanking two friends who have greatly lightened my labors. The first is Vernon Bartlet, M.A.; the second. Professor Sanday. Mr. Bartlet's part has been the heaviest; without him the work could never have been done. He labored at the MSS. till the broken sentences became whole, and the disconnected paragraphs wove themselves together; and then he transcribed the black and bewildering pages into clear and legible copy for the printer. He had heard the Lectures, and had happily taken a few notes, which, supplemented from other sources, proved most helpful, especially in the way of determining the order to be followed. He has indeed been in every way a most unwearied and diligent co-worker. To him we also owe the Synopsis of Contents and the Index. Professor Sanday has kindly read over all the Lectures that have passed under the hands of the editor, and has furnished him with most helpful criticisms, suggestions, and emendations.

The work is sent out with a sad gratitude. I am grateful that it has been possible so far to fulfil the author's design, but sad because he no longer lives to serve the cause he loved so well. This is not the place to say a word either in criticism or in praise of him or his work. Those of us who knew him know how little a book like this expresses his whole mind, or represents all that in this field he had it in him to do.

The book is an admirable illustration of his method; in order to be judged aright, it ought to be judged within the limits he himself has drawn. It is a study in historical development, an analysis of some of the formal factors that conditioned a given process and determined a given result; but it deals throughout solely with these formal factors and the historical conditions under which they operated. He never intended to discover or discuss the transcendental causes of the process on the one hand, or to pronounce on the value or validity of the result on the other. His purpose, like his method, was scientific; and as an attempt at the scientific treatment of the growth and formulation of ideas, of the evolution and establishment of usages within the Christian Church, it ought to be studied and criticized. Behind and beneath his analytical method was a constructive intellect, and beyond his conclusions was a positive and coordinating conception of the largest and noblest order. To his mind every species of mechanical Deism was alien; and if his method bears hardly upon the traditions and assumptions by which such a Deism still lives in the region of early ecclesiastical history, it was only that he might prepare the way for the coming of a faith and a society that should be worthier of the Master he loved and the Church he served.

A. M. Fairbaien. Oxford, July 1890.

SYNOPSIS OF CONTENTS.

Lecture I. INTRODUCTORY.

The Problem:

How the Church passed from the Sermon on the Mount to the Nicene Creed; the change in spirit coincident with a change in soil.

The need of caution: two preliminary considerations:

1. A religion relative to the whole mental attitude of an age: hence need to estimate the general attitude of the Greek mind during the first three centuries AD.
2. Every permanent change in religious belief and usage rooted in historical conditions: roots of the Gospel in Judaism, but of fourth century Christianity — the key to historical — in Hellenism.

The Method:

Evidence as to process of change scanty, but ample and representative as to ante -Nicene Greek thought and post-Nicene Christian thought. Respects in which evidence defective.

Two resulting tendencies:

1. To overrate the value of the surviving evidence.
2. To underestimate opinions no longer accessible or known only through opponents.

Hence method, the correlation of antecedents and consequents.

Antecedents: sketch of the phenomena of Hellenism.

Consequents: changes in original Christian ideas and usages.

Attitude of mind required:

1. Demand upon attention and imagination.
2. Personal prepossessions to be allowed for
3. Need to observe under-currents

History as a scientific study: the true apologia in religion

Lecture II. GREEK EDUCATION.

The first step a study of environment, particularly as literary. The contemporary Greek world an educated world in a special literary sense

    I. Its forms varied, but all literary: Grammar, Rhetoric, A "lecture-room" Philosophy

    II. Its influence shown by:

        1. Direct literary evidence

        2. Recognized and lucrative position of the teaching profession

        3. Social position of its professors

        4. Its persistent survival up to today in general education, in special terms and usages

Into such an artificial habit of mind Christianity came

Lecture III. GREEK AND CHRISTIAN EXEGESIS.

To the Greek the mystery of writing, the reverence for antiquity, the belief in inspiration, gave the ancient poets a unique value

Homer, his place in moral education; used by the Sophists in ethics, physics, metaphysics, &c.

    Apologies for this use culminate in allegory, especially among the Stoics

The Allegoric temper widespread, particularly in things religious

    Adopted by Hellenistic Jews, especially at Alexandria; Philo

    Continued by early Christian exegesis in varied schools, chiefly as regards the Prophets, in harmony with Greek thought, and as a main line of apologetic

Application to the New Testament writings by the Gnostics and the Alexandrines

Its aid as solution of the Old Testament problem, especially in Origen

Reactions both Hellenic and Christian: viz. in

    1. The Apologists' polemic against Greek mythology

2. The Philosophers' polemic against Christianity

3. Certain Christian Schools, especially the Antiochene

Here hampered by dogmatic complications

Use and abuse of allegory — the poetry of life

Alien to certain drifts of the modern spirit, viz.

1. Historic handling of literature

2. Recognition of the living voice of God

Lecture IV. GREEK AND CHRISTIAN RHETORIC.

The period one of widely diffused literary culture.

The Rhetorical Schools, old and new

Sophistic largely pursued the old lines of Rhetoric, but also philosophized and preached professionally

Its manner of discourse; its rewards

Objections of earnest men; reaction led by Stoics like Epictetus

Significance for Christianity

Primitive Christian "prophesying" v. later "preaching."

Preaching of composite origin: its essence and form, e.g. in fourth century, A.D.: preachers sometimes itinerant

Summary and conclusions

Lecture V. CHRISTIANITY AND GREEK PHILOSOPHY.

Abstract ideas among the Greeks, who were hardly aware of the different degrees of precision possible in mathematics and philosophy

Tendency to define strong with them, apart from any criterion; hence *dogmas*

Dogmatism, amid decay of originality: reaction towards doubt; yet Dogmatism regnant

"Palestinian Philosophy," a complete contrast

Fusion of these in the Old Catholic Church achieved through an underlying kinship of ideas

Explanations of this from both sides

Philosophical Judaism as a bridge, e.g., in allegorism and cosmology

Christian philosophy partly apologetic, partly speculative.
> Alarm of Conservatives: the second century one of transition and conflict

The issue, compromise, and a certain habit of mind
Summary answer to the main question
The Greek mind seen in:
> 1. The tendency to define
> 2. The tendency to speculate
> 3. The point of emphasis, i.e. Orthodoxy

Further development in the West. But Greece the source of the true *damnosa hereditas*

Lecture VI. GREEK AND CHRISTIAN ETHICS.
The average morality of the age: its moral philosophy
An age of moral reformation
> 1. Relation of ethics to philosophy and life
> Revived practical bent of Stoicism; Epictetus
> A moral gymnastic cultivated:
>> (1) *Askesis*: Philo, Epictetus, Dio Chrysostom
>> (2) The "philosopher" or moral reformer
> 2. The contents of ethical teaching, marked by a religious reference. Epictetus' two maxims, "Follow Nature," "Follow God"

Christian ethics show agreement amid difference; based upon the Divine command; idea of sin: agreement most emphasized at first, i.e. the importance of conduct
> 1. Tone of earliest Christian writings: the "Two "Ways:" Apostolical Constitutions, Bk. i.
> 2. Place of discipline in Christian life: Puritan ideal v. later *corpus permixtum*

Further developments due to Greece:
> 1. A Church within the Church: *askesis*, Monasticism
> 2. Resulting deterioration of average ethics: Ambrose of Milan

Complete victory of Greek ethics seen in the basis of modern society

Lecture VII. GREEK AND CHRISTIAN THEOLOGY.
I. The Creator.

The idea of One God, begotten of the unity and order of the world, and connected with the ideas of personality and mind. Three elements in the idea — Creator, Moral Governor, Absolute Being

Growth of idea of a beginning: Monism and Dualism

1. Monism of the Stoics: natura naturata and naturans: a beginning not necessarily involved
2. Dualism, Platonic: creation recognized

Syncretistic blending of these as to process: *Logos* idea common. Hence Philo's significance : God as Creator : Monistic and Dualistic aspects; his terms for the Forces in their plurality and unity : after all, God is Creator, even Father, of the world

Early Christian idea of a single supreme Artificer took permanent root; but questions as to mode emerged, and the first answers were tentative

1. Evolutional typo; supplemented by idea of a lapse
2. Creational type accepted

There remained:

(i.) The ultimate relation of matter to God : Dualistic solutions : Basilides' Platonic theory the basis of the later doctrine, though not at once recognized

(ii.) The Creator's contact with matter: Mediation hypothesis: the *Logos* solution

(iii.) Imperfection and evil: Monistic and Dualistic answers, especially Marcion's

But the Divine Unity overcomes all: position of Irenaeus, &c., widely accepted: Origen's cosmogony a theodicy. Prevalence of the simpler view seen in Monarchianism

Results

Lecture VIII. GREEK AND CHRISTIAN THEOLOGY.
II. The Moral Governor.

A. — *The Greek Idea.*

1. Unity of God and Unity of the world: will and order 209
   Order, number, necessity and destiny: intelligent force and law
   The Cosmos as a city-state (*polis*)
2. New conceptions of the Divine Nature : Justice and
   Goodness in connection with Providence

Thus about the Christian era we find Destiny and Providence, and a tendency to synthesis — through two stages — in the use of the terra God

3. The problem of evil emerges: attempts at solution.
   (a) Universality of Providence denied (Platonic and Oriental)
   (b) Reality of apparent evils denied (Stoic)
   This not pertinent to moral evil, hence:
   (c) Theory of human freedom
   Its relation to Universality of Providence: the Stoical theodicy
   exemplified in Epictetus

B. — *The Christian Idea.*

Primitive Christianity a contrast: two main conceptions.

1. Wages for work done
2. Positive Law — God a Lawgiver and Judge

Difficulties in fusing the two types.

(i.) Forgiveness and Law
Marcion's ditheism
Solution in Irenaeus, Tertullian, &c.: result

(ii.) The Moral Governor and Free-will.
Marcion's dualistic view of moral evil
Justin Martyr, Tatian, Irenaeus
Tertullian and the Alexandrines
Origen's comprehensive theodicy by aid of Stoicism and Neo-
Platonism

Lecture IX. GREEK AKD CHRISTIAN THEOLOGY.

III. God as the Supreme Being.

Christian Theology shaped by Greece, though on a Jewish basis

A. — *The Idea and its Development in Greek Philosophy.*

Parallel to Christian speculation in three stages.

1. Transcendence of God.

    History of the idea before and after Plato

    Its two forms, transcendent proper and supracosmic

    Blending with religious feeling, e.g. in Philo

2. Revelation of the Transcendent.

    Through intermediaries:

        (i.) Mythological

        (ii.) Philosophical, e.g. in Philo

3. Distinctions in the nature of God.

    Philo's *Logos*

        Conceived both monistically and dualistically in relation to God:

        But especially under metaphor of generation

    B. — *The Idea and its Development in Christian Theology.*

1. Here the idea of Transcendence is at first absent

    Present in the Apologists

    But God as transcendent (v, supra-cosmic) first emphasized by Basilides and the Alexandrines

2. Mediation (= Revelation) of the Transcendent, a vital problem

    Theories of *manifestation*

    Dominant idea that of modal existence:

        (i.) As manifold: so among certain Gnostics

        (ii.) As constituting a unity

    Its Gnostic forms

    Relation of the logoi to the *Logos*, especially in Justin

    The issue is the *Logos* doctrine of Irenaeus

3. Distinctions in the nature of God based on the *Logos*.

        (i.) Theories as to the genesis of the *Logos*, analogous to those as to the world

Theories guarding the "sole monarchy," thus endangered,
culminate in Origen's idea of eternal generation
(ii.) Theories of the nature of the *Logos* determined by either
the supra-cosmic or transcendental idea of God
Origen marks a stage — and but a stage — in the controversies

Greek elements in the subsequent developments.

Ousia; its history
Difficulty felt in applying it to God
As also with *homoousios*: need of another term
Hypostasis: its history
Comes to need definition by a third term (*prosopon*)
Resume of the use of these terms; the reign of dogmatism

Three underlying assumptions — a legacy of the Greek spirit

1. The importance of metaphysical distinctions.

2. Their absolute truth.

3. The nature of God's perfection.

Conclusion

Lecture X. THE INFLUENCE OF THE MYSTERIES UPON CHRISTIAN USAGES.

A.— *The Greek Mysteries and Related Cults.*

Mysteries and religious associations side by side with ordinary
Greek religion.

1. The Mysteries, e.g. at Eleusis
   (i.) Initial Purification, through confession and lustration
   (baptism)
   (ii.) Sacrifices, -with procession, &c.
   (iii.) Mystic Drama, of nature and human life
2. Other religious associations: condition of entrance, sacrifice
   and common meal
   Wide extent of the above

B. — *The Mysteries and the Church.*

Transition to the Christian Sacraments; influence, general and
special

1. Baptism:

Its primitive simplicity

Later period marked by:

   (i.) Change of *name*

   (ii.) Change of *time* and conception

Minor confirmations of the parallelism

2. The Lord's Supper:

Stages of extra-biblical development, e.g. in Didache, Apost. Const., the "altar," its offerings as "mysteries"

Culmination of tendency in fifth century in Dionysius

The tendency strongest in the most Hellenic circles, viz.

   Gnostics

Secrecy and long catechumenate

Anointing

Realistic change of conception

Conclusion

Lecture XI. THE INCORPORATION OF CHRISTIAN IDEAS, AS MODIFIED BY GREEK, INTO A BODY OF DOCTRINE.

"Faith" in Old Testament = trust — trust in a person.

In Greek philosophy = intellectual conviction

In Philo, these blend into trust in God — in His veracity, i.e. in the Holy Writings

Contemporary longing for certainty based on fact

Here we have the germs of (1) the Creed, (2) the New Testament Canon

1. At first emphasis on its ethical purpose and revealed basis; then the latent intellectual element emerges, though not uniformly

The baptismal formula becomes a test.

   Expansion by "apostolic teaching"

   The "Apostles' Creed" and the Bishops

2. Related question as to sources of the Creed and the materials for its interpretation.

Value of written tradition: influence of Old Testament and common idea of prophecy: apostolicity as limit

Marcion and the idea of a Canon

"Faith" assumes the sense it had in Philo

3. But the speculative temper remained active upon the "rule of faith:" *gnosis* alongside *pistis*, especially at Alexandria: Origen

Hence tendency to:

(1) Identify a fact with speculations upon it

(2) Check individual speculations in favor of those of the majority

Results:

(i.) Such speculations formulated and inserted in the Creed, formally as interpretations: belief changed, but not the importance attached to it

(ii.) Distinction between "majority" and " minority" views at a meeting, on points of metaphysical speculation

Resume of the stages of belief

Underlying conceptions to be noted

(1) Philosophic regard for exact definition.

(2) Political belief in a majority.

(3) Belief in the finality of the views of an age so ascertained.

Development, if admitted, cannot be arrested

Place of speculation in Christianity

Lecture XII. THE TRANSFORMATION OF THE BASIS OF CHRISTIAN UNION: DOCTRINE IN THE PLACE OF CONDUCT.

Association at first voluntary, according to the genius of Christianity

Its basis primarily moral and spiritual: Holiness its characteristic: the " Two Ways," Apost. Const. (Bk. i.), the Elchasaites

Also a common Hope: its changing form

Coincident relaxation of bonds of discipline and change in idea of the Church

Growing stress also upon the intellectual clement

Causes for this, primary and collateral

    (1) Importance given to Baptism realistically conceived : its relation to the ministrant

    (2) Intercommunion : the necessary test at first moral (e.g. Didache), subsequently a doctrinal formula

This elevation of doctrine due to causes internal to the Christian communities: but an external factor enters with case of Paul of Samosata: its results

Lines of reaction against this transformation:

    (1) Puritan or conservative tendency: Novatianism

    (2) Formation of esoteric class with higher moral ideal : Monachism

Conclusion:

    The Greek spirit still lives in Christian Churches: the vital question is its relation to Christianity

    Two theories — permanence of the primitive, assimilative development: no logical third

    On either theory, the Greek element may largely go

The problem pressing: our study a necessary preliminary and truly conservative

New ground here broken: a pioneer's forecast: the Christianity of the future

Lecture I. INTRODUCTORY.

It is impossible for anyone, whether he be a student of history or no, to fail to notice a difference of both form and content between the Sermon on the Mount and the Nicene Creed. The Sermon on the Mount is the promulgation of a new law of conduct; it assumes beliefs rather than formulates them; the theological conceptions which underlie it belong to the ethical rather than the speculative side of theology; metaphysics are wholly absent. The Nicene Creed is a statement partly of historical facts and partly of dogmatic inferences; the metaphysical terms which it contains would probably have been unintelligible to the first disciples; ethics have no place in it. The one belongs to a world of Syrian peasants, the other to a world of Greek philosophers.

The contrast is patent. If anyone thinks that it is sufficiently explained by saying that the one is a sermon and the other a creed, it must be pointed out in reply that the question why an ethical sermon stood in the forefront of the teaching of Jesus Christ, and a metaphysical creed in the forefront of the Christianity of the fourth century, is a problem which claims investigation.

It claims investigation but it has not yet been investigated. There have been inquiries, which in some cases have arrived at positive results, as to the causes of particular changes or developments in Christianity — the development, for example, of the doctrine of the Trinity, or of the theory of a Catholic Church. But the main question to which I invite your attention is antecedent to all such inquiries. It asks, not how did the Christian societies come to believe one proposition rather than another, but how did they come to the frame of mind which attached importance to either the one or the other, and made the assent to the one rather than the other a condition of membership.

In investigating this problem, the first point that is obvious to an inquirer is, that the change in the center of gravity from conduct to belief is coincident with the transference of Christianity from a Semitic to a Greek soil. The presumption is that it was the result of Greek influence. It will appear from the Lectures which follow that this presumption is true. Their general subject is, consequently, The Influence of Greece upon Christianity.

The difficulty, the interest, and the importance of the subject make it incumbent upon us to approach it with caution. It is necessary to bear many points in mind as we enter upon it; and I will begin by asking your attention to two considerations, which, being true of all analogous phenomena of religious development and change, may be presumed to be true of the particular phenomena before us.

1. The first is, that the religion of a given race at a given time is relative to the whole mental attitude of that time. It is impossible to separate the religious phenomena from the other phenomena, in the same way that you can separate a vein of silver from the rock in which it is embedded. They are as much determined by the general characteristics of the race as the fauna and flora of a geographical area are determined by its soil, its climate, and its cultivation; and they vary with the changing characteristics of the race as the fauna and flora of the tertiary system differ from those of the chalk. They are separable from the whole mass of phenomena, not in fact, but only in thought. We may

concentrate our attention chiefly upon them, but they still remain part of the whole complex life of the time, and they cannot be understood except in relation to that life. If anyone hesitates to accept this historical induction, I will ask him to take the instance that lies nearest to him, and to consider how he could understand the religious phenomena of our own country in our own time — its doubts, its hopes, its varied enterprises, its shifting enthusiasms, its noise, its learning, its aestheticism, and its philanthropies — unless he took account of the growth of the inductive sciences and the mechanical arts, of the expansion of literature, of the social stress, of the commercial activity, of the general drift of society towards its own improvement.

In dealing, therefore, with the problem before us, we must endeavor to realize to ourselves the whole mental attitude of the Greek world in the first three centuries of our era. We must take account of the breadth and depth of its education, of the many currents of its philosophy, of its love of literature, of its skepticism and its mysticism. We must gather together whatever evidence we can find, not determining the existence or measuring the extent of drifts of thought by their literary expression, but taking note also of the testimony of the monuments of art and history, of paintings and sculptures, of inscriptions and laws. In doing so, we must be content, at any rate for the present and until the problem has been more fully elaborated, with the broader features both of the Greek world and of the early centuries. The distinctions which the precise study of history requires us to draw between the state of thought of Greece proper and that of Asia Minor, and between the age of the Antonines and that of the Severi, are not necessary for our immediate purpose, and may be left to the minuter research which has hardly yet begun.

2. The second consideration is, that no permanent change takes place in the religious beliefs or usages of a race which is not rooted in the existing beliefs and usages of that race. The truth which Aristotle enunciated, that all intellectual teaching is based upon what is previously known to the person taught,[1] is applicable to a race as well as to an individual, and to beliefs even more than to knowledge. A religious change is, like a physiological change, of the nature of assimilation by, and absorption into, existing elements. The religion which our Lord preached was rooted in Judaism. It came "not to destroy, but to fulfil." It took the Jewish conception of a Father in heaven, and gave it a new meaning. It took existing moral precepts, and gave them a new application. The meaning and the application had already been anticipated in some degree by the Jewish prophets. There were Jewish minds which had been ripening for them; and so far as they were ripe for them, they received them. In a similar way we shall find that the Greek Christianity of the fourth century was rooted in Hellenism. The Greek minds which had been ripening for Christianity had absorbed new ideas and new motives; but there was a continuity between their present and their past; the new ideas and new motives mingled with the waters of existing currents; and it is only by examining the sources and the volume of the previous flow that we shall understand how it is that the Nicene Creed rather than the Sermon on the Mount has formed the dominant element in Aryan Christianity.

---

[1] Arist. *Anal. post.* i. 1, p. 71.

The method of the investigation, like that of all investigations, must be determined by the nature of the evidence. The special feature of the evidence which affects the method is, that it is ample in regard to the causes, and ample also in regard to the effects, but scanty in regard to the process of change.

We have ample evidence in regard to the state of Greek thought during the ante-Nicene period. The writers shine with a dim and pallid light when put side by side with the master-spirits of the Attic age; but their lesser importance in the scale of genius rather adds to than diminishes from their importance as representatives. They were more the children of their time. They are consequently better evidence as to the currents of its thought than men who supremely transcended it. I will mention those from whom we shall derive most information, in the hope that you will in course of time become familiar, not only with their names, but also with their works. Dio of Prusa, commonly known as Dio Chrysostom, "Dio of the golden mouth," who was raised above the class of travelling orators to which he belonged, not only by his singular literary skill, but also by the nobility of his character and the vigor of his protests against political unrighteousness. Epictetus, the lame slave, the Socrates of his time, in whom the morality and the religion of the Greek world find their sublimest expression, and whose conversations and lectures at Nicopolis, taken down, probably in short-hand, by a faithful pupil, reflect exactly, as in a photograph, the interior life of a great moralist's school. Plutarch, the prolific essayist and diligent encyclopedist, whose materials are far more valuable to us than the edifices which he erects with them. Maximus of Tyre, the eloquent preacher, in whom the cold metaphysics of the Academy are transmuted into a glowing mysticism. Marcus Aurelius, the imperial philosopher, in whose mind the fragments of many philosophies are lit by hope or darkened by despair, as the clouds float and drift in uncertain sunlight or in gathered gloom before the clearing rain. Lucian, the satirist and wit, the prose Aristophanes of later Greece. Sextus Empiricus, whose writings — or the collection of writings gathered under his name — are the richest of all mines for the investigation of later Greek philosophy. Philostratus, the author of a great religious romance, and of many sketches of the lives of contemporary teachers. It will hardly be an anachronism if we add to these the great syncretist philosopher, Philo of Alexandria; for, on the one hand, he was more Greek than Jew, and, on the other, several of the works which are gathered together under his name seem to belong to a generation subsequent to his own, and to be the only survivors of the Judeo-Greek schools which lasted on in the great cities of the empire until the verge of Christian times.

We have ample evidence also as to the state of Christian thought in the post-Nicene period. The Fathers Athanasius, Basil, Gregory of Nazianzus, Gregory of Nyssa, and Cyril of Jerusalem, the decrees of general and local Councils, the apocryphal and pseudonymous literature, enable us to form a clear conception of the change which Greek influences had wrought.

But the evidence as to the mode in which the causes operated within the Christian sphere before the final effects were produced is singularly imperfect. If we look at the literature of the schools of thought which ultimately became dominant, we find that it consists for the most part of some accidental survivals.[2] It tells us about some parts of the Christian world, but not about others. It represents a few phases of thought with adequate fulness, and of others it presents only a few fossils. In regard to Palestine, which in the third and fourth centuries was a great center of culture, we have only the evidence of Justin Martyr. In regard to Asia Minor, which seems to have been the chief crucible for the alchemy of transmutation, we have but such scanty fragments as those of Melito and Gregory of Neocaesarea. The largest and most important monuments are those of Alexandria, the works of Clement and Origen, which represent a stage of singular interest in the process of philosophical development. Of the Italian writers, we have little that is genuine besides Hippolytus. Of Galilean writers, we have chiefly Irenaeus, whose results are important as being the earliest formulating of the opinions which ultimately became dominant, but whose method is mainly interesting as an example of the dreary polemics of the rhetorical schools. Of African writers, we have Tertullian, a skilled lawyer, who would in modern times have taken high rank as a pleader at the bar or as a leader of Parliamentary debate; and Cyprian, who survives chiefly as a champion of the sacerdotal hypothesis, and whose vigorous personality gave him a moral influence which was far beyond the

---

[2] Tertullian (*adv. Valentin.* c. 5) singles out four writers of the previous generation whom he regards as standing on an equal footing: Justin, Miltiades, Irenaeus, Proculus. Of these, Proculus has entirely perished; of Miltiades, only a few fragments remain; Justin survives in only a single MS. and the greater part of Irenaeus remains only in a Latin translation,

measure of his intellectual powers. The evidence is not only imperfect, but also insufficient in relation to the effects that were produced. Writers of the stamp of Justin and Irenaeus are wholly inadequate to account for either the conversion of the educated world to Christianity, or for the forms which Christianity assumed when the educated world had molded it.

And if we look for the literature of the schools of thought which were ultimately branded as heretical, we look almost wholly in vain. What the earliest Christian philosophers thought, we know, with comparatively insignificant exceptions, only from the writings of their opponents. They were subject to a double hate — that of the heathen schools which they had left, and that of the Christians who were saying "Non possumus" to philosophy.[3] The little trust that we can place in the accounts which their opponents give of them is shown by the wide differences in those accounts. Each opponent, with the dialectical skill which was common at the time, selected, paraphrased, distorted, and re-combined the points which seemed to him to be weakest. The result is, naturally, that the accounts which the several opponents give are so different in form and feature as to be irreconcilable with one another.[4] It was so also with the

---

[3] Marcion, in the sad tone of one who bitterly felt that every man's hand was against him, addresses one of his disciples as "my partner in hate and wretchedness" (Tert. *adv. Marc.* 4. 9).

[4] Examples are the accounts of Basilides in Clement of Alexandria and Hippolytus, compared with those in Irenaeus and Epiphanius; and the accounts of the Ophites in Hippolytus, compared with those of Irenaeus and Epiphanius. The literature of the subject is considerable.

heathen opponents of Christianity.[5] With one important exception, we cannot tell how the new religion struck a dispassionate outside observer, or why it was that it left so many philosophers outside its fold. Then, as now, the forces of human nature were at work. The tendency to disparage and suppress an opponent is not peculiar to the early ages of Christianity. When the associated Christian communities won at length their hard-fought battle, they burned the enemy's camp.

This fact of the scantiness and inadequacy of the evidence as to the process of transformation has led to two results which constitute difficulties and dangers in our path.

1. The one is the tendency to overrate the value of the evidence that has survived. When only two or three monuments of a great movement remain, it is difficult to appreciate the degree in which those monuments are representative. We tend at almost all times to attach an exaggerated importance to individual writers; the writers who have molded the thoughts of their contemporaries, instead of being molded by them, are always few in number and exceptional. We tend also to attach an undue importance to phrases which occur in such writers; few, if any, writers write with the precision of a legal document, and the inverted pyramids which have been built upon chance phrases of Clement or Justin are monuments of caution which we shall do well to keep before our eyes.

---

[5] The very names of most of the heathen opponents are lost: cf Lactantius (5. 4).

2. The other is the tendency to underestimate the importance of the opinions that have disappeared from sight, or which we know only in the form and to the extent of their quotation by their opponents. If we were to trust the histories that are commonly current, we should believe that there was from the first a body of doctrine of which certain writers were the recognized exponents; and that outside this body of doctrine there was only the play of more or less insignificant opinions, like a fitful guerilla warfare on the flanks of a great army. Whereas what we really find on examining the evidence is, that out of a mass of opinions which for a long time fought as equals upon equal ground, there was formed a vast alliance which was strong enough to shake off the extremes at once of conservatism and of speculation, but in which the speculation whose monuments have perished had no less a share than the conservatism of which some monuments have survived.

This survey of the nature of the evidence enables us to determine the method which we should follow. We can trace the causes and we can see the effects; but we have only scanty information as to the intermediate processes. If the evidence as to those processes existed in greater mass, if the writings of those who made the first tentative efforts to give to Christianity a Greek form had been preserved to us, it might have been possible to follow in order of time and country the influence of the several groups of ideas upon the several groups of Christians. This method has been attempted, with questionable success, by some of those who have investigated the history of particular doctrines. But it is impossible to deprecate too strongly the habit of erecting theories upon historical quicksands; and I propose to pursue the surer path to which the nature of the evidence points, by stating the causes, by viewing them in relation to the effects, and by considering how far they were adequate in respect of both mass and complexity to produce those effects.

There is a consideration in favor of this method which is in entire harmony with that which arises from the nature of the evidence. It is, that the changes that took place were gradual and at first hardly perceptible. It would probably be impossible, even if we were in possession of ampler evidence, to assign a definite cause and a definite date for the introduction of each separate idea. For the early years of Christianity were in some respects like the early years of our lives. It has sometimes been thought that those early years are the most important years in the education of all of us. We learn then, we hardly know how, through effort and struggle and innocent mistakes, to use our eyes and our ears, to measure distance and direction, by a process which ascends by unconscious steps to the certainty which we feel in our maturity. We are helped in doing so, to an incalculable degree, by the accumulated experience of mankind which is stored up in language; but the growth is our own, the unconscious development of our own powers. It was in some such unconscious way that the Christian thought of the earlier centuries gradually acquired the form which we find when it emerges, as it were, into the developed manhood of the fourth century. Greek philosophy helped its development, as language helps a child; but the assimilation of it can no more be traced from year to year than the growth of the body can be traced from day to day.

We shall begin, therefore, by looking at the several groups of facts of the age in which Christianity grew, and endeavor, when we have looked at them, to estimate their influence upon it.

We shall look at the facts which indicate the state of education: we shall find that it was an age that was penetrated with culture, and that necessarily gave to all ideas which it absorbed a cultured and, so to speak, scholastic form.

We shall look at the facts which indicate the state of literature: we shall find that it was an age of great literary activity, which was proud of its ancient monuments, and which spent a large part of its industry in endeavoring to interpret and to imitate them.

We shall look at the facts which indicate the state of philosophy: we shall find that it was an age in which metaphysical conceptions had come to occupy relatively the same place which the conceptions of natural science occupy among ourselves; and that just as we tend to look upon external things in their chemical and physical relations, so there was then, as it were, a chemistry and physics of ideas.

We shall look at the facts which indicate the state of moral ideas: we shall find that it was an age in which the ethical forces of human nature were struggling with an altogether unprecedented force against the degradation of contemporary society and contemporary religion, and in which the ethical instincts were creating the new ideal of "following God," and were solving the old question whether there was or was not an art of life by practicing self-discipline.

We shall look at the facts which indicate the state of theological ideas: we shall find that it was an age in which men were feeling after God and not feeling in vain, and that from the domains of ethics, physics, metaphysics alike, from the depths of the moral consciousness, and from the cloud-lands of poets' dreams, the ideas of men were trooping in one vast host to proclaim with a united voice that there are not many gods, but only One, one First Cause by whom all things were made, one Moral Governor whose providence was over all His works, one Supreme Being "of infinite power, wisdom, and goodness."

We shall look at the facts which indicate the state of religion: we shall find that it was an age in which the beliefs that had for centuries been evolving themselves from the old religions were showing themselves in new forms of worship and new conceptions of what God needed in the worshipper; in which also the older animalism was passing into mysticism, and mysticism was the preparation of the soul for the spiritual religion of the time to come.

We shall then, in the case of each great group of ideas, endeavor to ascertain from the earliest Christian documents the original Christian ideas upon which they acted; and then compare the later with the earlier form of those Christian ideas; and finally examine the combined result of all the influences that were at work upon the mental attitude of the Christian world and upon the basis of Christian association.

I should be glad if I could at once proceed to examine some of these groups of facts. But since the object which I have in view is not so much to lead you to any conclusions of my own, as to invite you to walk with me in comparatively untrodden paths, and to urge those of you who have leisure for historical investigations to explore them for yourselves more fully than I have been able to do — and since the main difficulties of the investigation lie less in the facts themselves than in the attitude of mind in which they are approached — I feel that I should fail of my purpose if I did not linger still upon the threshold to say something of the "personal equation" that we must make before we can become either accurate observers or impartial judges. There is the more reason for doing so, because the study of Christian history is no doubt discredited by the dissonance in the voices of its exponents. An ill-informed writer may state almost any propositions he pleases, with the certainty of finding listeners; a well-informed writer may state propositions which are as demonstrably true as any historical proposition can be, with the certainty of being contradicted. There is no court of appeal, nor will there be until more than one generation has been engaged upon the task to which I am inviting you.

1. In the first place, it is necessary to take account of the demand which the study makes upon the attention and the imagination of the student. The scientific, that is the accurate, study of history is comparatively new. The minute care which is required in the examination of the evidence for the facts, and the painful caution which is required in the forming of inferences, are but inadequately appreciated. The study requires not only attention, but also imagination. A student must have something analogous to the power of a dramatist before he can realize the scenery of a vanished age, or watch, as in a moving panorama, the series and sequence of its events. He must have that power in a still greater degree before he can so throw himself into a bygone time as

to be able to enter into the motives of the actors, and to imagine how, having such and such a character, and surrounded by such and such circumstances, he would himself have thought and felt and acted. But the greatest demand that can be made upon either the attention or the imagination of a student is that which is made by such a problem as the present, which requires us to realize the attitude of mind, not of one man, but of a generation of men, to move with their movements, to float upon the current of their thoughts, and to pass with them from one attitude of mind into another.

2. In the second place, it is necessary to take account of our own personal prepossessions. Most of us come to the study of the subject already knowing something about it. It is a comparatively easy task for a lecturer to present, and for a hearer to realize, an accurate picture of, for example, the religion of Mexico or of Peru, because the mind of the student when he begins the study is a comparatively blank sheet. But most of us bring to the study of Christian history a number of conclusions already formed. We tend to beg the question before we examine it.

We have before us, on the one hand, the ideas and usages of early Christianity; on the other hand, the ideas and usages of imperial Greece.

We bring to the former the thoughts, the associations, the sacred memories, the happy dreams, which have been rising up round us, one by one, since our childhood. Even if there be some among us who in the maturity of their years have broken away from their earlier moorings, these associations still tend to remain. They are not confined to those of us who not only consciously retain them, but also hold their basis to be true. They linger unconsciously in the minds of those who seem most resolutely to have abandoned them.

We bring to the latter, most of us, a similar wealth of associations which have come to us through our education. The ideas with which we have to deal are mostly expressed in terms which are common to the early centuries of Christianity, and to the Greek literature of five centuries before. The terms are the same, but their meaning is different. Those of us who have studied Greek literature tend to attach to them the connotation which they had at Athens when Greek literature was in its most perfect flower. We ignore the long interval of time, and the new connotation which, by an inevitable law of language, had in the course of centuries clustered round the old nucleus of meaning. The terms have in some cases come down by direct transmission into our own language. They have in such cases gathered to themselves wholly new meanings, which, until we consciously hold them up to the light, seem to us to form part of the original meaning, and are with difficulty disentangled.

We bring to both the Christian and the Greek world the inductions respecting them which have been already made by ourselves and by others. We have in those inductions so many molds, so to speak, into which we press the plastic statements of early writers. We assume the primitiveness of distinctions which for the most part represent only the provisional conclusions of earlier generations of scholars, and stages in our own historical education; and we arrange facts in the categories which we find ready to hand, as Jewish or Gentile, orthodox or heretical, Catholic or Gnostic, while the question of the reality of such distinctions and such categories is one of the main points which our inquiries have to solve.

3. In the third place, it is necessary to take account of the undercurrents, not only of our own age, but of the past ages with which we have to deal. Every age has such undercurrents, and every age tends to be unconscious of them. We ourselves have succeeded to a splendid heritage. Behind us are the thoughts, the beliefs, the habits of mind, which have been in process of formation since the first beginning of our race. They are inwrought, for the most part, into the texture of our nature. We cannot transcend them. To them the mass of our thoughts are relative, and by them the thoughts of other generations tend to be judged. The importance of recognizing them as an element in our judgments of other generations increases in proportion as those generations recede from our own. In dealing with a country or a period not very remote, we may not go far wrong in assuming that its inheritance of ideas is cognate to our own. But in dealing with a remote country, or a remote period of time, it becomes of extreme importance to allow for the difference, so to speak, of mental longitude. The men of earlier days had other mental scenery round them. Fewer streams of thought had converged upon them. Consequently, many ideas which were in entire harmony with the mental fabric of their time, are unintelligible when referred to the standard of our own; nor can we understand them until we have been at the pains to find out the underlying ideas to which they were actually relative.

I will briefly illustrate this point by two instances:

(a) "We tend to take with us, as we travel into bygone times, the dualistic hypothesis — which to most of us is no hypothesis, but an axiomatic truth — of the existence of an unbridged chasm between body and soul, matter and spirit. The relation in our minds of the idea of matter to the idea of spirit is such, that though we readily conceive matter to act upon matter, and spirit upon spirit, we find it difficult or impossible to conceive a direct action either of matter upon spirit or of spirit upon matter. When, therefore, in studying, for example, the ancient rites of baptism, we find expressions which seem to attribute a virtue to the material element, we measure such expressions by a modern standard, and regard them as containing only an analogy or a symbol. They belong, in reality, to another phase of thought than our own. They are an outflow of the earlier conception of matter and spirit as varying forms of a single substance.[6] "Whatever acts, is body," it was said. Mind is the subtlest form of body, but it is body nevertheless. The conception of a direct action of the one upon the other presented no difficulty. It was imagined, for instance that demons might be the direct causes of diseases, because the extreme tenuity of their substance enabled them to enter, and to exercise a malignant influence upon, the bodies of men. So water, when exorcized from all the evil influences which might reside in it, actually cleansed the soul.[7] The conception of the

---

[6] This was the common view of the Stoics, probably following Anaxagoras or his school; cf. Plutarch [Aetius], de Plac. Philos. 4. 3 (Diels, Doxographi Greci, p. 387), (Chrysipp. Fragm. ap. Nemes. de Nat. Hom. 33), by Zeno, in Cic. Academ. 1.11.39; by their followers, Plutarch [Aetius], de Plac. Philos. 1.11.4 (Diels, p. 310), so by Seneca, Epist. 117.2, so among some Christian writers, e.g. Tertullian, de Anima, 5.

process as symbolical came with the growth of later ideas of the relation of matter to spirit. It is, so to speak, a rationalizing explanation of a conception which the world was tending to outgrow.

(b) We take with us in our travels into the past the underlying conception of religion as a personal bond between God and the individual soul. We cannot believe that there is any virtue in an act of worship in which the conscience has no place. We can understand, however much we may deplore, such persecutions as those of the sixteenth century, because they ultimately rest upon the same conception: men were so profoundly convinced of the truth of their own personal beliefs as to deem it of supreme importance that other men should hold those beliefs also. But we find it difficult to understand why, in the second century of our era, a great emperor who was also a great philosopher should have deliberately persecuted Christianity. The difficulty arises from our overlooking the entirely different aspect under which religion presented itself to a Roman mind. It was a matter which lay, not between the soul and God, but between the individual and the State. Conscience had no place in it. Worship was an ancestral usage which the State sanctioned and enforced. It was one of the ordinary duties of life.[8] The neglect of it, and still more

---

[7] The conception underlies the whole of Tertullian's treatise, *de Baptismo*: it accounts for the rites of exorcism and benediction of both the oil and the water which are found in the older Latin service-books, e.g. in what is known as the Gelasian Sacramentary, 1.73 (in Muratori, Liturgia *Romana vetus*, vol. i. p. 594).

the disavowal of it, was a crime. An emperor might pity the offender for his obstinacy, but he must necessarily either compel him to obey or punish him for disobedience.

It is not until we have thus realized the fact that the study of history requires as diligent and as constant an exercise of the mental powers as any of the physical sciences, and until we have made what may be called the "personal equation," disentangling ourselves as far as we can from the theories which we have inherited or formed, and recognizing the existence of undercurrents of thought in past ages widely different from those which flow in our own, that we shall be likely to investigate with success the great problem that lies before us. I lay stress upon these points, because the interest of the subject tends to obscure its difficulties. Literature is full of fancy sketches of early Christianity; they are written, for the most part, by enthusiasts whose imagination soars by an easy flight to the mountain-tops which the historian can only reach by a long and rugged road; they are read, for the most part, by those who give them only the attention which they would give to a shilling hand-book or to an article in a review. I have no desire, and I am sure that you have no desire, to add one more to such fancy sketches. The time has come for a precise study. The materials for such a study are

---

[8] These conceptions are found in Xenophon's account of Socrates, who quotes more than once the Delphic oracle. Xen. *Mem*. 1.3.1, and again 4.3.16: in Epictet. *Ench*. 31, repeatedly in Plutarch, e.g. *de Defect. Orac.* 12, p. 416, *de Comm. Notit.* 31.1, p. 1074: in the *Aureum Carmen* of the later Pythagoreans, and in the Neoplatonist Porphyry (*ad Marcell.* 18, p. 286, ed. Nauck). The intellectual opponents of Christianity laid stress upon its desertion of the ancestral religion; e.g. Caecilius in Minucius Felix, *Octav.* 5. and Celsus in Origen, *c. Cels.* 5.25, 35; 8.57.

available. The method of such a study is determined by canons which have been established in analogous fields of research. The difficulties of such a study come almost entirely from ourselves, and it is a duty to begin by recognizing them.

For the study is one not only of living interest, but also of supreme importance. Other history may be more or less antiquarian. Its ultimate result may be only to gratify our curiosity and to add to the stores of our knowledge. But Christianity claims to be a present guide of our lives. It has been so large a factor in the moral development of our race, that we cannot set aside its claim unheard. Neither can we admit it until we know what Christianity is. A thousand dissonant voices are each of them professing to speak in its name. The appeal lies from them to its documents and to its history. In order to know what it is, we must first know both what it professed to be and what it has been. The study of the one is the complement of the other; but it is with the latter only that we have at present to do. We may enter upon the study with confidence, because it is a scientific inquiry. We may hear, if we will, the solemn tramp of the science of history marching slowly, but marching always to conquest. It is marching in our day, almost for the first time, into the domain of Christian history. Upon its flanks, as upon the flanks of the physical sciences, there are scouts and skirmishers, who venture sometimes into morasses where there is no foothold, and into ravines from which there is no issue. But the science is marching on. "Vestigia nulla retrorsum." It marches, as the physical sciences have marched, with the firm tread of certainty. It meets, as the physical sciences have met, with opposition, and even with contumely. In front of it, as in front of the physical sciences, is chaos; behind it is order. We may march in its progress, not only with the confidence of scientific certainty, but also with the confidence of Christian faith. It may show some things to be derived which we thought to be original; and some things to be compound which we thought to be incapable of analysis; and some things to be phantoms which we thought to be realities. But it will add a new chapter to Christian apologetics; it will confirm the divinity of Christianity by showing it to be in harmony with all else that we believe to be divine; its results will take their place among those truths which burn in the souls of men with a fire that cannot be quenched, and light up the darkness of this stormy sea with a light that is never dim.

Lecture II. GREEK EDUCATION.

The general result of the considerations to which I have already invited your attention is, that a study of the growth and modifications of the early forms of Christianity must begin with a study of their environment. For a complete study, it would be necessary to examine that environment as a whole. In some respects all life hangs together, and no single element of it is in absolute isolation. The political and economical features of a given time affect more or less remotely its literary and philosophical features, and a complete investigation would take them all into account. But since life is short, and human powers are limited, it is necessary in this, as in many other studies, to be content with something less than ideal completeness. It will be found sufficient in practice to deal only with the proximate causes of the phenomena into which we inquire; and in dealing, as we shall mainly do, with literary effects, to deal also mainly with those features of the age which were literary also.

The most general summary of those features is, that the Greek world of the second and third centuries was, in a sense which, though not without some just demur, has tended to prevail ever since, an educated world. It was reaping the harvest which many generations had sown. Five centuries before, the new elements of knowledge and cultured speech had begun to enter largely into the simpler elements of early Greek life. It had become no longer enough for men to till the ground, or to pursue their several handicrafts, or to be practiced in the use of arms. The word *sophos*, which in earlier times had been applied to one who was skilled in any of the arts of life, who could string a bow or tune a lyre or even trim a hedge, had come to be applied, if not exclusively, yet at least chiefly, to one who was shrewd with practical wisdom, or who knew the thoughts and sayings of the ancients. The original reasons, which lay deep in the Greek character, for the element of knowledge assuming this special form, had been accentuated by the circumstances of later Greek history. There seems to be little reason in the nature of things why Greece should not have anticipated modern Europe in the study of nature, and why knowledge should not have had for its chief meaning in earlier times that which it is tending to mean now, the knowledge of the phenomena and laws of the physical world. The tendency to collect and colligate and compare the facts of nature appears to be no less instinctive than the tendency to become acquainted with the thoughts of those who have gone before us. But Greece on the one hand had lost political power, and on the other hand possessed in her splendid literature an inalienable heritage. She could acquiesce with the greater equanimity in political subjection, because in the domain of letters she was still supreme with an indisputable supremacy. It was natural that she should turn to letters. It was natural also that the study of letters should be reflected upon speech. For the lore of speech had become to a large proportion of Greeks a second nature. They were a nation of talkers. They were almost the slaves of cultivated expression. Though the public life out of which orators had grown had passed away with political freedom, it had left behind it a habit which in the second century of our era was blossoming into a new spring. Like children playing at "make-believe," when real speeches in real assemblies became impossible, the Greeks revived the old practice of public speaking by addressing fictitious assemblies and arguing in fictitious courts. In the absence of the distractions of either keen political struggles at home or wars abroad, these tendencies had spread themselves over the large surface of general Greek society. A kind of literary instinct had come to exist. The mass of men in the Greek world tended to lay stress on that acquaintance with the literature of bygone generations, and that habit of cultivated speech, which has ever since been commonly spoken of as education.

Two points have to be considered in regard to that education before it can be regarded as a cause in relation to the main subject which we are examining: we must look first at its forms, and secondly at its mass. It is not enough that it should have corresponded in kind to certain effects; it must be shown to have been adequate in amount to account for them.

I. The education was almost as complex as our own. If we except only the inductive physical sciences, it covered the same field. It was, indeed, not so much analogous to our own as the cause of it. Our own comes by direct tradition from it. It set a fashion which until recently has uniformly prevailed over the whole civilized world. We study literature rather than nature because the Greeks did so, and because when the Romans and the Roman provincials resolved, to educate their sons, they employed Greek teachers and followed in Greek paths.

The two main elements were those which have been already indicated, Grammar and Rhetoric.

1. By Grammar was meant the study of literature.[9] In its original sense of the art of reading and writing, it began as

early as that art begins among ourselves. "We are given over to Grammar," says Sextus Empiricus[10], "from childhood, and almost from our baby-clothes." But this elementary part of it was usually designated by another name, and Grammar itself had come to include all that in later times has been designated Belles Lettres. This comprehensive view of it was of slow growth; consequently, the art is variously defined and divided. The division which Sextus Empiricus[11] speaks of as most free from objection, and which will sufficiently indicate the general limits of the subject, is into the technical, the historical, and the exegetical elements. The first of these was the study of diction, the laying down of canons of correctness, the distinction between Hellenisms and Barbarisms. Upon this as much stress was laid as was laid upon academic French in the age of Boileau. "I owe to Alexander," says Marcus Aurelius[12], "my habit of not finding fault, and of not using abusive language to those who utter a barbarous or awkward or unmusical phrase." "I must apologize for the style of this letter," says the Christian Father Basil two centuries afterwards, in writing to his old teacher Libanius; "the truth is, I have been in the company of Moses and Elias, and men of that kind, who tell us no doubt what is true, but in a barbarous dialect, so that your instructions have quite gone out of my head."[13] The second

---

[9] Quintil. 2.1.4.

[10] *Adv Gramm.* 1.44.

[11] *Adv Gramm.* 1.91. This is quoted as being most representative of the period with which these Lectures have mainly to do. With it may be compared the elaborate account given by Quintilian, 1. 4 sqq.

[12] 1.10.

element of Grammar was the study of the antiquities of an author: the explanation of the names of the gods and heroes, the legends and histories, which were mentioned. It is continued to this day in most notes upon classical authors. The third element was partly critical, the distinguishing between true and spurious treatises, or between true and false readings; but chiefly exegetical, the explanation of an author's meaning. It is spoken of as the prophetess of the poets,[14] standing to them in the same relation as the Delphian priestess to her inspiring god.

The main subject-matter of this literary education was the poets. They were read, not only for their literary, but also for their moral value.[15] They were read as we read the Bible. They were committed to memory. The minds of men were saturated with them. A quotation from Homer or from a tragic poet was apposite on all occasions and in every kind of society. Dio Chrysostom, in an account of his travels, tells how he came to the Greek colony of the Borysthenes, on the farthest borders of the empire, and found that even in those remote settlements almost all the inhabitants knew the Iliad by heart, and that they did not care to hear about anything else.[16]

---

[13] The substance of Basil's letter, *Ep.* 339 (146), *tom.* iii. p. 455. There is a charming irony in Libanius' answer, Ep. 340 (147), *ibid.*

[14] Sext. Emp. *Adv. Gramm.* 1.279.

[15] Strabo, 1.2.3.

[16] Dio Chrys. *Orat.* xxxvi. vol. ii. p. 51, ed. Dind.

2. Grammar was succeeded by Rhetoric — the study of literature by the study of literary expression and quasi-forensic argument. The two were not sharply distinguished in practice, and had some elements in common. The conception of the one no less than of the other had widened with time, and Rhetoric, like Grammar, was variously defined and divided. It was taught partly by precept, partly by example, and partly by practice. The professor either dictated rules and gave lists of selected passages of ancient authors, or he read such passages with comments upon the style, or he delivered model speeches of his own. The first of these methods has its literary monument in the handbooks which remain.[17] The second survives as an institution in modern times, and on a large scale, in the University "lecture," and it has also left important literary monuments in the Scholia upon Homer and other great writers. The third method gave birth to an institution which also survives in modern times. Each of these methods was followed by the student. He began by committing to memory both the professor's rules and also selected passages of good authors: the latter he recited, with appropriate modulations and gestures, in the presence of the professor. In the next stage, he made his comments upon them. Here is a short example which is embedded in Epictetus:[18] the student reads the first

---

[17] These are printed in Walz, *Rhetores Graeci*, vol. i.: There is a letter of Dio Chrysostom, printed among his speeches, *Orat.* xvii. ed. Dind. i. 279, consisting of advice to a man who was beginning the study of Rhetoric late in life, which, without being a formal treatise, gives as good a view as could be found of the general course of training.

[18] *Diss.* 3.23.20.

sentence of Xenophon's Memorabilia and makes his criticism upon it:

> "'I have often wondered what in the world
> were the grounds on which …'
> Rather, … 'the ground on which …' It is
> neater."

From this, or concurrently with this, the student proceeded to compositions of his own. Beginning with mere imitation of style, he was gradually led to invent structure as well as the style of what he wrote, and to vary both the style and the subject-matter. Sometimes he had the use of the professor's library;[19] and though writing in his native language, he had to construct his periods according to rules of art, and to avoid all words for which an authority could not be quoted, just as if he were an English undergraduate writing his Greek prose. The crown of all was the acquisition of the art of speaking extempore. A student's education in Rhetoric was finished when he had the power to talk off-hand on any subject that might be proposed. But whether he recited a prepared speech or spoke off-hand, he was expected to show the same artificiality of structure and the same pedantry of diction. "You must strip off all that boundless length of sentences that is wrapped round you," says Charon to the rhetorician who is just stepping into his boat, "and those antitheses of yours, and balancings of clauses, and strange expressions, and all the other heavy weights of speech (or you will make my boat too heavy)."[20]

---

[19] *Philostr.* V.S. 2.21.3, of Proclus.

[20] Lucian, *Dial. Mort.* 10.10.

To a considerable extent there prevailed, in addition to Belles Lettres and Rhetoric, a teaching of Philosophy. It was the highest element in the education of the average Greek of the period. Logic, in the form of Dialectic, was common to Philosophy and Rhetoric. Everyone learnt to argue: a large number learnt, in addition, the technical terms of Philosophy and the outlines of its history. Lucian tells a tale of a country gentleman of the old school, whose nephew went home from lecture night after night, and regaled his mother and himself with fallacies and dilemmas, talking about "relations" and "comprehensions" and "mental presentations," and jargon of that sort; nay, worse than that, saying, "that God does not live in heaven, but goes about among stocks and stones and such-like." As far as Logic was concerned, it was almost natural to a Greek mind: Dialectic was but the conversation of a sharp-witted people conducted under recognized rules. But it was a comparatively new phase of Philosophy that it should have a literary side. It had shared in the common degeneracy. It had come to take wisdom at second-hand. It was not the evolution of a man's own thoughts, but an acquaintance with the recorded thoughts of others. It was divorced from practice. It was degraded to a system of lectures and disputations. It was taught in the same general way as the studies which preceded it. But lectures had a more important place. Sometimes the professor read a passage from a philosopher, and gave his interpretation of it; sometimes he gave a discourse of his own. Sometimes a student read an essay of his own, or interpreted a passage of a philosopher, in the presence of the professor, and the professor afterwards pronounced his opinion upon the correctness of the reasoning or the interpretation.[21] The

Discourses of Epictetus have a singular interest in this respect, apart from their contents; for they are in great measure notes of such lectures, and form, as it were, a photograph of a philosopher's lecture-room.

Against this degradation of Philosophy, not only the Cynics, but almost all the more serious philosophers protested. Though Epictetus himself was a professor, and though he followed the current usages of professorial teaching, his life and teaching alike were in rebellion against it. "If I study Philosophy," he says, "with a view only to its literature, I am not a philosopher, but a *litterateur*, the only difference is, that I interpret Chrysippus instead of Homer."[22] They sometimes protested not only against the degradation of Philosophy, but also against the whole conception of literary education. "There are two kinds of education," says Dio Chrysostom,[23] " the one divine, the other human; the divine is great and powerful and easy; the human is mean and weak, and has many dangers and no small deceitfulness. The mass of people call it education (*paideian*), as being, I suppose, an amusement (*paidian*) and think that a man who knows most literature — Persian and Greek and Syrian and Phoenician — is the wisest and best-educated man; and then, on the other hand, when they find a man of this sort to be vicious and cowardly and fond of money, they think the education to be as worthless as the man himself. The other

---

[21] There is a good example of the former of these methods in Maximus of Tyre, *Dissert*. 33.

[22] *Enchir*. 49: see also *Diss*. 3. 21.

[23] *Orat*. iv. vol i. p 69, ed. Dind.

kind they call sometimes education, and sometimes manliness and high-mindedness. It was thus that the men of old used to call those who had this good kind of education — men with manly souls, and educated as Herakles was — sons of God." And not less significant as an indication not only of the reaction against this kind of education but also of its prevalence, is the deprecation of it by Marcus Aurelius: "I owe it to Rusticus," he says,[24] " that I formed the idea of the need of moral reformation, and that I was not diverted to literary ambition, or to write treatises on philosophical subjects, or to make rhetorical exhortations .... and that I kept away from rhetoric and poetry and foppery of speech."

II. I pass from the forms of education to its extent. The general diffusion of it, and the hold which it had upon the mass of men, are shown by many kinds of evidence.

1. They are shown by the large amount of literary evidence as to scholars and the modes of obtaining education. The exclusiveness of the old aristocracy had broken down. Education was no longer in the hands of " private tutors" in the houses of the great families. It entered public life, and in doing so left a record behind it. It may be inferred from the extant evidence that there were grammar-schools in almost every town. At these all youths received the first part of their education. But it became a common practice for youths to supplement this by attending the lectures of an eminent professor elsewhere. They went, as we might say, from school to a University.[25] The students who so went away

---

[24] i.7.

[25] This higher education was not confined to Rome or Athens, but was found in many parts of the empire: Marseilles in the

from home were drawn from all classes of the community. Some of them were very poor, and, like the "*bettelstudenten*" of the medieval Universities, had sometimes to beg their bread.[26] "You are a miserable race," says Epictetus[27] to some students of this kind; "when you have eaten your fill today, you sit down whining about to-morrow, where to-morrow's dinner will come from." Some of them went because it was the fashion. The young sybarites of Rome or Athens complained bitterly that at Nicopolis, where they had gone to listen to Epictetus, lodgings were bad, and the baths were bad, and the gymnasium was bad, and "society" hardly existed.[28] Then, as now, there were home-sick students, and mothers weeping over their absence, and letters that were looked for but never came, and letters that brought bad

---

time of Strabo was even more frequented than Athens. There were other great schools at Antioch and Alexandria, at Rhodes and Smyrna, at Ephesus and Byzantium, at Naples and Nicopolis, at Bordeaux and Autun. The practice of resorting to such schools lasted long. In the fourth century and among the Christian Fathers, Basil and Gregory Nazianzen, Augustine and Jerome, are recorded to have followed it: the general recognition of Christianity did not seriously affect the current educational system: "Through the whole world," says Augustine, "the schools of the rhetoricians are alive with the din of crowds of students."

[26] There is an interesting instance, at a rather later time, of the poverty of two students, one of whom afterwards became famous, Prohaeresius and Hephaestion: they had only one ragged gown between them, so that while one went to lecture, the other had to stay at home in bed (Eunap. *Prohaeres*, p. 78).

[27] *Diss*. 1.9.19.

[28] *Ib*. 2.21.12; 3.24.54

news; and young men of promise who were expected to return home as living encyclopedias, but who only raised doubts when they did return home whether their education had done them any good.[29] Then, as now, they went from the lecture-room to athletic sports or the theatre; "and the consequence is," says Epictetus,[30] "that you don't get out of your old habits or make moral progress." Then, as now, some students went, not for the sake of learning, but in order to be able to show off. Epictetus draws a picture of one who looked forward to airing his logic at a city dinner, astonishing the "alderman" who sat next to him with the puzzles of hypothetical syllogisms.[31] And then, as now, those who had followed the fashion by attending lectures showed by their manner that they were there against their will. "You should sit upright," says Plutarch,[32] in his advice to hearers in general, "not lolling, or whispering, or smiling, or yawning as if you were asleep, or fixing your eyes on the ground instead of on the speaker." In a similar way Philo,[33] also speaking of hearers in general, says: "Many persons who come to a lecture do not bring their minds inside with them, but go wandering about outside, thinking ten thousand things about ten thousand different subjects — family affairs, other people's affairs, private affairs, ... and the professor talks to an audience, as it were, not of men but of statues, which have ears but hear not."

---

[29] *Ib*. 2.21.12, 13, 15; 3.24.22, 24.

[30] *Ib*. 3.16.14, 15.

[31] *Ib*. 1.26.9.

[32] *De audiendo*, 13, vol. ii. p. 45. The passage is abridged above.

[33] *Quis rer. Div. heres* 3, vol. i. p. 474.

2. A second indication of the hold which education had upon the age is the fact that teaching had come to be a recognized and lucrative profession. This is shown not so much by the instances of individual teachers,[34] who might be regarded as exceptional, as by the fact of the recognition of teachers by the State and by municipalities.

The recognition by the State took the double form of endowment and of immunities from public burdens.

(a) Endowments probably began with Vespasian, who endowed teachers of Rhetoric at Rome with an annual grant of 100,000 sesterces from the imperial treasury. Hadrian founded an Athenaeum or University at Rome, like the Museum or University at Alexandria, with an adequate income, and with a building of sufficient importance to be sometimes used as a Senate-house. He also gave large sums to the professors at Athens: in this he was followed by Antoninus Pius: but the first permanent endowment at Athens seems to have been that of Marcus Aurelius, who founded two chairs in each of the four great philosophical schools of Athens, the Academic, the Peripatetic, the Epicurean, and the Stoic, and added one of the new or literary Rhetoric, and one of the old or forensic Rhetoric.

----

[34] For example, Verrius Flaccus, the father of the system of "prize essays," who received an annual salary of 100,000 sesterces from Augustus (*Suet. de illustr. Gramm.* 17). The inscriptions of Asia Minor furnish several instances of teachers who had left their homes to teach in other provinces of the Empire, and had returned rich enough to make presents to their native cities.

(b) The immunities of the teaching classes began with Julius Caesar, and appear to have been so amply recognized in the early empire that Antoninus Pius placed them upon a footing which at once established and limited them. He enacted that small cities might place upon the free list five physicians, three teachers of rhetoric, and three of literature; that assize towns might so place seven physicians, three teachers of rhetoric, and three of literature; and that metropolitan cities might so place ten physicians, five teachers of rhetoric, and five of literature; but that these numbers should not be exceeded. These immunities were a form of indirect endowment.[35] They exempted those whom they affected from all the burdens which tended in the later empire to impoverish the middle and upper classes. They were consequently equivalent to the gift from the municipality of a considerable annual income.

3. A third indication of the hold of education upon contemporary society is the place which its professors held in social intercourse. They were not only a recognized class; they also mingled largely, by virtue of their profession, with ordinary life. If a dinner of any pretensions were given, the professor of Belles Lettres must be there to recite and expound passages of poetry, the Professor of Rhetoric to speak upon any theme which might be proposed to him, and the professor of Philosophy to read a discourse upon morals. A "sermonette" from one of these professional philosophers after dinner was as much in fashion as a piece of vocal or instrumental music is with us.[36] All three kinds of professors

---

[35] The edict of Antoninus Pius is contained in L. 6, § 2, D. *de excusat.* 27.1.

were sometimes part of the permanent retinue of a great household. But the philosophers were even more in fashion than their brother professors. They were petted by great ladies. They became "domestic chaplains."[37] They were sometimes, indeed, singularly like the chaplains of whom we read in novels of the last century. Lucian, in his essay "On Persons who give their Society for Pay," has some amusing vignettes of their life. One is of a philosopher who has to accompany his patroness on a tour: he is put into a wagon with the cook and the lady's-maid, and there is but a scanty allowance of leaves thrown in to ease his limbs against the jolting.[38] Another is of a philosopher who is summoned by his lady and complimented, and asked as an especial favor, "You are so very kind and careful: will you take my lapdog into the wagon with you, and see that the poor creature does not want for anything?"[39] Another is of a philosopher who has to discourse on temperance while his lady is having her hair braided: her maid comes in with a *billet-doux* and the discourse on temperance is suspended until she has written

---

[36] Lucian's *Convivium* is a humorous and satirical description of such a dinner. The philosopher reads his discourse from a small, finely-written manuscript, c. 17. The *Deipnosophistae* of Athenaeus, and the *Questiones Conviviales* of Plutarch, are important literary monuments of the practice.

[37] An interesting corroboration of the literary references is afforded by the mosaic pavement of a large villa at Hammam Grous, near Milev, in North Africa, where "the philosopher's apartment," or "chaplain's room, is specially marked, and near it is a lady (the mistress of the house) sitting under a palm-tree.

[38] Lucian, *de merc. cond.* 32.

[39] *Ib.* 34.

an answer to her lover.[40] Another is of a philosopher who only gets his pay in doles of two or three pence at a time, and is thought a bore if he asks for it, and whose tailor or shoemaker is meanwhile waiting to be paid, so that even when the money comes it seems to do him no good.[41] It is natural to find that Philosophy, which had thus become a profession, had also become degenerate. It afforded an easy means of livelihood. It was natural that some of those who adopted it should be a disgrace to their profession. And although it would be unsafe to take every description of the great satirist literally, yet it is difficult to believe that there is not a substantial foundation of truth in his frequent caricatures. The fact of their frequency, and also the fact that such men as he describes could exist, strengthen the inference which other facts enable us to draw, as to the large place which the professional philosophers occupied in contemporary society. The following is his picture of Thrasycles:[42]

> "He comes along with his beard spread out and his eyebrows raised, talking solemnly to himself, with a Titan-like look in his eyes, with his hair thrown back from his forehead, the very picture of Boreas or Triton, as Zeuxis painted them. This is the man who in the morning dresses himself simply, and walks sedately, and wears a sober gown, and preaches long sermons about virtue, and inveighs against the votaries of pleasure: then he has his bath

---

[40] *Ib.* 36.

[41] *Ib.* 38.

[42] *Timon*, 50, 51.

and goes to dinner, and the butler offers him a
large goblet of wine, and he drinks it down
with as much gusto as if it were the water of
Lethe: and he behaves in exactly the opposite
way to his sermons of the morning, for he
snatches all the tit-bits like a hawk, and elbows
his neighbor out of the way, and he peers into
the dishes with as keen an eye as if he were
likely to find Virtue herself in them; and he
goes on preaching all the time about
temperance and moderation, until he is so
dead-drunk that the servants have to carry him
out. Nay, besides this, there is not a man to
beat him in the way of lying and braggadocio
and avarice: he is the first of flatterers and the
readiest of perjurers: chicanery leads the way,
and impudence follows after: in fact, he is
clever all round, doing to perfection whatever
he touches."

4. But nothing could more conclusively prove the great
hold which these forms of education had upon their time
than the fact of their persistent survival. It might be
maintained that the prominence which is given to them in
literature, their endowment by the State, and their social
influence, represented only a superficial and passing phase.
But when the product of one generation spreads its branches
far and wide into the generations that succeed, its roots must
be deep and firm in the generation from which it springs. No
lasting element of civilization grows upon the surface. Greek
education has been almost as permanent as Christianity
itself, and for similar reasons. It passed from Greece into
Africa and the West. It had an especial hold first on the
Roman and then upon the Celtic and Teutonic populations

of Gaul; and from the Galilean schools it has come, probably by direct descent, to our own country and our own time.

Two things especially have come:

(i.) The place which literature holds in general education. We educate our sons in grammar, and in doing so we feed them upon ancient rather than upon English literature, by simple continuation of the first branch of the medieval *trivium*, which was itself a continuation of the Greek habit which has been described above.

(ii.) The other point, though less important in itself, is even more important as indicating the strength of the Greek educational system. It is that we retain still its technical terms and many of its scholastic usages, either in their original Greek form or as translated into Latin and modified by Latin habits, in the schools of the West.

The designation "professor" comes to us from the Greek sophists, who drew their pupils by promises: to "profess" was to "promise," and to promise was the characteristic of the class of teachers with whom in the fourth century B.C. Greek education began. The title lost its original force, and became the general designation of a public teacher, superseding the special titles, "philosopher," "sophist," "rhetorician," "grammarian," and ending by being the synonym of "doctor."[43]

The practice of lecturing, that is of giving instruction by reading an ancient author, with longer or shorter comments

---

[43] Pliny, *Ep*. 4. 11. 1.

upon his meaning, comes to us from the schools in which a passage of Homer or Plato or Chrysippus was read and explained. The "lecture" was probably in the first instance a student's exercise: the function of the teacher was to make remarks or to give his judgment upon the explanation that was given: it was not so much *legere* as *praelegere*, whence the existing title of "praelector."[44]

The use of the word "chair" to designate the teacher's office, and of the word "faculty" to denote the branch of knowledge which he teaches, are similar survivals of Greek terms.

The use of academical designations as titles is also Greek: it was written upon a man's tombstone that he was "philosopher" or "sophist," "grammarian" or "rhetorician," as in later times he would be designated M.A. or D.D.[45] The most interesting of these designations is that of "sophist." The long academical history of the word only ceased at Oxford a few years ago, when the clauses relating to "sophistae generales" were erased as obsolete from the statute-book.

The restriction of the right to teach, and the mode of testing a man's qualifications to teach, have come to us from the same source. The former is probably a result of the fact

---

[44] an early use of praelector in this sense is Quintil. 1.8.13.

[45] Hispania Tarraconensis, *Corpus Inscr*. Lat. ii. 2892, 5079; *ibid*. 3872; *ibid*. 2236; *Corpus Inser. Graec*. 1253; *ibid*. 3163 (dated a.d. 211), 3198, 3865, add. 4366; *ibid*. 4817; *ibid*. 1628; *ibid*. 5783.

which has been mentioned above, that the teachers of liberal arts were privileged and endowed. The State guarded against the abuse of the privilege, as in subsequent times for similar reasons it put limitations upon the appointment of the Christian clergy. In the case of some of the professors at Athens who were endowed from the imperial chest, the Emperors seem to have exercised a certain right of nomination, as in our own country the Crown nominates a "Regius Professor;"[46] but in the case of others of those professors, the nomination was in the hands of "the best and oldest and wisest in the city," that is, either the Areopagus, or the City Council, or, as some have thought, a special Board.[47] Elsewhere, and apparently without exception in later times, the right of approval of a teacher was in the hands of the City Council,[48] the ordinary body for the administration of municipal affairs.[49] The authority which conferred the right might also take it away: a teacher who proved incompetent might have his license withdrawn.[50] The

[46] Marcus Aurelius himself nominated Theodotus to be "Regius Professor of Rhetoric," but he entrusted the nomination of the Professors of Philosophy to Herodes Atticus, Philostrat. V.S.2.3, p. 240; and Commodus nominated Polydeuces, *ibid.* 2.12, p. 258.

[47] Lucian, *Eunuchus*, 3.

[48] The existence of a competition appears in Lucian, *Eunuchus*, 8, 5: the fullest account is that of Eunapius, *Prohcaeres.* pp. 79 sqq.

[49] This was fixed by a law of Julian in 362.

[50] This is mentioned in a law of Gordian: *Cod. Justin.* 10.52, 2. A professor was sometimes removed for other reasons besides incompetency, e.g. Prohraesius was removed by Julian for being a Christian, Eunap. *Prohaeres.* p. 92.

testing of qualifications preceded the admission to office. It was sometimes superseded by a sort of *congé d'élire* from the Emperor;[51] but in ordinary cases it consisted in the candidate's giving a lecture or taking part in a discussion before either the Emperor's representative or the City Council. It was the small beginning of that system of "examination" which in our own country and time has grown to enormous proportions. The successful candidate was sometimes escorted to his house, as a mark of honor, by the proconsul and the "examiners," just as in Oxford, until the present generation, a "grand compounder" might claim to be escorted home by the Vice-chancellor and Proctors.[52] In the fourth century appear to have come restrictions not only upon teaching, but also upon studying: a student might probably go to a lecture, but he might not formally announce his devotion to learning by putting on the student's gown without the leave of the professors, as in a modern University a student must be formally enrolled before he can assume the academical dress.[53]

---

[51] Alexander of Aphrodisias, *de Fato*, 1, says that he obtained his professorship on the testimony of Severus and Caracalla.

[52] Eunapius, *ibid*. p. 84.

[53] Olympiodorus, ap. Phot. *Biblioth*. 80; S. Greg. Naz. *Orat*. 43 (20). 15, vol. i. p. 782; Liban. *de fort. sua*, vol. i. p. 14. The admission was probably the occasion of some academical sport: the novice was marched in mock procession to the baths, whence he came out with his gown on. It was something like initiation into a religious guild or order. There was a law against anyone who assumed the philosopher's dress without authority, *Cod. Theodos*. 13.3.7.

The survival of these terms and usages, as indicating the strength of the system to which they originally belonged, is emphasized by the fact that for a long interval of time there are few, if any, traces of them.[54] They are found in full force in Gaul in the fifth and sixth centuries: they are found again when education began to revive on a large scale in the tenth century: they then appear, not as new creations, but as terms and usages which had lasted all through what has been called "the Benedictine era,"[55] without special nurture and without literary expression, by the sheer persistency of their original roots.

This is the feature of the Greek life into which Christianity came to which I first invite your attention. There was a complex system of education, the main elements in which were the knowledge of literature, the cultivation of literary expression, and a general acquaintance with the rules of argument. This education was widely diffused, and had a great hold upon society. It had been at work in its main outlines for several centuries. Its effect in the second century of our era had been to create a certain habit of mind. When Christianity came into contact with the society in which that habit of mind existed, it modified, it reformed, it elevated, the ideas which it contained and the motives which stimulated it to action; but in its turn it was itself profoundly modified by the habit of mind of those who accepted it. It was impossible for Greeks, educated as they were with an

---

[54] The last traces are in the Christian poets: for example, in Sidonius Apollinaris (482), *Carm.* xxiii. 211, ed. Luetjohann.

[55] Leon Maitre, *Les ecoles episcopales et monastiques de l'Occident*, p. 173.

education which penetrated their whole nature, to receive or to retain Christianity in its primitive simplicity. Their own life had become complex and artificial: it had its fixed ideas and its permanent categories: it necessarily gave to Christianity something of its own form. The world of the time was a world, I will not say like our own world, which has already burst its bonds, but like the world from which we are beginning to be emancipated — a world which had created an artificial type of life, and which was too artificial to be able to recognize its own artificiality — a world whose schools, instead of being the laboratories of the knowledge of the future, were forges in which the chains of the present were fashioned from the knowledge of the past. And if, on the one hand, it incorporated Christianity with the larger humanity from which it had at first been isolated, yet, on the other hand, by crushing uncultivated earnestness, and by laying more stress on the expression of ideas than upon ideas themselves, it tended to stem the very forces which had given Christianity its place, and to change the rushing torrent of the river of God into a broad but feeble stream.

Lecture III. GREEK AND CHRISTIAN EXEGESIS.

Two thousand years ago, the Greek world was nearer than we are now to the first wonder of the invention of writing. The mystery of it still seemed divine. The fact that certain signs, of little or no meaning in themselves, could communicate what a man felt or thought, not only to the generation of his fellows, but also to the generations that came afterwards, threw a kind of glamour over written words. It gave them an importance and an impressiveness which did not attach to any spoken words. They came in time to have, as it were, an existence of their own. Their precise relation to the person who first uttered them, and their literal meaning at the time of their utterance, tended to be overlooked or obscured.

In the case of the ancient poets, especially Homer, this glamour of written words was accompanied, and perhaps had been preceded, by two other feelings.

The one was the reverence for antiquity. The voice of the past sounded with a fuller note than that of the present. It came from the age of the heroes who had become divinities. It expressed the national legends and the current mythology, the primitive types of noble life and the simple maxims of awakening reflection, the "wisdom of the ancients," which has sometimes itself taken the place of religion. The other was the belief in inspiration. With the glamour of writing was blended the glamour of rhythm and melody. When the gods spoke, they spoke in verse.[56] The poets sang under the impulse of a divine enthusiasm. It was a god who gave the words: the poet was but the interpreter.[57] The belief was not merely popular, but was found in the best minds of the imperial age. "Whatever wise and true words were spoken in the world about God and the universe, came into the souls of men not without the Divine will and intervention through the agency of divine and prophetic men."[58] "To the poets sometimes, I mean the very ancient poets, there came a brief utterance from the Muses, a kind of inspiration of the divine nature and truth, like a flash of light from an unseen fire."[59]

The combination of these three feelings, the mystery of writing, the reverence for antiquity, the belief in inspiration, tended to give the writings of the ancient poets a unique value. It lifted them above the common limitations of place and time and circumstance. The verses of Homer were not simply the utterances of a particular person with a particular meaning for a particular time. They had a universal validity. They were the voice of an undying wisdom. They were the Bible of the Greek races.[60]

---

[56] Hor. *A. P.* 403.

[57] Cf. e.g. Pindar, *Frag.* 127 (118), and, in later times, Aelius Aristides, vol. iii. P. 22, ed. Cant.

[58] Dio Chrysostom, *Orat.* i. vol. i. p. 12, ed. Dind.

[59] Id. *Orat.* xxxvi. vol. ii. p. 99.

[60] It was a natural result of the estimation in which he was held that he should sometimes have been regarded as being not only inspired, but divine: the passages which refer to this are collected in G. Cuper, *Apotheosis vel consecratio Homeri* (in vol. ii. of Polenus' Supplement. to Gronovius' *Thesaurus*), which is primarily a commentary on the bas-relief by Archelaus

When the unconscious imitation of heroic ideals passed into a conscious philosophy of life, it was necessary that that philosophy should be shown to be consonant with current beliefs, by being formulated, so to speak, in terms of the current standards; and when, soon afterwards, the conception of education, in the sense in which the term has ever since been understood, arose, it was inevitable that the ancient poets should be the basis of that education. Literature consisted, in effect, of the ancient poets. Literary education necessarily meant the understanding of them. "I consider," says Protagoras, in the Platonic dialogue which bears his name,[61] "that the chief part of a man's education is to be skilled in epic poetry; and this means that he should be able to understand what the poets have said, and whether they have said it rightly or not, and to know how to draw distinctions, and to give an answer when a question is put to him." The educators recognized in Homer one of themselves: he, too, was a "sophist," and had aimed at educating men.[62] Homer was the common text-book of the grammar-schools as long as Greek continued to be taught, far on into imperial times. The study of him branched out in more than one direction. It was the beginning of that study

---

of Priene, now in the British Museum. The idea has existed in much more recent times, not indeed that he was divine, but that so much truth and wisdom could not have existed outside Judea. There is, for example, a treatise by G. Croesus which endeavors to prove both that the name Homer is a Hebrew word, that the Iliad is an account of the conquest of Canaan, and 'that the Odyssey is a narrative of the wanderings of the children of Israel up to the death of Moses.

[61] Plat. *Protag.* 72, p. 339 a.

[62] *Ibid.* 22, p. 5170.

of literature for its own sake which still holds its ground. It was continued until far on in the Christian era, partly by the schools of textual critics, and partly by the successors of the first sophists, who sharpened their wits by disputations as to Homer's meaning, posing difficulties and solving them: of these disputations some relics survive in the Scholia, especially such as are based upon the *Questions* of Porphyry. But in the first conception, literary and moral education had been inseparable. It was impossible to regard Homer simply as literature. Literary education was not an end in itself, but a means. The end was moral training. It was imagined that virtue, no less than literature, could be taught, and Homer was the basis of the one kind of education no less than of the other. Nor was it difficult for him to become so. For though the thoughts of men had changed, and the new education was bringing in new conceptions of morals, Homer was a force which could easily be turned in new directions. All imaginative literature is plastic when it is used to enforce a moral; and the sophists could easily preach sermons of their own upon Homeric texts. There was no fixed traditional interpretation; and they were but following a current fashion in drawing their own meanings from him. He thus became a support, and not a rival. The *Hippias Minor* of Plato furnishes as pertinent instances as could be mentioned of this educational use of Homer.

The method lasted as long as Greek literature. It is found in full operation in the first centuries of our era. It was explicitly recognized, and most of the prominent writers of the time supply instances of its application. "In the childhood of the world," says Strabo,[63] "men, like children, had to be taught by tales;" and Homer told tales with a moral purpose. "It has been contended," he says again,[64] "that poetry was meant only to please:" on the contrary, the ancients looked upon poetry as a form of philosophy, introducing us early to the facts of life, and teaching us in a pleasant way the characters and feelings and actions of men. It was from Homer that moralists drew their ideals: it was his verses that were quoted, like verses of the Bible with us, to enforce moral truths. There is in Dio Chrysostom[65] a charming "imaginary conversation" between Philip and Alexander. "How is it," said the father, "that Homer is the only poet you care for: there are others who ought not to be neglected?" "Because," said the son, "it is not every kind of poetry, just as it is not every kind of dress, that is fitting for a king; and the poetry of Homer is the only poetry that I see to be truly noble and splendid and regal, and fit for one who will someday rule over men." And Dio himself reads into Homer many a moral meaning. When, for example,[66] the poet speaks of the son of Kronos having given the staff and rights of a chief that he might take counsel for the people, he meant to imply that not all kings, but only those who have a special gift of God, had that staff and those rights, and that they had them, moreover, not for their own gratification, but for the general good; he meant, in fact, that no bad man can be a true master either of himself or of others — no, not if all the Greeks and all the barbarians join in calling him king.

---

[63] Strab. 1.2.8.

[64] Id. 1.2.3.

[65] Dio Chrys. *Orat.* 2, vol. i. pp. 19, 20.

[66] Dio Chrys. *Orat.* 1, vol. i. p. 3.

It was not only the developing forms of ethics that were thus made to find a support in Homer, but all the varying theories of physics and metaphysics, one by one. The Heracliteans held, for example, that when Homer spoke of "Ocean, the birth of gods, and Tethys their mother," he meant to say that all things are the offspring of flow and movement.[67] The Platonists held that when Zeus reminded Hera of the time when he had hung her trembling by a golden chain in the vast concave of heaven, it was God speaking to matter which he had taken and bound by the chains of laws.[68] The Stoics read into the poets so much Stoicism, that Cicero says, in good-humored banter, that you would think the old poets, who had really no suspicion of such things, to have been Stoical philosophers.[69] Sometimes Homer was treated as a kind of encyclopedia. Xenophon, in his *Banquet*,[70] makes one of the speakers, who could repeat Homer by heart, say that "the wisest of mankind had written about almost all human things;" and there is a treatise by an unknown author of imperial times which endeavors to show in detail that he contains the beginning of every one of the later sciences, historical, philosophical, and political.[71] When

---

[67] Plat. *Theat*. 9, p. 152d, quoting Hom. *Il*. 14. 201—302. In later times, the same verse was quoted as having suggested and supported the theory of Thales, Irenaeus, 2.14 ; Theodoret, *Grac. Affect. Cur.* 2. 9.

[68] Celsus in Origen, *c. Cels*. 6. 42, referring to Hom. *Il*. 15. 18 sqq.

[69] Cic. *N. D.* 1.15.

[70] Xen. *Sympos*. 4.6; 3. 5.

[71] Ps-Plutarch, *de vita et poesi Homeri*, vol. v. pp. 1056 sqq.,

he calls men deep-voiced and women high-voiced, he shows his knowledge of the distinctions of music. When he gives to each character its appropriate style of speech, he shows his knowledge of rhetoric. He is the father of political science, in having given examples of each of the three forms of government — monarchy, aristocracy, democracy. He is the father of military science, in the information which he gives about tactics and siege-works. He knew and taught astronomy and medicine, gymnastics and surgery; "nor would a man be wrong if he were to say that he was a teacher of painting also."

This indifference to the actual meaning of a writer, and the habit of reading him by the light of the reader's own fancies, have a certain analogy in our own day in the feeling with which we sometimes regard other works of art. We stand before some great masterpiece of painting — the St. Cecilia or the Sistine Madonna — and are, as it were, carried off our feet by the wonder of it. We must be cold critics if we simply ask ourselves what Raffaele meant by it. We interpret it by our own emotions. The picture speaks to us with a personal and individual voice. It links itself with a thousand memories of the past and a thousand dreams of the future. It translates us into another world — the world of a lost and impossible love, the dreamland of achieved aspirations, the tender and half-tearful heaven of forgiven sins: we are ready to believe, if only for a moment, that Raffaele meant by it all that it means to us; and for what he did actually mean, we have but little care.

---

chapters 148, 164, 182, 192, 216.

But these tendencies to draw a moral from all that Homer wrote, and to read philosophy into it, though common and permanent, were not universal. There was an instinct in the Greek mind, as there is in modern times, which rebelled against them. There were literalists who insisted that the words should be taken as they stood, and that some of the words as they stood were clearly immoral.[72] There were, on the other hand, apologists who said sometimes that Homer reflected faithfully the checkered lights and shadows of human life, and sometimes that the existence of immorality in Homer must clearly be allowed, but that if a balance were struck between the good and the evil, the good would be found largely to predominate.[73] There were other apologists who made a distinction between the divine and the human elements: the poets sometimes spoke, it was said, on their own account: some of their poetry was inspired, and some was not: the Muses sometimes left them: "and they may very properly be forgiven if, being men, they made mistakes when the divinity which spoke through their mouths had gone away from them." [74]

But all these apologies were insufficient. The chasm between the older religion which was embodied in the poets, and the new ideas which were marching in steady progress away from the Homeric world, was widening day by day. A

---

[72] The earliest expression of this feeling is that of Xenophanes, which is twice quoted by Sextus Empiricus, *adv. Gramm.* 1. 288, *adv. Phys.* 9 193.

[73] Plutarch, *de aud. poet.* c. 4, pp. 24, 25.

[74] Lucian, *Jupit confut.* 2.

reconciliation had to be found which had deeper roots. It was found in a process of interpretation whose strength must be measured by its permanence. The process was based upon a natural tendency. The unseen working of the will which lies behind all voluntary actions, and the unseen working of thought which by an instinctive process causes some of those actions to be symbolical, led men in comparatively early times to find a meaning beneath the surface of a record or representation of actions. A narrative of actions, no less than the actions themselves, might be symbolical. It might contain a hidden meaning. Men who retained their reverence for Homer, or who at least were not prepared to break with the current belief in him, began to search for such meanings. They were assisted in doing so by the concomitant development of the "mysteries." The mysteries were representations of passages in the history of the gods which, whatever their origin, had become symbolical. It is possible that no words of explanation were spoken in them; but they were, notwithstanding, habituating the Greek mind both to symbolical expression in general, and to the finding of physical or religious or moral truths in the representation of fantastic or even immoral actions.[75]

---

[75] The connection of allegory with the mysteries was recognized: Heraclitus Ponticus, c. 6, justifies his interpretation of Apollo as the sun, ps-Demetrius Phalereus, *de interpret*. c. 99, 101, ap. Walz, *Rhett. Gr.* ix. p. 47, so Macrobius, in *Somn. Scip.* 1.2, after an account of the way in which the poets veiled truths in symbols. That a physical explanation lay behind the scenery of the mysteries is stated elsewhere, e.g. by Theodoret, *Grec. Affect. Cur.* i. vol. iv. p. 721, without being connected with the allegorical explanation of the poets.

It is uncertain when this method of interpretation began to be applied to ancient literature. It was part of the general intellectual movement of the fifth century B.C. It is found in one of its forms in Hecataeus, who explained the story of Cerberus by the existence of a poisonous snake in a cavern on the headland of Tainaron.[76] It was elaborated by the sophists. It was deprecated by Plato. "If I disbelieved it," he makes Socrates say,[77] in reference to the story of Boreas and Oreithyia, "as the philosophers do, I should not be unreasonable: then I might say, talking like a philosopher, that Oreithyia was a girl who was caught by a strong wind and carried off while playing on the cliffs yonder; … but it would take a long and laborious and not very happy lifetime to deal with all such questions: and for my own part I cannot investigate them until, as the Delphian precept bids me, I first Know myself." Nor will he admit allegorical interpretation as a sufficient vindication of Homer:[78] "The chaining of Hera, and the flinging forth of Hephoestus by his father, and all the fightings of gods which Homer has described, we shall not admit into our state, whether with allegories or without them." But the direct line of historical tradition of the method seems to begin with Anaxagoras and his school.[79] In Anaxagoras himself the allegory was probably ethical: he found in Homer a symbolical account of

---

[76] Pausan. 3.25.4—6.

[77] Plat. *Phedr*. p. 329 c.

[78] Plat. *Resp*. p. 378 d.

[79] Diogenes Laertius, 2. 11, quotes Favorinus as saying that Anaxagoras was the first who showed that the poems of Homer had virtue and righteousness for their subject.

the movements of mental powers and moral virtues: Zeus was mind, Athene was art. But the method which, though it is found in germ among earlier or contemporary writers, seems to have been first formulated by his disciple Metrodorus, was not ethical but physical.[80] By a remarkable anticipation of a modern science, possibly by a survival of memories of an earlier religion, the Homeric stories were treated as a symbolical representation of physical phenomena. The gods were the powers of nature: their gatherings, their movements, their loves, and their battles, were the play and interaction and apparent strife of natural forces. The method had for many centuries an enormous hold upon the Greek mind; it lay beneath the whole theology of the Stoical schools; it was largely current among the scholars and critics of the early empire.[81]

Its most detailed exposition is contained in two writers of both of whom so little is personally known that there is a division of opinion whether the name of the one was Heraclitus or Heraclides,[82] and of the other Cornutus or

---

[80] Diog. Laert. 2. 11: Tatian, *Orat. ad Gracos*, c. 21. A later tradition used the name of Pherecydes: Isidore, son of Basilides, in Clem. Alex. *Strom.* 6, p. 767.

[81] On the general subject of allegorical interpretation, especially in regard to Homer, reference may be made to N. Schow in the edition of Heraclitus Ponticus mentioned below.

[82] The most recent edition is Heracliti *Allegorie Homerice*, ed. E. Mehler, Leyden, 1851: that of N. Schow, Gottingen, 1782, contains a Latin translation, a good essay on Homeric allegory, and a critical letter by Heyne. It seems probable that the treatise is really anonymous, and that the name Heraclitus was intended to be that of the philosopher of Ephesus: see Diels, *Doxographi Graci*, p. 95 n.

Phornutus;[83] but both were Stoics, both are most probably assigned to the early part of the first century of our era, and in both of them the physical is blended with an ethical interpretation.

1. Heraclitus begins by the definite avowal of his apologetic purpose. His work is a vindication of Homer from the charge of impiety. "He would unquestionably be impious if he were not allegorical;"[84] but as it is, "there is no stain of unholy fables in his words: they are pure and free from impiety."[85] Apollo is the sun; the "far-darter" is the sun sending forth his rays: when it is said that Apollo slew men with his arrows, it is meant that there was a pestilence in the heat of summertime.[86] Athene is thought: when it is said that Athene came to Telemachus, it is meant only that the young man then first began to reflect upon the waste and profligacy of the suitors: a thought, shaped like a wise old man, came, as it were, and sat by his side.[87] The story of Proteus and Eidothea is an allegory of the original formless matter taking many shapes:[88] the story of Ares and Aphrodite and

---

[83] The most recent, and best critical, edition is by C. Lang, ed. 1881, in Teubner's series. More help is afforded to an ordinary student by that which was edited from the notes of de Villoison by Osann, Gittingen, 1844.

[84] c. 1.

[85] c. 2.

[86] c. 8.

[87] c. 61.

[88] c. 66.

Hephaestus is a picture of iron subdued by fire, and restored to its original hardness by Poseidon, that is by water.[89]

2. Cornutus writes in vindication not so much of the piety of the ancients as of their knowledge: they knew as much as men of later times, but they expressed it at greater length and by means of symbols. He rests his interpretation of those symbols to a large extent upon etymology. The science of religion was to him, as it has been to some persons in modern days, an extension of the science of philology. The following are examples: Hermes (from *erein*, "to speak") is the power of speech which the gods sent from heaven as their peculiar and distinguishing gift to men. He is called the "conductor," because speech conducts one man's thought into his neighbor's soul. He is the "brightshiner," because speech makes dark things clear. His winged feet are the symbols of "winged words." He is the "leader of souls," because words soothe the soul to rest; and the "awakener from sleep," because words rouse men to action. The serpents twined round his staff are a symbol of the savage natures that are calmed by words, and their discords gathered into harmony.[90] The story of Prometheus ("forethought"), who made a man from clay, is an allegory of the providence and forethought of the universe: he is said to have stolen fire, because it was the forethought of men found out its use: he is said to have stolen it from heaven, because it came down in a lightning-flash: and his being chained to a rock is a picture of the quick inventiveness of

---

[89] c. 69.

[90] c. 16.

human thought chained to the painful necessities of physical life, its liver gnawed at unceasingly by petty cares.[91]

Two other examples of the method may be given from later writers, to show the variety of its application.

The one is from Sallust, a writer of the fourth century of our era. He thus explains the story of the judgment of Paris. The banquet of the gods is a picture of the vast supra-mundane Powers, who are always in each other's society. The apple is the world, which is thrown from the banquet by Discord, because the world itself is the play of opposing forces; and different qualities are given to the world by different Powers, each trying to win the world for itself; and Paris is the soul in its sensuous life, which sees not the other Powers in the world, but only Beauty, and says that the world is the property of Love.[92]

The other is from a writer of a late but uncertain age. He deals only with the Odyssey. Its hero is the picture of a man who is tossed upon the sea of life, drifted this way and that by adverse winds of fortune and of passion: the companions who were lost among the Lotophagi are pictures of men who are caught by the baits of pleasure and do not return to reason as their guide: the Sirens are the pleasures that tempt and allure all men who j)ass over the sea of life, and against which the only counter-charm is to fill one's senses and powers of mind full of divine words and actions, as

---

[91] c. 18.

[92] Sallust, *de diis et mundo*, c. 4, in Mullach, *Fragmenta Philosophorum Grecorum*, vol. iii. p. 32.

Odysseus filled his ears with wax, that, no part of them being left empty pleasure may knock at their doors in vain.[93]

The method survived as a literary habit long after its original purpose failed. The mythology which it had been designed to vindicate passed from the sphere of religion into that of literature; but in so passing, it took with it the method to which it had given rise. The habit of trying to find an *arriere pensee* beneath a man's actual words had become so inveterate, that all great writers without distinction were treated as writers of riddles. The literary class insisted that their functions were needed as interpreters, and that a plain man could not know what a great writer meant. "The use of symbolical speech," said Didymus, the great grammarian of the Augustan age, "is characteristic of the wise man, and the explanation of its meaning."[94] Even Thucydides is said by his biographer to have purposely made his style obscure that he might not be accessible except to the truly wise.[95] It tended to become a fixed idea in the minds of many men that religious truth especially must be wrapped up in symbol, and that symbol must contain religious truth. The idea has so far descended to the present day, that there are, even now, persons who think that a truth which is obscurely stated is more worthy of respect, and more likely to be divine, than a truth which "he that runs may read."

---

[93] *Incerti Scriptoris Graci Fabule aliquot Homerice de Ulixis erroribus ethice explicate,* ed. J. Columbus, Leiden, 1745.

[94] Clem. Alex. *Strom.* 5. 8, p. 673.

[95] Marcellinus, *Vita Thucydidis*, c. 35

The same kind of difficulty which had been felt on a large scale in the Greek world in regard to Homer, was felt in no less a degree by those Jews who had become students of Greek philosophy in regard to their own sacred books. The Pentateuch, in a higher sense than Homer, was regarded as having been written under the inspiration of God. It, no less than Homer, was so inwrought into the minds of men that it could not be set aside. It, no less than Homer, contained some things which, at least on the surface, seemed inconsistent with morality. To it, no less than to Homer, was applicable the theory that the words were the veils of a hidden meaning. The application fulfilled a double purpose: it enabled educated Jews, on the one hand, to reconcile their own adoption of Greek philosophy with their continued adhesion to their ancestral religion, and, on the other hand, to show to the educated Greeks with whom they associated, and whom they frequently tried to convert, that their literature was neither barbarous, nor unmeaning, nor immoral. It may be conjectured that, just as in Greece proper the adoption of the allegorical method had been helped by the existence of the mysteries, so in Egypt it was helped by the large use in earlier times of hieroglyphic writing, the monuments of which were all around them, though the writing itself had ceased.[96]

The earliest Jewish writer of this school of whom any remains have come down to us, is reputed to be Aristobulus (about B.C. 170 — 150).[97] In an exposition of the

---

[96] The analogy is drawn by Clem. Alex. *Strom.* 5, chapters 4 and 7.

Pentateuch which he is said to have addressed to Ptolemy Philometor, he boldly claimed that, so far from the Mosaic writings being outside the sphere of philosophy, the Greek philosophers had taken their philosophy from them. "Moses," he said, "using the figures of visible things, tells us the arrangements of nature and the constitutions of important matters." The anthropomorphisms of the Old Testament were explained on this principle. The "hand" of God, for example, meant His power. His "feet," the stability of the world.

Put by far the most considerable monument of this mode of interpretation consists of the works of Philo. They are based throughout on the supposition of a hidden meaning. Put they carry us into a new world. The hidden meaning is not physical, but metaphysical and spiritual. The seen is the veil of the unseen, a robe thrown over it which marks its contour, "and half conceals and half reveals the form within."

It would be easy to interest you, perhaps even to amuse you, by quoting some of the strange meanings which Philo gives to the narratives of familiar incidents. Put I deprecate the injustice which has sometimes been done to him by taking such meanings apart from the historical circumstances out of which allegorical interpretation grew, and the purpose which it was designed to serve. I will give only one passage,

---

[97] It is impossible not to mention Aristobulus: he is quoted by Clement of Alexandria (*Strom.* 1.15, 22; 5.14; 6.3), and extracts from him are given by Eusebius (*Prep. Evang.* 8.10; 13.12; but the genuineness of the information that we possess about him is much controverted and has given rise to much literature.

which I have chosen because it shows as well as any other the contemporary existence of both, the methods of interpretation of which I have spoken — that of finding a moral in every narrative, and that of interpreting the narrative symbolically: the former of these Philo calls the literal, the latter the deeper meaning. The text is Gen. xxviii. 11, "He took the stones of that place and put them beneath his head;" the commentary is:[98]

> "The words are wonderful, not only because of their allegorical and physical meaning, but also because of their literal teaching of trouble and endurance. The writer does not think that a student of virtue should have a delicate and luxurious life, imitating those who are called fortunate, but who are in reality full of misfortunes, eager anxieties and rivalries, whose whole life the Divine Lawgiver describes as a sleep and a dream. These are men who, after spending their days in doing injuries to others, return to their homes and upset them — I mean, not the houses they live in, but the body which is the home of the soul — by immoderate eating and drinking, and at night lie down in soft and costly beds. Such men are not the disciples of the sacred word. Its disciples are real men, lovers of temperance and sobriety and modesty, who make self-restraint and contentment and endurance the corner-stones, as it were, of their lives: who rise superior to money and pleasure and fame: who are ready, for the sake of acquiring virtue, to

---

[98] Philo, *de somniis*, i. 20, vol. i. p. 639.

endure hunger and thirst, heat and cold: whose costly couch is a soft turf, whose bedding is grass and leaves, whose pillow is a heap of stones or a hillock rising a little above the ground. Of such men, Jacob is an example: he put a stone for his pillow: a little while afterwards (v. 20), we find him asking only for nature's wealth of food and raiment: he is the archetype of a soul that disciplines itself, one who is at war with every kind of effeminacy.

"But the passage has a further meaning, which is conveyed in symbol. You must know that the divine place and the holy ground is full of incorporeal Intelligences, who are immortal souls. It is one of these that Jacob takes and puts close to his mind, which is, as it were, the head of the combined person, body and soul. He does so under the pretext of going to sleep, but in reality to find repose in the Intelligence which he has chosen, and to place all the burden of his life upon it."

In all this, Philo was following not a Hebrew but a Greek method. He expressly speaks of it as the method of the Greek mysteries. He addresses his hearers by the name which was given to those who were being initiated. He bids them be purified before they listen. And in this way it was possible for him to be a Greek philosopher without ceasing to be a Jew.

The earliest methods of Christian exegesis were continuations of the methods which were common at the time to both Greek and Greco-Judean writers. They were employed on the same subject matter. Just as the Greek philosophers had found their philosophy in Homer, so Christian writers found in him Christian theology. "When he represents Odysseus as saying,[99] "The rule of many is not good: let there be one ruler," he means to indicate that there should be but one God; and his whole poem is designed to show the mischief that comes of having many gods.[100] When he tells us that Hephaestus represented on the shield of Achilles "the earth, the heaven, the sea, the sun that rests not, and the moon full-orbed,"[101] he is teaching us the divine order of creation which he learned in Egypt from the books of Moses.[102] So Clement of Alexandria interprets the withdrawal of Oceanus and Tethys from each other to mean the separation of land and sea;[103] and he holds that Homer, when he makes Apollo ask Achilles, "Why fruitlessly pursue him, a god," meant to show that the divinity cannot be apprehended by the bodily powers.[104] Some of the philosophical schools which hung upon the skirts of Christianity mingled such interpretations of Greek mythology with similar interpretations of the Old Testament. For example, the writer to whom the name Simon Magus is given, is said to have "interpreted in whatever way he wished both the writings of Moses and also those of the (Greek) poets;"[105] and the Ophite writer, Justin, evolves an elaborate

---

[99] Hom. *Il*, 2.204.

[100] Ps-Justin, c. 17.

[101] Hom. *Il*, 18.483.

[102] Ps-Justin, c. 28.

[103] Hom. *Il*. 14.206; Clem. Al. *Strom*. 5.14, p. 708.

[104] *Il*. 22.8; Clem. Al. *Strom*. 5.14, p. 719; but it sometimes required a keen eye to see the Gospel in Homer.

[105] Hippol. *Philosophumena*, 6.14.

cosmogony from a story of Herakles narrated in Herodotus,[106] combined with the story of the garden of Eden.[107] But the main application was to the Old Testament exclusively. The reasons given for believing that the Old Testament had an allegorical meaning were precisely analogous to those which had been given in respect to Homer. There were many things in the Old Testament which jarred upon the nascent Christian consciousness. "Far be it from us to believe," says the writer of the Clementine Homilies,[108] "that the Master of the universe, the Maker of heaven and earth, 'tempts' men as though He did not know — for who then does foreknow? and if He 'repents,' who is perfect in thought and firm in judgment? and if He 'hardens' men's hearts, who makes them wise? and if He 'blinds' them, who makes them to see? and if He desires 'a fruitful hill,' whose then are all things? and if He wants the savor of sacrifices, who is it that needeth nothing? and if He delights in lamps, who is it that set the stars in heaven?"

One early answer to all such difficulties was, like a similar answer to difficulties about the Homeric mythology, that there was a human as well as a divine element in the Old Testament: some things in it were true, and some were false: and "this was indeed the very reason why the Master said, 'Be genuine money-changers,'[109] testing the Scriptures like coins, and separating the good from the bad." But the answer did not generally prevail. The more common

---

[106] Herod. 4. 8—10.

[107] Hippol. 5. 21.

[108] *Clementin. Hom*, 2.48, 44.

[109] *Ib*, 2.51.

solution, as also in the case of Homer, was that Moses had written in symbols in order to conceal his meaning from the unwise; and Clement of Alexandria, in an elaborate justification of this method, mentions as analogies not only the older Greek poetry, but also the hieroglyphic writing of the Egyptians.[110] The Old Testament thus came to be treated allegorically. A large part of such interpretation was inherited. The coincidences of mystical interpretation between Philo and the Epistle of Barnabas show that such interpretations were becoming the common property of Jews and Judeo-Christians.[111] But the method was soon applied to new data. Exegesis became apologetic. Whereas Philo and his school had dealt mainly with the Pentateuch, the early Christian writers came to deal mainly with the prophets and poetical books; and whereas Philo was mainly concerned to show that the writings of Moses contained Greek philosophy, the Christian writers endeavored to show that the writings of the Hebrew preachers and poets contained Christianity; and whereas Philo had been content to speak of the writers of the Old Testament as Dio Chrysostom spoke of the Greek poets, as having been stirred by a divine enthusiasm, the Christian writers soon came to construct an elaborate theory that the poets and preachers were but as the flutes through which the Breath of God flowed in divine music into the souls of men.[112]

---

[110] Clem. Alex. *Strom.* 5.4, p. 237.

[111] These are given by J. G. Rosenmiiller, *Historia Interpretationis librorum sacrorum in ecclesia Christiana*, vol. i. p. 63.

[112] Athenag. *Legat.* c. 19: ps-Justin (Apollonius), *Cohort. ad.*

The prophets, even more than the poets, lent themselves easily to this allegorical method of interpretation. The *nabi* was in an especial sense the messenger of God and an interpreter of His will. But his message was often a parable. He saw visions and dreamed dreams. He wrote, not in plain words, but in pictures. The meaning of the pictures was often purposely obscure. The Greek word "prophet" sometimes properly belonged not to the *nabi* himself, but to those who, in his own time or in after time, explained the riddle of his message. When the message passed into literature, the interpretation of it became linked with the growing conception of the foreknowledge and providence of God: it was believed that He not only knew all things that should come to pass, but also communicated His knowledge to men. The *nabi*, through whom He revealed His will as to the present, was also the channel through whom He revealed His intention as to the future. The prophetic writings came to be read in the light of this conception. The interpreters wandered, as it were, along vast corridors whose walls were covered with hieroglyphs and paintings. They found in them symbols which might be interpreted of their own times. They went on to infer the divine ordering of the present from the coincidence of its features with features that could be traced in the hieroglyphs of the past. A similar conception prevailed in the heathen world. It lay beneath the many forms of divination. Hence Tertullian[113] speaks of Hebrew prophecy as a special form of divination, "*divinatio prophetica*." So far from being strange to the Greek world, it was

---

Grac. c. 8, uses the analogous metaphor of a harp of which the Divine Spirit is the *plectrum*.

[113] Tertull. *adv. Marc.* 3. 5,

accepted. Those who read the Old Testament without accepting Christianity, found in its symbols prefigurings, not of Christianity, but of events recorded in the heathen mythologies. The Shiloh of Jacob's song was a foretelling of Dionysus: the virgin's son of Isaiah was a picture of Perseus: the Psalmist's "strong as a giant to run his course" was a prophecy of Herakles.[114]

The fact that this was an accepted method of interpretation enabled the Apologists to use it with great effect. It became one of the chief evidences of Christianity. Explanations of the meaning of historical events and poetical figures which sound strange or impossible to modern ears, so far from sounding strange or impossible in the second century, carried conviction with them. When it was said, "The government shall be upon his shoulder," it was meant that Christ should be extended on the cross;[115] when it was said, "He shall dip his garment in the blood of the grape," it was meant that his blood should be, not of human origin, but, like the red juice of the grape, from God;[116] when it was said that "He shall receive the power of Damascus," it was meant that the power of the evil demon who dwelt at Damascus should be overcome, and the prophecy was fulfilled when the Magi came to worship Christ.[117] The convergence of a large number of such interpretations upon the Gospel history was a powerful argument against both

---

[114] Justin M. *Apol.* i, 54.

[115] *Ib.* i. 35.

[116] *Ib.* i. 32.

[117] *Ib. Tryph.* 78.

Jews and Greeks. I need not enlarge upon them. They have formed part of the general stock of Christian teaching ever since. But I will draw your attention to the fact that the basis of this use of the Old Testament was not so much the idea of prediction as the prevalent practice of treating ancient literature as symbolical or allegorical.

The method came to be applied to the books which were being formed into a new volume of sacred writings, side by side with the old. It was so applied, in the first instance, not by the Apologists, but by the Gnostics. It was detached from the idea of prediction. It was linked with the idea of knowledge as a secret. This extension of the method was inevitable. The earthly life of Christ presented as many difficulties to the first Christian philosophers as the Old Testament had done. The conception of Christ as the Wisdom and the Power of God seemed inconsistent with the meanness of a common human life; and that life resolved itself into a series of symbolic representations of superhuman movements, and the record of it was written in hieroglyphs. When Symeon took the young child in his arms and said the *Nunc dimittis*, he was a picture of the Demiurge who had learned his own change of place on the coming of the Savior, and who gave thanks to the Infinite Depth.[118] The raising of Jairus' daughter was a type of Achamoth, the Eternal Wisdom, the mother of the Demiurge, whom the Savior led anew to the perception of the light which had forsaken her. Even the passion on the Cross was a setting forth of the anguish and fear and perplexity of the Eternal Wisdom.[119]

---

[118] Iren, 1.8.4, of the Valentinians.

The method was at first rejected with contumely. Irenaeus and Tertullian bring to bear upon it their batteries of irony and denunciation. It was a blasphemous invention. It was one of the arts of spiritual wickedness against which a Christian must wrestle. But it was deep-seated in the habits of the time; and even while Tertullian was writing, it was establishing a lodgment inside the Christian communities which it has never ceased to hold. It did so first of all in the great school of Alexandria, in which it had grown up as the reconciliation of Greek philosophy and Hebrew theology. The methods of the school of Philo were applied to the New Testament even more than to the Old. When Christ said, "The foxes have holes, but the Son of Man hath not where to lay his head," he meant that on the believer alone, who is separated from the rest, that is from the wild beasts of the world, rests the Head of the universe, the kind and gentle Word.[120] When he is said to have fed the multitude on five barley-loaves and two fishes, it is meant that he gave mankind the preparatory training of the Law, for barley, like the Law, ripens sooner than wheat, and of philosophy, which had grown, like fishes, in the waves of the Gentile world.[121] When we read of the anointing of Christ's feet, we read of both his teaching and his passion; for the feet are a symbol of divine instruction travelling to the ends of the earth, or, it may be, of the Apostles who so travelled, having received the fragrant unction of the Holy Ghost; and the ointment, which is adulterated oil, is a symbol of the traitor Judas, "by

---

[119] *Ib.* 1.8.2.

[120] Clem. Al. *Strom.* 1.3, p. 329.

[121] *Ib.* 6.11, p. 787.

whom the Lord was anointed on the feet, being released from his sojourn in the world: for the dead are anointed."[122]

But it may reasonably be doubted whether the allegorical method would have obtained the place which it did in the Christian Church if it had not served an other-than-exegetical purpose. It is clear that after the first conflicts with Judaism had subsided, the Old Testament formed a great stumbling block in the way of those who approached Christianity on its ideal side, and viewed it by the light of philosophical conceptions. Its anthropomorphisms, its improbabilities, the sanction which it seemed to give to immoralities, the dark picture which it sometimes presented of both God and the servants of God, seemed to many men to be irreconcilable with both the theology and the ethics of the Gospel. An important section of the Christian world rejected its authority altogether: it was the work, not of God, but of His rival, the god of this world: the contrast between the Old Testament and the New was part of the larger contrast between matter and spirit, darkness and light, evil and good.[123] Those who did not thus reject it were still conscious of its difficulties. There were many solutions of those difficulties. Among them was that which had been the Greek solution of analogous difficulties in Homer. It was adopted and elaborated by Origen expressly with an apologetic purpose. He had been trained in current methods of Greek interpretation. He is expressly said to have studied

---

[122] Id. *Padag.* 2.8, p. 76.

[123] This was the contention of Marcion, whose influence upon the Christian world was far larger than is commonly supposed. By far the best account of him, in both this and other respects, is that of Harnack, *Dogmengeschichte*, ler Th. B. i. c. 5.

the books of Cornutus.[124] He found in the hypothesis of a
spiritual meaning as complete a vindication of the Old
Testament as Cornutus had found of the Greek mythology.
The difficulties which men find, he tells us, arise from their
lack of the spiritual sense. Without it he himself would have
been a sceptic.

> "What man of sense," he asks,[125] "will
> suppose? that the first and the second and the
> third day, and the evening and the morning,
> existed without a sun and moon and stars?
> Who is so foolish as to believe that God, like a
> husbandman, planted a garden in Eden, and
> placed in it a tree of life, that might be seen and
> touched, so that one who tasted of the fruit by
> his bodily lips obtained life? or, again, that one
> was partaker of good and evil by eating that
> which was taken from a tree? And if God is
> said to have walked in a garden in the evening,
> and Adam to have hidden under a tree, I do
> not suppose that anyone doubts that these
> things figuratively indicate certain mysteries,
> the history being apparently but not literally
> true Nay, the Gospels themselves are filled
> with the same kind of narratives. Take, for
> example, the story of the devil taking Jesus up
> into a high mountain to show him from thence
> the kingdoms of the world and the glory of
> them: what thoughtful reader would not
> condemn those who teach that it was with the
> eye of the body — which needs a lofty height

---

[124] Euseb. *H. E.* 6.19.8.

[125] Origen, *de princip.* 1.16.

that even the near neighborhood may be seen
— that Jesus beheld the kingdoms of the
Persians, and Scythians, and Indians, and
Parthians, and the manner in which their rulers
were glorified among men?"

The spirit intended, in all such narratives, on the one hand to reveal mysteries to the wise, on the other hand to conceal them from the multitude. The whole series of narratives is constructed with a purpose, and subordinated to the exposition of mysteries. Difficulties and impossibilities were introduced in order to prevent men from being drawn into adherence to the literal meaning. Sometimes the truth was told by means of a true narrative which yielded a mystical sense: sometimes, when no such narrative of a true history existed, one was invented for the purpose.[126]

In this way, as a rationalizing expedient for solving the difficulties of Old Testament exegesis, the allegorical method established for itself a place in the Christian Church: it largely helped to prevent the Old Testament from being discarded: and the conservation of the Old Testament was the conservation of allegory, not only for the Old Testament, but also for the New.

Against the whole tendency of symbolical interpretation there was more than one form of reaction in both the Greek and the Christian world.

1. It was attacked by the Apologists in its application to Greek mythology. "With an inconsequence which is remarkable, though not singular, they found in it a weapon

---

[126] *Ib.* c. 15.

of both defense and offence. They used it in defense of Christianity, not only because it gave them the evidence of prediction, but also because it solved some of the difficulties which the Old Testament presented to philosophical minds. They used it, on the other hand, in their attack upon Greek religion. Allegories are an after-thought, they said sometimes, a mere pious gloss over unseemly fables.[127] Even if they were true, they said again, and the basis of Greek belief were as good as its interpreters alleged it to be, it was a work of wicked demons to wrap round it a veil of dishonorable fictions.[128] The myth and the god who is supposed to be behind it vanish together, says Tatian: if the myth be true, the gods are worthless demons; if the myth be not true, but only a symbol of the powers of nature, the godhead is gone, for the powers of nature are not gods since they constrain no worship.[129] In a similar way, in the fourth century, Eusebius treats it as a vain attempt of a younger generation to explain away (*therapeusai*) the mistakes of their fathers.[130]

2. It was attacked by the Greek philosophers in its application to Christianity. There are some persons, says Porphyry,[131] who being anxious to find, not a way of being rid of the immorality of the Old Testament, but an explanation of it, have recourse to interpretations which do not hold together nor fit the words which they interpret,

---

[127] Clement. *Recogn.* 10.36.

[128] Clement. *Hom.* 6.18.

[129] Tatian, *Orat. ad. Grec.* 21.

[130] Euseb. *Prep. Evang.* 2.6, vol. iii. p. 74.

[131] Porphyr. ap. Euseb. *H. E.* 6. 19. 5.

which serve not so much as a defense of Jewish doctrines as to bring approbation and credit for their own. It is a delusive evasion of your difficulties, said in effect Celsus;[132] you find in your sacred books narratives which shock your moral sense; you think that you get rid of the difficulty by having recourse to allegory; but you do not: in the first place, your scriptures do not admit of being so interpreted; in the second place, the explanation is often more difficult than the narrative which it explains. The answer of Origen is weak: it is partly a *Tu quoque*: Homer is worse than Genesis, and if allegory will not explain the latter, neither will it the former: it is partly that, if there had been no secret, the Psalmist would not have said, "Open thou mine eyes, that I may see the wondrous things of thy law."

3. The method had opponents even in Alexandria itself. Origen[133] more than once speaks of those who objected to his "digging wells below the surface;" and Eusebius mentions a lost work of the learned Kepos of Arsinoe, entitled "A Refutation of the Allegorists."[134] But it found its chief antagonist in the school of interpretation which arose at the end of the fourth century at Antioch. The dominant philosophy of Alexandria had been a fusion of Platonism with some elements of both Stoicism and revived Pythagoreanism: that of Antioch was coming to be Aristotelianism. The one was idealistic, the other realistic: the one was a philosophy of dreams and mystery, the other of

---

[132] Origen, *c. Cels.* 4.48—50.

[133] Origen, *in Gen. Hom.* 13.3, vol. ii. p. 94; *in Joann. Hom.* 10.13, vol. iv. p. 178.

[134] Euseb. *H. E.* 7. 24.

logic and system: to the one, Revelation was but the earthy foothold from which speculation might soar into infinite space; to the other, it was "a positive fact given in the light of history."[135] Allegorical interpretation was the outcome of the one; literal interpretation of the other. The precursor of the Antiochene school, Julius Africanus, of Emmaus, has left behind a letter which has been said "to contain in its two short pages more true exegesis than all the commentaries and homilies of Origen."[136] The chief founder of the school was Lucian, a scholar who shares with Origen the honor of being the founder of Biblical philology, and whose lifetime, which was cut short by martyrdom in 311, just preceded the great Trinitarian controversies of the Nicene period. His disciples came to be leaders on the Arian side: among them were Eusebius of Nicomedia and Arius himself. The question of exegesis became entangled with the question of orthodoxy. The greatest of Greek interpreters, Theodore of Mopsuestia, followed, a hundred years afterwards, in the same path; but in his day also questions of canons of interpretation were so entangled with questions of Christology, and the Christology of the Antiochene school was so completely outvoted at the great ecclesiastical assemblies by the Christology of the Alexandrian school, that his reputation for scholarship has been almost wholly obscured by the ill-fame of his leanings towards

---

[135] Kihn, *Theodor von Mopsuestia und Junilius Africanus als Exegeten*, Freib. im Breisg. 1880, p. 7.

[136] J.G. Rosenmiiller, *Hist. Interpret.* iii. p. 161. The letter is printed, with the other remains of Julius Africanus, in Routh, *Reliquie Sacre*, vol, 11.

Nestorianism. It has been one of the many results of the controversies into which the metaphysical tendencies of the Greeks led the churches of the fourth and fifth centuries, to postpone almost to modern times the acceptance of "the literal grammatical and historical sense" as the true sense of Scripture.

The allegorical method of interpretation has survived the circumstances of its birth and the gathered forces of its opponents. It has filled a large place in the literature of Christianity. But by the irony of history, though it grew out of a tendency towards rationalism, it has come in later times to be vested like a saint, and to wear an aureole round its head. It has been the chief instrument by which the dominant beliefs of every age have constructed their strongholds. It was harmless so long as it was free. It was the play of innocent imagination on the surface of great truths. But when it became authoritative, when the idea prevailed that only that poetical sense was true of which the majority approved, and when moreover it became traditional, so that one generation was bound to accept the symbolical interpretations of its predecessors, it became at once the slave of dogmatism and the tyrant of souls. Outside its relation to dogmatism, it has a history and a value which rather grow than diminish with time. It has given to literature books which, though of little value for the immediate purpose of interpretation, are yet monuments of noble and inspiring thoughts. It has contributed even more to art than to literature. The poetry of life would have been infinitely less rich without it. For though without it Dante might have been stirred to write, he would not have written the Divine Comedy; and though without it Raffaele would have painted, he would not have painted the St. Cecilia; and though without it we should have had Gothic cathedrals, we should not have had that sublime symbolism of their structure which is of itself a religious education. It survives because it is based upon an element in human nature which is not likely to pass away: whatever be its value in relation to the literature of the past, it is at least the expression in relation to the present that our lives are hedged round by the unknown, that there is a haze about both our birth and our departure, and that even the meaner facts of life are linked to infinity.

But two modern beliefs militate against it.

1. The one belief affects all literature, religious and secular alike. It is that the thoughts of the past are relative to the past, and must be interpreted by it. The glamor of writing has passed away. A written word is no more than a spoken word; and a spoken word is taken in the sense in which the speaker used it, at the time at which he used it. There have been writers of enigmas and painters of emblems, but they have formed an infinitesimal minority. There have been those who, as Cicero says of himself in writing to Atticus, have written allegorically lest open speech should betray them; but such cryptograms have only a temporary and transient use. The idea that ancient literature consists of riddles which it is the business of modern literature to solve, has passed for ever away.

2. The other belief affects specially religious literature. It is that the Spirit of God has not yet ceased to speak to men, and that it is important for us to know, not only what He told the men of other days, but also what He tells us now. Interpretation is of the present as well as of the past. We can believe that there is a Divine voice, but we find it hard to

believe that it has died away to an echo from the Judean hills. We can believe in religious as in other progress, but we find it hard to believe that that progress was suddenly arrested fifteen hundred years ago. The study of nature and the study of history have given us another maxim for religious conduct and another axiom of religious belief. They apply to that which is divine within us the inmost secret of our knowledge and mastery of that which is divine without us: *man, the servant and interpreter of nature, is also, and is thereby the servant and interpreter of the living God.*

Lecture IV. GREEK AND CHRISTIAIN RHETORIC.

It is customary to measure the literature of an age by its highest products and to measure the literary excellence of one age as compared with that of another by the highest products of each of them. We look, for example, upon the Periclean age at Athens, or the Augustan age at Rome, or the Elizabethan age in our own country, as higher than the ages respectively of the Ptolemies, the Caesars, or the early Georges. The former are "golden;" the latter, "silver." Nor can it be doubted that from the point of view of literature in itself, as distinguished from literature in its relation to history or to social life, such a standard of measurement is correct. But the result of its application has been the doing of a certain kind of injustice to periods of history in which, though the highwater mark has been lower, there has been a wide diffusion of literary culture. This is the case with the period with which we are dealing. It produced no writer of the first rank. It was artificial rather than spontaneous. It was imitative more than original. It was appreciative rather than constructive. Its literature was born, not of the enthusiasm of free activity, but rather of the passivity which comes when there is no hope. But as to a student of science the afterglow is an object of study no less than the noon-day, so to a student of the historical development of the world the silver age of a nation's literature is an object of study no less than its golden age.

Its most characteristic feature was one for which it is difficult to find any more exact description than the paradoxical phrase, "a *viva-voce* literature." It had its birth and chief development in that part of the Empire in which Christianity and Greek life came into closest and most frequent contact. It was the product of the rhetorical schools which have been already described. In those schools the professor had been in the habit of illustrating his rules and instructing his students by model compositions of his own.[137] Such compositions were in the first instance exercises in the pleading of actual causes, and accusations or defenses of real persons. The cases were necessarily supposed rather than actual, but they had a practical object in view, and came as close as possible to real life. The large growth of the habit of studying Rhetoric as a part of the education of a gentleman, and the increased devotion to the literature of the past, which came partly from the felt loss of spontaneity and partly from national pride, caused these compositions in the rhetorical schools to take a wider range. They began on the one hand to be divorced from even a fictitious connection with the law-courts, and on the other to be directly imitative of the styles of ancient authors. From the older Rhetoric, the study of forensic logic and speech with a view to the actual practice in the law-courts, which necessarily still went on, there branched out the new Rhetoric, which was sometimes specially known as Sophistic.

Sophistic proceeded for the most part upon the old lines. Its literary compositions preserved the old name, "exercises" (*meletai*), as though they were still the rehearsals of actual pleadings. They were divided into two kinds, *Theses* and

---

[137] I have endeavored to confine the above account to what is true of *Greek* Rhetoric: the accounts which are found in Roman writers, especially in Quintilian, though in the main agreeing with it, differ in some details.

Hypotheses, according as a subject was argued in general terms or names were introduced. The latter were the more common. Their subjects were sometimes fictitious, sometimes taken from real history. Of the first of these there is a good example in Lucian's *Tyrannicide*: the situation is, that a man goes into the citadel of a town for the purpose of killing a tyrant: not finding the tyrant, the man kills the tyrant's son: the tyrant coming in and seeing his son with the sword in his body, stabs himself: the man claims the reward as a tyrannicide. Of the second kind of subjects, there are such instances as "Demosthenes defending himself against the charge of having taken the bribe which Demades brought,"[138] and "The Athenians wounded at Syracuse beg their comrades who are returning to Athens to put them to death."[139] The Homeric cycle was an unfailing mine of subjects: the Persian wars hardly less so. "Would you like to hear a sensible speech about Agamemnon, or are you sick of hearing speeches about Agamemnon, Atreus' son?" asks Dio Chrysostom in one of his Dialogues.[140] "I should not take amiss even a speech about Adrastus or Tantalus or Pelops, if I were likely to get good from it," is the polite reply. In the treatment of both kinds of subjects, stress was laid on dramatic consistency. The character, whether real or supposed, was required to speak in an appropriate style.[141] The "exercise" had to be recited with an appropriate

---

[138] Philostr. *V. S.* 1.25.7, 16.

[139] *Ib.* 2.5.3.

[140] Dio Chrysost. lvi. vol. ii. p. 176.

[141] see Theon. *Progymnasmata*, c. 10, ed. Spengel, vol. ii. 115: Quintil. 3.8.49; 9.2.29.

intonation.[142] Sometimes the dramatic effect was heightened "by the introduction of two or more characters: for example, one of the surviving pieces of Dio Chrysostom[143] consists of a wrangle in tragic style, and with tragic diction, between Odysseus and Philoctetes.

This kind of Sophistic has an interest in two respects, apart from its relation to contemporary life. It gave birth to the Greek romance, which is the progenitor of the medieval romance and of the modern novel:[144] a notable example of such a sophistical romance in Christian literature is the Clementine Homilies and Recognitions; in non-Christian literature, Philostratus' Life of Apollonius of Tyana. It gave birth also to the writings in the style of ancient authors which, though commonly included in the collected works of those authors, betray their later origin by either the poverty of their thought or inadvertent neologisms of expression: for example, the Eryxias of Plato.[145]

But though Sophistic grew mainly out of Rhetoric, it had its roots also in Philosophy. It was defined as Rhetoric

---

[142] "They made their voice sweet with musical cadences, and modulations of tone, and echoed resonances:" Plut. *de aud.* 7, p. 41. So at Rome Favorinus is said to have "charmed even those who did not know Greek by the sound of his voice, and the significance of his look, and the cadence of his sentences:" Philostr. *V. S.* 1.7, p. 208.

[143] Orat. lix.

[144] Rohde, pp. 336 sqq.

[145] This trained habit of composing in different styles is of importance in relation to Christian as well as to non-Christian literature.

philosophizing.[146] It threw off altogether the fiction of a law-court or an assembly, and discussed in continuous speech the larger themes of morality or theology. Its utterances were not "exercises" but "discourses" (*dialexeis*).[147] It preached sermons. It created not only a new literature, but also a new profession. The class of men against whom Plato had inveighed had become merged in the general class of educators: they were specialized partly as grammarians, partly as rhetoricians: the word "sophist," to which the invectives had failed to attach a permanent stigma, remained partly as a generic name, and partly as a special name for the new class of public talkers. They differed from philosophers in that they did not mark themselves off from the rest of the world, and profess their devotion to a higher standard of living, by wearing a special dress.[148] They were a notable feature of their time. Some of them had a fixed residence and gave discourses regularly, like the "stated minister" of a modern congregation: some of them travelled from place to place. The audience was usually gathered by invitation. There were no newspaper advertisements in those days, and no bells; consequently the invitations were personal. They were made sometimes by a "card" or "programme," sometimes by word

---

[146] Philostratus, *V. S.* 1. p. 202,

[147] On the distinction, see Kayser's preface to his editions of Philostratus, p. vii.

[148] Philostratus, *V.S.* 2.3, p. 245, says that the famous sophist Aristocles lived the earlier part of his life as a Peripatetic philosopher, "squalid and unkempt and ill-clothed," but that when he passed into the ranks of the sophists he brushed off his squalor, and brought luxury and the pleasures of music into his life. On the philosopher's dress, see below, Lecture VI. p. 151.

of mouth: "Come and hear me lecture today."[149] Sometimes a messenger was sent round; sometimes the sophist would go round himself and knock at people's doors and promise them a fine discourse.[150]

The audience of a travelling sophist was what might be expected among a people who lived very much out of doors. When a stranger appeared who was known by his professional dress, and whose reputation had preceded him, the people clustered round him — like iron filings sticking to a magnet, says Themistius.[151] If there was a resident sophist, the two were pitted together; just as if, in modern times, a famous violinist from Paris or Vienna might be asked to play at the next concert with the leading violinist in London. It was a matter not only of professional honor, but also of obligation. A man could not refuse. There is a story in Plutarch[152] about a sophist named Niger who found himself in a town in Galatia which had a resident professor. The resident made a discourse. Niger had, unfortunately, a fishbone in his throat and could not easily speak; but he had either to speak or to lose his reputation: he spoke, and an inflammation set in which killed him. There is a much longer story in Philostratus[153] of Alexander Peloplato going to

---

[149] Epictetus, *Diss.* 3.21.6; 3.23.6, 23, 28: Pliny, *Epist.* 3.18: Cf. Lucian, *Hermotimus*, 11.

[150] Philostratus, *V. S.* 2.10.5, says that the enthusiasm at Rome about the sophist Adrian was such that when his messenger appeared on the scene with a notice of lecture, the people rose up, whether from the senate or the circus, and flocked to the Athenaeum to hear him.

[151] *Orat.* 23, p. 360, ed. Dind.

[152] *De sanit. prec.* 16, p. 131.

Athens to discourse in a friendly contest with Herodes
Atticus. The audience gathered together in a theatre in the
Ceramicus, and waited a long time for Herodes to appear:
when he did not come, they grew angry and thought that it
was a trick, and insisted on Alexander coming forward to
discourse before Herodes arrived. And when Herodes did
arrive, Alexander suddenly changed his style — sang tenor,
so to speak, instead of bass — and Herodes followed him,
and there was a charming interchange of compliments: "We
sophists," said Alexander, "are all of us only slices of you,
Herodes."

Sometimes they went to show their skill at one of the great
festivals, such as that of Olympia. Lucian[154] tells a story of
one who had plucked feathers from many orators to make a
wonderful discourse about Pythagoras. His object was to
gain the glory of delivering it as an extempore oration, and
he arranged with a confederate that its subject should be the
subject selected for him by the audience. But the imposture
was too barefaced: some of the hearers amused themselves
by assigning the different passages to their several authors;
and the sophist himself at last joined in the universal
laughter. And Dio Chrysostom[155] draws a picture of a public
place at Corinth during the Isthmian games, which he alleges
to be as true of the time of Diogenes as of his own: "You
might hear many poor wretches of sophists shouting and
abusing one another, and their disciples, as they call them,

---

[153] *V. S.* 2.5.3.

[154] *Pseudolog.* 5 sqq.

[155] *Orat.* viii, vol. i. 145.

squabbling, and many writers of books reading their stupid compositions, and many poets singing their poems, and many jugglers exhibiting their marvels, and many soothsayers giving the meaning of prodigies, and ten thousand rhetoricians twisting lawsuits, and no small number of traders driving their several trades."

Of the manner of the ordinary discourse there are many indications. It was given sometimes in a private house, sometimes in a theatre, sometimes in a regular lecture room. The professor sometimes entered already robed in his "pulpit-gown," and sometimes put it on in the presence of his audience. He mounted the steps to his professorial chair, and took his seat upon its ample cushion.[156] He sometimes began with a preface, sometimes he proceeded at once to his discourse. He often gave the choice of a subject to his audience.[157] He was ready to discourse on any theme; and it was part of his art either to force the choice of a subject, or so to turn the subject as to bring in something which he had already prepared. "His memory is incredible," says Pliny of Isaeus; "he repeats by heart what he appears to say extempore; but he does not falter even in a single word."[158] "When your audience have chosen a subject for you," says Lucian,[159] in effect, in his satirical advice to rhetoricians, "go

---

[156] Epict. *Diss*. 3.23.35.

[157] Pliny, *Epist*. 2.3.

[158] Plin. *Epist*. 2.3.4; cf. Philostr. *V.S.* 1.20.2. His disciple Dionysius of Miletus had so wonderful a memory, and so taught his pupils to remember, as to be suspected of sorcery: Philostr. *V. S.* 1.22.3.

[159] *Rhet. prec*. 18,

straight at it and say without hesitation whatever words come to your tongue, never minding about the first point coming first and the second second: the great thing is to go right on and not have any pauses. If you have to talk at Athens about adultery, bring in the customs of the Hindus and Persians: above all, have passages about Marathon and Cynaegirus — that is indispensable. And Athos must always be turned into sea, and the Hellespont into dry land, and the sun must be darkened by the clouds of Median arrows .... and Salamis and Artemisium and Platcea, and so forth, must come in pretty frequently; and, above all, those little Attic words I told you about must blossom on the surface of your speech — *atta* and *depouthen* — must be sprinkled about freely, whether they are wanted or not: for they are pretty words, even when they do not mean anything."

It was a disappointment if he was not interrupted by applause. "A sophist is put out in an extempore speech," says Philostratus,[160] "by a serious-looking audience and tardy praise and no clapping." " They are all agape," says Dio Chrysostom,[161] " for the murmur of the crowd .... like men walking in the dark, they move always in the direction of the clapping and the shouting." "I want your praise," said one of them to Epictetus.[162] "What do you mean by my praise?" asked the philosopher. "Oh, I want you to say Bravo! and Wonderful!" replied the sophist. These were the common cries; others were not infrequent — "Divine!" "Inspired!"

---

[160] *V.S.* 2.26.3.

[161] *Orat.* xxxiii. vol. 1. p. 422.

[162] Epict. *Diss.* 3.23.24.

"Unapproachable !"[163] They were accompanied by clapping of the hands and stamping of the feet and waving of the arms. "If your friends see you breaking down," says Lucian in his satirical advice to a rhetorician,[164] "let them pay the price of the suppers you give them by stretching out their arms and giving you a chance of thinking of something to say in the interval between the rounds of applause." Sometimes, of course, there were signs of disapproval. "It is the mark of a good hearer," says Plutarch,[165] "that he does not howl out like a dog at everything of which he disapproves, but at any rate waits until the end of the discourse."

After the discourse, the professor would go round: " 'What did you think of me today?' "says one in Epictetus.[166] " 'Upon my life, sir, I thought you were admirable.' 'What did you think of my best passage? 'Which was that?' 'Where I described Pan and the Nymphs.' 'Oh, it was excessively well done." "Again, to quote another anecdote from Epictetus:[167] " 'A much larger audience today, I think,' says the professor. 'Yes; much larger.' 'Five hundred, I should guess.' 'Oh, nonsense; it could not have been less than a thousand.' 'Why that is more than Dio ever had: I wonder why it was: they appreciated what I said, too.' 'Beauty, sir, can move even a stone.' "

---

[163] Plut. *de audiendo*, 15, p. 46, speaks of the strange and extravagant words which had thus come into use.

[164] *Rhet. prac.* 21.

[165] *De audiendo*, 4, p. 39.

[166] *Diss.* 3.23.11.

[167] *Diss.* 3.23.19.

They made both money and reputation. The more eminent of them were among the most distinguished men of the time. They were the pets of society, and sometimes its masters.[168] They were employed on affairs of state at home and on embassies abroad.[169] They were sometimes placed on the free list of their city, and lived at the public expense. They were sometimes made senators — raised, as we might say, to the House of Lords — and sometimes governors of provinces.[170] When they died, and sometimes before their death, public statues were erected in their honor.[171] The inscriptions of some of them are recorded by historians, and some remain: "The Queen of Cities to the King of Eloquence," was inscribed on the statue of Prohaeresius at Rome.[172] "One of the Seven Wise Men, though he had not fulfilled twenty-five years," is inscribed on an existing base of a statue at Attaleia;[173] and, beneath a representation of crowning, the words, "He subjects all things to eloquence," are found on a similar base at Parion.[174]

---

[168] Eunapius, *Vit. Julian*, p. 68.

[169] Philostr. *V. S.* 1.21.6, 1.24.2, 1.2.1, 5, 2.5.2.

[170] Philostr. *V. S.* 1.22, 1.25.3.

[171] The inscription of one of the statues which are mentioned by Philostratus, *V. S.* 1. 23. 2, as having been erected to Lollianus at Athens, was found a few years ago near the Propylea.

[172] Eunap. *Vit. Proheres*. p. 90.

[173] *Bulletin de correspondence Hellénique*, 1886, p. 157.

[174] *Mittheilungen des deutsches archeol. Institut*, 1884, p. 61.

They naturally sometimes gave themselves great airs. There are many stories about them. Philostratus tells one of the Emperor Antoninus Pius on arriving at Smyrna going, in accordance with imperial custom, to spend the night at the house which was at once the best house in the city and the house of the most distinguished man. It was that of the sophist Polemo, who happened on the Emperor's arrival to be away from home; but he returned from his journey at night, and with loud exclamations against being kept out of his own, turned the Emperor out of doors.[175] The common epithet for them is *alaxon* — a word with no precise English equivalent, denoting a cross between a braggart and a mountebank.

But the real grounds on which the more earnest men objected to them were those upon which Plato had objected to their predecessors: their making a trade of knowledge, and their unreality.

1. The making of discourses, whether literary or moral, was a thriving trade.[176] The fees given to a leading sophist were on the scale of those given to a prima donna in our own day.[177] But the objection to it was not so much the fact

---

[175] Philostratus, *V. S.* 1. 25. 3, p. 228, narrates the incident with graphic humor, and adds two anecdotes which show that the Emperor was rather amused than annoyed by it. It was said of the same sophist that "he used to talk to cities as a superior, to kings as not inferior, and to gods as an equal," ibid. 4.

[176] Dio Cassius, 71.35.2.

[177] For example, the father of Herodes Atticus gave Scopelianus a fee of twenty-five talents, to which Atticus himself added another twenty five: Philostr. *V.S.* 1.21.7, p. 222.

of its thriving, as the fact of its being a trade at all. "If they do what they do," says Dio Chrysostom,[178] "as poets and rhetoricians, there is no harm perhaps; but if they do it as philosophers, for the sake of their own personal gain and glory, and not for the sake of benefiting you, there is harm." The defense which Themistius[179] makes for himself is more candid than effective: " I do make money," he says; "people give me sometimes one mina, sometimes two, sometimes as much as a talent: but, since I must speak about myself, let me ask you this — Did anyone ever come away the worse for having heard me? Mark, I charge nothing: it is a voluntary contribution."

2. The stronger ground of objection to them was their unreality. They had lost touch with life. They had made philosophy itself seem unreal. "They are not philosophers, but fiddlers," said the sturdy old Stoic Musonius.[180] It is not necessary to suppose that they were all charlatans. There was then, as now, the irrepressible young man of good morals who wished to air his opinions. But the tendency to moralize had become divorced from practice. They preached, not because they were in grim earnest about the reformation of the world, but because preaching was a respectable profession, and the listening to sermons a fashionable diversion. "The mass of men," says Plutarch,[181] "enjoy and

---

[178] Dio Chrysost. *Orat.* xxxii. p. 403.

[179] *Orat.* xxiii. p. 861, The whole speech is a plea against the disrepute into which the profession had fallen.

[180] *ap.* Aul. Gell. 5.1.1.

[181] *De audiendo*, 12, p. 43.

admire a philosopher when he is discoursing about their neighbors; but if the philosopher, leaving their neighbors alone, speaks his mind about things that are of importance to the men themselves, they take offence and vote him a bore; for they think that they ought to listen to a philosopher in his lecture-room in the same bland way that they listen to tragedians in the theatre. This, as might be expected, is what happens to them in regard to the sophists; for when a sophist gets down from his pulpit and puts aside his MSS., in the real business of life he seems but a small man, and under the thumb of the majority. They do not understand about real philosophers that both seriousness and play, grim looks and smiles, and above all the direct personal application of what they say to each individual, have a useful result for those who are in the habit of giving a patient attention to them."

Against this whole system of veneering rhetoric with philosophy, there was a strong reaction. Apart from the early Christian writers, with whom "sophist" is always a word of scorn, there were men, especially among the new school of Stoics, who were at open war with its unreality.[182] I will ask

---

[182] It is clear that the word "sophist" had under the Early Empire, as in both earlier and later times, two separate streams of meaning. It was used as a title of honor, e.g. Lucian, *Rhet. Prec.* 1; Philostr. *V.S.* 2. 31. 1; Eunap. *Vit. Liban.* p. 100. But the disparagement of the class to whom the word was applied runs through a large number of writers, e.g. Dio Chrys. *Orat.* iv. vol. i. 70; ib. viii. vol. i. 151; ib. x. vol. i. 166; ib. xii. vol. i, 214; Epict. *Diss.* 2.20, 23; M. Aurel. 1.16; 6.30. Lucian, *Fugitiv.* 10; Maximus Tyr. *Diss.* 33.8; Among the Christian Fathers, especial reference may be made to Clem. Alex. *Strom.* 1, chapters 3 and 8, pp. 328, 343.

you to listen to the expostulation which the great moral reformer Epictetus addresses to a rhetorician who came to him:

> "First of all, tell yourself what you want to be, and then act accordingly. For this is what we see done in almost all other cases. Men who are practicing for the games first of all decide what they mean to be, and then proceed to do the things that follow from their decision… So then when you say, Come and listen to my lecture, first of all consider whether your action be not thrown away for want of an end, and then consider whether it be not a mistake, on account of your real end being a wrong one. Suppose I ask a man, 'Do you wish to do good by your expounding, or to gain applause?' There-upon straightway you hear him saying, 'What do I care for the applause of the multitude?' And his sentiment is right: for in the same way, applause is nothing to the musician (*qua* musician, or to the geometrician *qua* geometrician.

> "You wish to do good, then," I continue; "in what particular respect? tell me, that I too may hasten to your lecture-room. But can a man impart good to others without having previously received good himself? "No: just as a man is of no use to us in the way of carpentering unless he is himself a carpenter. "Would you like to know, then, whether you have received good yourself? Bring me your convictions, philosopher. (Let us take an example.) Did you not the other day praise so-and-so more than you really thought he deserved? Did you not flatter that senator's

son? — and yet you would not like your own sons to be like him, would you?

"God forbid!

"Then why did you flatter him and toady to him?

"He is a clever young fellow, and a good student.

"How do you know that?

"He admires my lectures.

"Yes; that is the real reason. But don't you think that these very people despise you in their secret hearts? I mean that when a man who is conscious that he has neither done nor thought any single good thing, finds a philosopher who tells him that he is a man of great ability, sincerity, and genuineness, of course he says to himself, 'This man wants to get something out of me!' Or (if this is not the case with you), tell me what proof he has given of great ability. No doubt he has attended you for a considerable time: he has heard you discoursing and expounding: but has he become more modest in his estimate of himself — or is he still looking for someone to teach him?

"Yes, he is looking for someone to teach him.

"To teach him how to live? No, fool; not how to live, but how to talk: which also is the reason why he admires you.

...

"[The truth is, you like applause: you care more for that than for doing good, and so you invite people to come and hear you.]

"But does a philosopher invite people to come and hear him? Is it not that as the sun, or as food, is its own sufficient attraction, so the philosopher also is his own sufficient attraction to those who are to be benefited by him? Does a physician invite people to come and let him heal them? . . . . (Imagine what a genuine philosopher's invitation would be) — 'I invite you to come and be told that you are in a bad way — that you care for everything except what you should care for — that you do not know what things are good and what evil — and that you are unhappy and unfortunate.' A nice invitation! and yet if that is not the result of what a philosopher says, he and his words alike are dead. (Musonius) Rufus used to say, 'If you have leisure to praise me, my teaching has been in vain.' Accordingly he used to talk in such a way that each individual one of us who sat there thought that someone had been telling Rufus about him: he so put his finger upon what we had done, he so set the individual faults of each one of us clearly before our eyes.

"The philosopher's lecture-room, gentlemen, is a surgery: when you go away you ought to have felt not pleasure but pain. For when you come in, something is wrong with you: one man has put his shoulder out, another has an abscess, another a headache. Am I — the surgeon — then, to sit down and give you a string of fine sentences, that you may praise me — and then go away — the man with the dislocated arm, the man with the abscess, the man with the headache — just as you came? Is it for this that young men come away from home, and leave their parents and their kinsmen and their property, to say 'Bravo' to you for your fine moral conclusions? Is this what Socrates did — or Zeno — or Cleanthes?

"Well, but is there no such class of speeches as exhortations?

"Who denies it? But in what do exhortations consist? In, being able to show, whether to one man or to many men, the contradiction in which they are involved, and that their thoughts are given to anything but what they really mean. For they mean to give them to the things that really tend to happiness, but they look for those things elsewhere than where they really are. (That is the true aim of exhortation): but to show this, is it necessary to place a thousand chairs, and invite people to come and listen, and dress yourself up in a fine gown, and ascend the pulpit — and describe the death of Achilles? Cease, I implore you, from bringing dishonor, as far as you can, upon noble words and deeds. There can be no stronger exhortation to duty, I suppose, than for a speaker to make it clear to his audience that he wants to get something out of them! Tell me who, after hearing you lecture or discourse, became anxious about or reflected upon himself? or who, as he went out of the room, said, 'The philosopher put his finger upon my faults: I must not behave in that way again'?

"You cannot: the utmost praise you get is when
a man says to another, 'That was a beautiful
passage about Xerxes,' and the other says, ' No,
I liked best that about the battle of
Thermopylae.'

"This is a philosopher's sermon !"[183]

I have dwelt on this feature of the Greek life of the early
Christian centuries, not with the view of giving a complete
picture of it, which would be impossible within the compass
of a lecture, but rather with the view of establishing a
presumption, which you will find amply justified by further
researches, that it was sufficient, not only in its quality and
complexity, but also in its mass, to account for certain
features of early Christianity.

In passing from Greek life to Christianity, I will ask you, in
the first instance, to note the broad distinction which exists
between what in the primitive churches was known as
"prophesying," and that which in subsequent times came to
be known as "preaching." I lay the more stress upon the
distinction for the accidental reason that, in the first reaction
against the idea that "prophecy" necessarily meant
"prediction," it was maintained — and with a certain
reservation the contention was true — that a "prophet"
meant a "preacher." The reservation is, that the prophet was
not merely a preacher but a spontaneous preacher. He
preached because he could not help it, because there was a
divine breath breathing within him which must needs find an
utterance. It is in this sense that the prophets of the early

---

[183] Epict. *Diss*, 3, 23.

churches were preachers. They were not church officers appointed to discharge certain functions. They were the possessors of a *charisma*, a divine gift which was not official but personal. "No prophecy ever came by the will of man; but men spake from God, being moved by the Holy Ghost." They did not practice beforehand how or what they should say; for "the Holy Ghost taught them in that very hour what they should say." Their language was often, from the point of view of the rhetorical schools, a barbarous patois. They were ignorant of the rules both of style and of dialectic. They paid no heed to refinements of expression. The greatest preacher of them all claimed to have come among his converts, in a city in which Rhetoric flourished, not with the persuasiveness of human logic, but with the demonstration which was afforded by spiritual power.

Of that "prophesying" of the primitive churches it is not certain that we possess any monument. The Second Epistle of Peter and the Epistle of Jude are perhaps representatives of it among the canonical books of the New Testament. The work known as the Second Epistle of Clement is perhaps a representative of the form which it took in the middle of the second century; but though it is inspired by a genuine enthusiasm, it is rather more artistic in its form than a purely prophetic utterance is likely to have been.

In the course of the second century, this original spontaneity died almost entirely away. It may almost be said to have died a violent death. The dominant parties in the Church set their faces against it. The survivals of it in Asia Minor were formally condemned. The Montanists, as they were called, who tried to fan the lingering sparks of it into a flame, are ranked among heretics. And Tertullian is not even now admitted into the calendar of the Saints, because he believed the Montanists to be in the right.

It was inevitable that it should be so. The growth of a confederation of Christian communities necessitated the definition of a basis of confederation. Such a definition, and the further necessity of guarding it, were inconsistent with that free utterance of the Spirit which had existed before the confederation began. Prophesying died when the Catholic Church was formed.

In place of prophesying came preaching. And preaching is the result of the gradual combination of different elements. In the formation of a great institution it is inevitable that, as time goes on, different elements should tend to unite. To the original functions of a bishop, for example, were added by degrees the functions — which had originally been separate — of teacher.[184] In a similar way were fused together, on the one hand, teaching — that is, the tradition and exposition of the sacred books and of the received doctrine; and, on the other hand, exhortation — that is, the endeavor to raise men to a higher level of moral and spiritual life. Each of these was a function which, assuming a certain natural aptitude, could be learned by practice. Each of them was consequently a function which might be discharged by the permanent officers of the community, and discharged habitually at regular intervals without waiting for the fitful flashes of the prophetic fire. We consequently find that with the growth of organization there grew up also, not only a fusion of

---

[184] The functions are clearly separable in the Teaching of the Apostles, 15.

teaching and exhortation, but also the gradual restriction of the liberty of addressing the community to the official class.

It was this fusion of teaching and exhortation that constituted the essence of the homily: its form came from the sophists. For it was natural that when addresses, whether expository or hortatory, came to prevail in the Christian communities, they should be affected by the similar addresses which filled a large place in contemporary Greek life. It was not only natural but inevitable that when men who had been trained in rhetorical methods came to make such addresses, they should follow the methods to which they were accustomed. It is probable that Origen is not only the earliest example whose writings have come down to us, but also one of the earliest who took into the Christian communities these methods of the schools. He lectured, as the contemporary teachers seem to have lectured, every day: his subject matter was the text of the Scriptures, as that of the rhetoricians and sophists by his side was Homer or Chrysippus: his addresses, like those of the best professors, were carefully prepared: he was sixty years of age, we are told, before he preached an extempore sermon.[185]

When the Christian communities emerge into the clearer light of the fourth century, the influence of the rhetorical schools upon them begins to be visible on a large scale and with permanent effects. The voice of the prophet had ceased, and the voice of the preacher had begun. The greatest Christian preachers of the fourth century had been trained to rhetorical methods, and had themselves taught rhetoric. Basil and Gregory Nazianzen studied at Athens

[185] Euseb. *H. E.* 6.36.1.

under the famous professors Himerius and Prohaeresius: Chrysostom studied under the still more famous Libanius, who on his death-bed said of him that he would have been his worthiest successor "if the Christians had not stolen him."[186] The discourses came to be called by the same names as those of the Greek professors. They had originally been called homilies — a word which was unknown in this sense in pre-Christian times, and which denoted the familiar intercourse and direct personal addresses of common life. They came to be called by the technical terms of the schools — discourses, disputations, or speeches.[187] The distinction between the two kinds of terms is clearly shown by a later writer, who, speaking of a particular volume of Chrysostom's addresses, says, "They are called 'speeches' (*logoi*), but they are more like homilies, for this reason, above others, that he again and again addresses his hearers as actually present before his eyes."[188] The form of the discourses tended to be the same: if you examine side by side a discourse of Himerius or Themistius or Libanius, and one of Basil or Chrysostom or Ambrose, you will find a similar artificiality of structure, and a similar elaboration of phraseology. They were delivered under analogous circumstances. The preacher sat in his official chair: it was an exceptional thing for him to ascend the reader's *ambo*, the modern "pulpit:"[189] the audience crowded in front of him, and frequently interrupted

---

[186] Sozom. *H. E.* 8.2.

[187] Eusebius, *H. E.* 6.36.1; Aug, *Confess.* 5, 13, vol. i. 118; *Tract.* lxxxix. in *Johann, Evang.* c. 5, vol. iii. pars 2, p. 719.

[188] Phot. *Biblioth.* 172.

[189] Sozomen. *H. E.* 8.5.

him with shouts of acclamation. The greater preachers tried to stem the tide of applause which surged round them: again and again Chrysostom begs his hearers to be silent: what he wants is, not their acclamations, but the fruits of his preaching in their lives.[190] There is one passage which not only illustrates this point, but also affords a singular analogy to the remonstrance of Epictetus which was quoted just now:

"There are many preachers who make long sermons: if they are well applauded, they are as glad as if they had obtained a kingdom: if they bring their sermon to an end in silence, their despondency is worse, I may almost say, than hell. It is this that ruins churches, that you do not seek to hear sermons that touch the heart, but sermons that will delight your ears with their intonation and the structure of their phrases, just as if you were listening to singers and lute-players. And we preachers humor your fancies, instead of trying to crush them. We act like a father who gives a sick child a cake or an ice, or something else that is merely nice to eat — just because he asks for it; and takes no pains to give him what is good for him; and then when the doctors blame him says, 'I could not bear to hear my child cry.' That is what we do when we elaborate beautiful sentences, fine combinations and harmonies, to please and not to profit, to be admired and not to instruct, to delight and not to touch you, to go away with your applause in our ears, and not to better your conduct. Believe me, I am not speaking at

---

[190] *Adv. Jud.* 7. 6, vol. i. 671;

random: when you applaud me as I speak, I
feel at the moment as it is natural for a man to
feel. I will make a clean breast of it. Why
should I not? I am delighted and overjoyed.
And then when I go home and reflect that the
people who have been applauding me have
received no benefit, and indeed that whatever
benefit they might have had has been killed by
the applause and praises, I am sore at heart,
and I lament and fall to tears, and I feel as
though I had spoken altogether in vain, and I
say to myself. What is the good of all your
labors, seeing that your hearers don't want to
reap any fruit out of all that you say? And I
have often thought of laying down a rule
absolutely prohibiting all applause, and urging
you to listen in silence."[191]

And there is a passage near the end of Gregory
Nazianzen's greatest sermon, in which the human nature of
which Chrysostom speaks bursts forth with striking force:
after the famous peroration in which after bidding farewell
one by one to the church and congregation which he loved,
to the several companies of his fellow-workers, and to the
multitudes who had thronged to hear him preach, he turns
to the court and his opponents the Arian courtiers —

"Farewell, princes and palaces, the royal court
and household — whether ye be faithful to the
king I know not, ye are nearly all of you
unfaithful to God." (There was evidently a
burst of applause, and he interrupts his
peroration with an impromptu address.) "Yes

---

[191] S. Chrys. *Hom*, xxx. in *Act, Apost.* c. 3, vol. ix.

— clap your hands, shout aloud, exalt your
orator to heaven: your malicious and chattering
tongue has ceased: it will not cease for long: it
will fight (though I am absent) with writing and
ink: but just for the moment we are silent."
(Then the peroration is resumed.) "Farewell,
great and Christian city…"[192]

I will add only one more instance of the way in which the
habits of the sophists flowed into the Christian churches.
Christian preachers, like the sophists, were sometimes
peripatetic; they went from place to place, delivering their
orations and making money by delivering them. The
historians Socrates and Sozomen[193] tell an instructive story
of two Syrian bishops, Severianus of Gabala and Antiochus
of Ptolemais (St. Jean d'Acre). They were both famous for
their rhetoric, though Severianus could not quite get rid of
his Syrian accent. Antiochus went to Constantinople, and
stayed there a long time, preaching frequently in the
churches, and making a good deal of money thereby. On his
return to Syria, Severianus, hearing about the money,
resolved to follow his example; he waited for some time,
exercised his rhetoric, got together a large stock of sermons,
and thou went to Constantinople. He was kindly received by
the bishop, and soon became both a great popular preacher
and a favorite at court. The fate of many preachers and court
favorites overtook him: he excited great jealousy, was
accused of heresy and banished from the city; and only by
the personal intercession of the Empress Eudoxia was he
received back again into ecclesiastical favor.

---

[192] Greg. *Naz. Oral.* xiii.

[193] Socrates, *H. E.* 6.11; Sozomen, *H. E.* 8.10.

Such are some of the indications of the influence of Greek Rhetoric upon the early churches. It created the Christian sermon. It added to the functions of church officers a function which is neither that of the exercise of discipline, nor of administration of the funds, nor of taking the lead in public worship, nor of the simple tradition of received truths, but that of either such an exegesis of the sacred books as the Sophists gave of Homer, or such elaborated discourses as they also gave upon the speculative and ethical aspects of religion. The result was more far-reaching than the creation of either an institution or a function. If you look more closely into history, you will find that Rhetoric killed Philosophy. Philosophy died, because for all but a small minority it ceased to be real. It passed from the sphere of thought, and conduct to that of exposition and literature. Its preachers preached, not because they were bursting with truths which could not help finding expression, but because they were masters of fine phrases and lived in an age in which fine phrases had a value. It died, in short, because it had become sophistry. But sophistry is of no special age or country. It is indigenous to all soils upon which literature grows. No sooner is any special form of literature created by the genius of a great writer than there arises a class of men who cultivate the style of it for the style's sake. No sooner is any new impulse given either to philosophy or to religion than there arises a class of men who copy the form without the substance, and try to make the echo of the past sound like the voice of the present. So it has been with Christianity. It came into the educated world in the simple dress of a Prophet of Righteousness. It won that world by the stern reality of its life, by the subtle bonds of its brotherhood, by its divine message of consolation and of hope. Around it thronged the race of eloquent talkers who persuaded it to change its dress and to assimilate its language to their own. It seemed thereby to win a speedier and completer victory. But it purchased conquest at the price of reality. With that its progress stopped. There has been an element of sophistry in it ever since; and so far as in any age that element has been dominant, so far has the progress of Christianity been arrested. Its progress is arrested now, because many of its preachers live in an unreal world. The truths they set forth are truths of utterance rather than truths of their lives. But if Christianity is to be again the power that it was in its earliest ages, it must renounce its costly purchase. A class of rhetorical chemists would be thought of only to be ridiculed: a class of rhetorical religionists is only less anomalous because we are accustomed to it. The hope of Christianity is, that the class which was artificially created may ultimately disappear; and that the sophistical element in Christian preaching will melt, as a transient mist, before the preaching of the prophets of the ages to come, who, like the prophets of the ages that are long gone by, will speak only "as the Spirit gives them utterance."

Lecture V. CHRISTIANITY AND GREEK PHILOSOPHY.

The power of generalizing and of forming abstract ideas exists, or at least is exercised, in varying degrees among different races and at different times. The peculiar feature of the intellectual history of the Greeks is the rapidity with which the power was developed, and the strength of the grasp which it had upon them.

The elaboration of one class of such ideas, those of form and quantity, led to the formation of a group of sciences, the mathematical sciences, which hold a permanent place. The earliest and most typical of these sciences is geometry. In it, the attention is drawn away from all the other characteristics of material things, and fixed upon the single characteristic of their form. The forms are regarded in themselves. The process of abstraction or analysis reaches its limit in the point, and from that limit the mind, making a new departure, begins the process of construction or synthesis. Complex ideas are formed by the addition of one simple idea to another, and having been so formed can be precisely defined. Their constituent elements can be distinctly stated, and a clear boundary drawn round the whole. They can be so marked off from other ideas that the idea which one man has formed can be communicated to and represented in another man's mind. The inferences which, assuming certain "axioms" to be true and certain "postulates" to be granted, are made by one man, are accepted by another man or at once disproved. There is no question of mere probability, nor any halting between two opinions. The inferences are not only true but certain.

The result is, that there are not two sciences of geometry, but one: all who study it are agreed as to both its definitions and its inferences.

The elaboration of another class of abstract ideas, those of quality, marched at first by a parallel road. To a limited extent such a parallel march is possible. The words which are used to express sensible qualities suggest the same ideas to different minds. They are applied by different minds to the same objects. But the limits of such an agreement are narrow. When we pass from the abstract ideas of qualities, or generalizations as to substances, which can be tested by the senses, to such ideas as those, for example, of courage or justice, law or duty, though the words suggest, on the whole, the same ideas to one man as to another, not all men would uniformly apply the same words to the same actions. The phenomena which suggest such ideas assume a different form and color as they are regarded from different points of view. They enter into different combinations. They are not sharply marked out by lines which would be universally recognized. The attention of different men is arrested by different features. There is consequently no universally recognized definition of them. 'Nor is such a definition possible. The ideas themselves tend to shade off into their contraries. There is a fringe of haze round each of them. The result is that assertions about them vary. There is not one system of philosophy only; there are many.

Between these two classes of generalizations and abstractions, those of quantity and those of quality or substance, many Greek thinkers do not appear to have made any clear distinction. Ideas of each class were regarded as equally capable of being defined; the canons of inference which were applicable to the one were conceived to be equally applicable to the other: and the certainty of inference and exactness of demonstration which were possible in regard to the ideal forms of geometry, were supposed to be also possible in regard to the conceptions of metaphysics and ethics.[194]

The habit of making definitions, and of drawing deductions from them, was fostered by the habit of discussion. Discussion under the name of dialectic, which implies that it was but a regulated conversation, had a large place, not only in the rhetorical and philosophical schools, but also in ordinary Greek life. It was like a game of cards. The game, so to speak, was conducted under strict and recognized rules; but it could not proceed unless each card had a determined and admitted value. The definition of terms was its necessary preliminary; and dialectic helped to spread the habit of requiring definitions over a wider area and to give it a deeper root.

There was less divergence in the definitions themselves than there was in the propositions that were deduced from them. That is to say, there was a verbal agreement as to definitions which was not a real agreement of ideas: the same words were found on examination to cover different areas of thought. But whether the difference lay in the definitions themselves or in the deductions made from them, there was

---

[194] An indication of this may be seen in the fact that words which have come down to modern times as technical terms of geometry were used indifferently in the physical and moral sciences.

nothing to determine which of two contrary or contradictory propositions was true. There was no universally recognized standard of appeal, or *criterion*, as it was termed. Indeed, the question of the nature of the criterion was one of the chief questions at issue. Consequently, assertions about abstract ideas and wide generalizations could only be regarded as the affirmations of a personal conviction. The making of such an affirmation was expressed by the same phrase which was used for a resolution of the will — "It seems to me," or "It seems (good) to me" (*dokei moi*): the affirmation itself, by the corresponding substantive, *dogma*. But just as the resolutions of the will of a monarch were obeyed by his subjects, that is, were adopted as resolutions of the will of other persons, so the affirmations of a thinker might be assented to by those who listened to him, that is, might become affirmations of other persons. In the one case as in the other, the same word *dogma* was employed.[195] It thus came to express (1) a decree, (2) a doctrine. The latter use tended to predominate. The word came ordinarily to express an affirmation made by u philosopher which was accepted as true by those who, from the fact of so accepting it, became his followers and formed his school. The acquiescence of a large number of men in the same affirmation gave to such an affirmation a high degree of probability; but it did not cause it to lose its original character of a personal conviction, nor did it afford any guarantee that the coincidence of expression was also a coincidence of ideas either between the original thinker and his disciples, or between the disciples themselves.[196]

---

[195] Dio Chrys. vol. i. p. 46, ed. Dind.

[196] The use of the word in Epictetus is especially instructive: *dogmata* fill a large place in his philosophy. They are the inner

Within these limits of its original and proper use, and as
expressing a fact of mind, the word has an indisputable
value. But the fact of the personal character of a dogma soon
became lost to sight. Two tendencies which grew with a
parallel growth dominated the world in place of the
recognition of it. It came to be assumed that certain
convictions of certain philosophers were not simply true in
relation to the philosophers themselves, and to the state of
knowledge in their time, but had a universal validity:
subjective and temporary convictions were thus elevated to
the rank of objective and eternal truths. It came also to be
assumed that the processes of reason so closely followed the
order of nature, that a system of ideas constructed in strict
accordance with the laws of reasoning corresponded exactly
with the realities of things. The unity of such a system
reflected, it was thought, the unity of the world of objective
fact. It followed that the truth or untruth of a given
proposition was thought to be determined by its logical
consistency or inconsistency with the sum of previous
inferences.

These tendencies were strongly accentuated by the decay
of original thinking. Philosophy in later Greece was less
thought than literature. It was the exegesis of received
doctrines. Philosophers had become professors. The

---

judgments of the mind (*Diss*. 4. 11. 7) in regard to both
intellectual and moral phenomena. They are especially relative
to the latter. They are the convictions upon which men act, the
moral maxims which form the ultimate motives of action and the
resolution to act or not act in a particular case. They are the most
personal and inalienable part of us. See especially, *Diss*. 1.11.33,
35, 38; 17.26; 29.11,12; 2.1.21, 32; 3.2.12; 9.2; Euch. 45.

question of what was in itself true had become entangled with the question of what the Master had said. The moral duty of adherence to the traditions of a school was stronger than the moral duty of finding the truth at all hazards. The literary expression of a doctrine came to be more important than the doctrine itself. The differences of expression between one thinker and another were exaggerated. Words became fetishes. Outside the schools were those who were litterateurs rather than philosophers, and who fused different elements together into systems which had a greater unity of literary form than of logical coherence. But these very facts of the literary character of philosophy, and of the contradictions in the expositions of it, served to spread it over a wider area. They tended on the one hand to bring a literary acquaintance with philosophy into the sphere of general education, and on the other hand to produce a propaganda. Sect rivalled sect in trying to win scholars for its school. The result was that the ordinary life of later Greece was saturated with philosophical ideas, and that the discordant theories of rival schools were blended together in the average mind into a syncretistic dogmatism.

Against this whole group of tendencies there was more than one reaction. The tendency to dogmatize was met by the tendency to doubt; and the tendency to doubt flowed in many streams, which can with difficulty be traced in minute detail, but whose general course is sufficiently described for the ordinary student in the Academics of Cicero. In the second and third centuries of our era there had come to be three main groups of schools. "Some men," writes Sextus Empiricus,[197] " say that they have found the truth; some say that it is impossible for truth to be apprehended; some still search for it. The first class consists of those who are specially designated Dogmatics, the followers of Aristotle and Epicurus, the Stoics, and some others: the second class consists of the followers of Clitomachus and Carneades, and other Academics: the third class consists of the Sceptics." They may be distinguished as the philosophy of assertion, the philosophy of denial, and the philosophy of research.[198] But the first of these was in an overwhelming majority. The Dogmatics, especially in the form either of pure Stoicism or of Stoicism largely infused with Platonism, were in possession of the field of educated thought. It is a convincing proof of the completeness with which that thought was saturated with their methods and their fundamental conceptions, that those methods and conceptions are found even among the philosophers of research who claimed to have wholly disentangled themselves from them.[199]

The philosophy of assertion, the philosophy of denial, and the philosophy of research, were all alike outside the earliest forms of Christianity. In those forms the moral and spiritual elements were not only supreme but exclusive. They reflected the philosophy, not of Greece, but of Palestine. That philosophy was almost entirely ethical. It dealt with the problems, not of being in the abstract, but of human life. It was stated for the most part in short antithetical sentences,

---

[197] Sext. Empir. *Pyrrh. Hypot* 1.3.

[198] *Ibid.* 4.

[199] Sext. Empir. *Pyrrh. Hypot.* 3.2, 3.

with a symbol or parable to enforce them. It was a philosophy of proverbs. It had no eye for the minute anatomy of thought. It had no system, for the sense of system was not yet awakened. It had no taste for verbal distinctions. It was content with the symmetry of balanced sentences, without attempting to construct a perfect whole. It reflected as in a mirror, and not unconsciously, the difficulties, the contradictions, the unsolved enigmas of the world of fact.

When this Palestinian philosophy became more self-conscious than it had been, it remained still within its own sphere, the enigmas of the moral world were still its subject-matter, and it became in the Fathers of the Talmud on the one hand fatalism, and on the other casuistry.

The earliest forms of Christianity were not only outside the sphere of Greek philosophy, but they also appealed, on the one hand, mainly to the classes which philosophy did not reach, and, on the other hand, to a standard which philosophy did not recognize. "Not many wise men after the flesh" were called in St. Paul's time: and more than a century afterwards, Celsus sarcastically declared the law of admission to the Christian communities to be — "Let no educated man enter, no wise man, no prudent man, for such things we deem evil; but whoever is ignorant, whoever is unintelligent, whoever is uneducated, whoever is simple, let him come and be welcome."[200] It proclaimed, moreover, that "the philosophy of the world was foolishness with God." It appealed to prophecy and to testimony. "Instead of logical demonstration, it produced living witnesses of the words and

[200] Origen, *c. Cels*. 3.44.

wonderful doings of Jesus Christ." The philosophers from the point of view of "worldly education" made sport of it: Celsus[201] declared that the Christian teachers were no better than the priests of Mithra or of Hekate, leading men wherever they willed with the maxims of a blind belief.

It is therefore the more remarkable that within a century and a half after Christianity and philosophy first came into close contact, the ideas and methods of philosophy had flowed in such mass into Christianity, and filled so large a place in it, as to have made it no less a philosophy than a religion.

The question which arises, and which should properly be discussed before the influences of particular ideas are traced in particular doctrines, is, how this result is to be accounted for as a whole. The answer must explain both how Christianity and philosophy came into contact, and how when in contact the one exercised upon the other the influence of a molding force.

The explanation is to be found in the fact that, in spite of the apparent and superficial antagonism, between certain leading ideas of current philosophy and the leading ideas of Christianity there was a special and real kinship. Christianity gave to the problems of philosophy a new solution which was cognate to the old, and to its doubts the certainty of a revelation. The kinship of ideas is admitted, and explanations of it are offered by both Christian writers and their opponents. "We teach the same as the Greeks," says Justin

---

[201] Origen, *c. Cels.* 1.9.

Martyr,[202] "though we alone are hated for what we teach." "Some of our number," says Tertullian,[203] "who are versed in ancient literature, have composed books by means of which it may be clearly seen that we have embraced nothing new or monstrous, nothing in which we have not the support of common and public literature." Elsewhere[204] the same writer founds an argument for the toleration of Christianity on the fact that its opponents maintained it to be but a kind of philosophy, teaching the very same doctrines as the philosophers — innocence, justice, endurance, soberness, and chastity: he claims on that ground the same liberty for Christians which was enjoyed by philosophers.

The general recognition of this kinship of ideas is even more conclusively shown by the fact that explanations of it were offered on both the one side and the other.

(a) It was argued by some Christian apologists that the best doctrines of philosophy were due to the inworking in the world of the same Divine Word who had become incarnate in Jesus Christ. "The teachings of Plato," says Justin Martyr,[205] "are not alien to those of Christ, though not in all respects similar... For all the writers (of antiquity) were able to have a dim vision of realities by means of the indwelling seed of the implanted Word." It was argued by others that philosophers had borrowed or "stolen" their doctrines from the Scriptures. "From the divine preachings of the prophets,"

---

[202] *Apol.* i. 20.

[203] *De testim. Animae*, 1.

[204] *Apol.* 46.

[205] *Apol* 2.13.

says Minucius Felix,[206] "they imitated the shadow of half-truths." "What poet or sophist," says Tertullian,[207] "has not drunk at the fountain of the prophets? From thence it is, therefore, that philosophers have quenched the thirst of their minds, so that it is the very things which they have of ours which bring us into comparison with them." "They have borrowed from our books," says Clement of Alexandria,[208] "the chief doctrines they hold, both on faith and knowledge and science, on hope and love, on repentance and temperance and the fear of God:" and he goes in detail through many doctrines, speculative as well as ethical, either to show that they were borrowed from revelation, or to uphold the truer thesis that philosophy was no less the schoolmaster of the Greeks than the Law was of the Jews to bring them to Christ.

(b) It was argued, on the other hand, by the opponents of Christianity that it was a mere mimicry of philosophy or a blurred copy of it. "They weave a web of misunderstandings of the old doctrine," says Celsus,[209] "and sound them forth with a loud trumpet before men, like hierophants booming round those who are being initiated in mysteries." Christianity was but a misunderstood Platonism. Whatever in it was true had been better expressed before.[210] Even the striking and distinctive saying of the Sermon on the Mount,

[206] *Octav.* 34.

[207] *Apol.* 47.

[208] *Strom.* 2. 1.

[209] Origen, *c. Cels.* 3.16.

[210] Origen, *c. Cels.* 5.65; 6.1,7,15,19

"Whosoever shall smite thee on thy right cheek, turn to him the other also," was but a coarser and more homely way of saying what had been extremely well said by Plato's Socrates.[211]

It was through this kinship of ideas that Christianity was readily absorbed by some of the higher natures in the Greek world. The two classes of ideas probably came into contact in philosophical Judaism. For it is clear on the one hand that the Jews of the dispersion had a literature, and on the other hand that that literature was clothing itself in Greek forms and attracting the attention of the Greek world. Some of that literature was philosophical. In the Sibylline verses, the poem of Phocylides, and the letters of Heraclitus, there is a blending of theology and ethics: in some of the writings which are ascribed to Philo, but which in reality bridge the interval between Philo and the Christian Fathers, there is a blending of theology and metaphysics. None of them are "very far from the kingdom of God." The hypothesis that they paved the way for Christian philosophy is confirmed by the fact that in the first articulate expressions of that philosophy precisely those elements are dominant which were dominant in Jewish philosophy. Two such elements may specially be mentioned: (1) the allegorical method of interpretation which was common to both Jews and Greeks, and by means of which both the Gnostics who were without, and the Alexandrians who were within, the pale of the associated communities, were able to find their philosophy in the Old Testament as well as in the New; (2) the cosmological speculations, which occupied only a small space in the thoughts of earlier Greek thinkers, but which

---

[211] *Ibid.* 7. 58.

were already widening to a larger circle on the surface of Greek philosophy, and which became so prominent in the first Christian philosophies as to have thrust aside almost all other elements in the current representations of them.

The Christian philosophy which thus rose out of philosophical Judaism was partly apologetic and partly speculative. The apologetic part of it arose from the necessity of defense. The educated world tended to scout Christianity when it was first presented to them, as an immoral and barbarous atheism. It was necessary to show that it was neither the one nor the other. The defense naturally fell into the hands of those Christians who were versed in Greek methods; and they not less naturally sought for points of agreement rather than of difference, and presented Christian truths in a Greek form. The speculative part of it arose from some of its elements having found an especial affinity with some of the new developments of Pythagoreanism and Platonism. Inside the original communities were men who began to build great edifices of speculation upon the narrow basis of one or other of the pinnacles of the Christian temple; and outside those communities were men who began to coalesce into communities which had the same moral aims as the original communities, and which appealed in the main to the same authorities, but in which the simpler forms of worship were elaborated into a thaumaturgic ritual, and the solid facts of Scripture history evaporated into mist. They were linked on the one hand with the cults of the Greek mysteries, and on the other with philosophical idealism. The tendency to conceive of abstract ideas as substances, with form and real existence, received in them its extreme development.

Wisdom and vice, silence and desire, were real beings: they were not, as they had been to earlier thinkers, mere thin vapors which had floated upwards from the world of sensible existences, and hung like clouds in an uncertain twilight. The real world was indeed not the world of sensible existences, of thoughts and utterances about sensible things, but a world in which sensible existences were the shadows and not the substance, the waves and not the sea.[212]

It was natural that those who held to the earlier forms of Christianity should take alarm. "I am not unaware," says Clement of Alexandria, in setting forth the design of his *Stromateis*,[213] "of what is dinned in our ears by the ignorant timidity of those who tell us that we ought to occupy ourselves with the most necessary matters, those in which the Faith consists: and that we should pass by the superfluous matters that lie outside them, which vex and detain us in vain over points that contribute nothing to the end in view. There are others who think that philosophy will prove to have been introduced into life from an evil source, at the hands of a mischievous inventor, for the ruin of men."

---

[212] The above slight sketch of some of the leading tendencies which have been loosely grouped together under the name of Gnosticism has been left unelaborated, because a fuller account, with the distinctions which must necessarily be noted, would lead us too far from the main track of the Lecture: some of the tendencies will reappear in detail in subsequent Lectures, and students will no doubt refer to the brilliant exposition of Gnosticism in Harnack, *Dogmengeschichte*, i. pp. 186— 226, ed. 2.

[213] *Strom*. 1.1: almost the whole of the first book is valuable as a vindication of the place of culture in Christianity.

"The simpler-minded," says Tertullian,[214] "not to say ignorant and unlearned men, who always form the majority of believers, are frightened at the Economy" [the philosophical explanation of the doctrine of the Trinity]. "These men," says a contemporary writer,[215] of some of the early philosophical schools at Rome, "have fearlessly perverted the divine Scriptures, and set aside the rule of the ancient faith, and have not known Christ, seeking as they do, not what the divine Scriptures say, but what form of syllogism may be found to support their godlessness; and if one advances any express statement of the divine Scripture, they try to find out whether it can form a conjunctive or a disjunctive hypothetical. And having deserted the holy Scriptures of God, they study geometry, being of the earth and speaking of the earth, and ignoring Him who comes from above. Some of them, at any rate, give their minds to Euclid: some of them are admiring disciples of Aristotle and Theophrastus: as for Galen, some of them go so far as actually to worship him."

The history of the second century is the history of the clash and conflict between these new mystical and philosophical elements of Christianity and its earlier forms. On the one hand were the majority of the original communities, holding in the main the conception of Christianity which probably finds its best contemporary exposition in the first two books of the Apostolical Constitutions, a religion of stern moral practice and of strict

---

[214] *Adv. Prax.* 3.

[215] Quoted by Euseb. *H. E.* 5.28.13.

moral discipline, of the simple love of God and the unelaborated faith in Jesus Christ. On the other hand were the new communities, and the new members of the older communities, with their conception of knowledge side by side with faith, and with their tendency to speculate side by side with their acceptance of tradition. The conflict was inevitable. In the current state of educated opinion it would have been as impossible for the original communities to ignore the existence of philosophical elements either in their own body, or in the new communities which were growing up around them, as it would be for the Christian churches of our own day to ignore physical science. The result of the conflict was, that the extreme wing of each of the contending parties dropped off from the main body. The old-fashioned Christians, who would admit of no compromise, and maintained the old usages unchanged, were gradually detached as Ebionites, or Nazaraeans. The old orthodoxy became a new heresy. In the lists of the early handbooks they are ranked as the first heretics. The more philosophical Gnostics also passed one by one outside the Christian lines. Their ideas gradually lost their Christian color. They lived in another, but non-Christian, form. The true Gnostic, though he repudiates the name, is Plotinus. The logical development of the thoughts of Basilides and Justin, of Valentinus and the Naassenes, is to be found in Neo-Platonism — that splendid vision of incomparable and irrecoverable cloudland in which the sun of Greek philosophy set.

The struggle really ended, as almost all great conflicts end, in a compromise. There was apparently so complete a victory of the original communities and of the principles which they embodied, that their opponents seem to vanish from Christian literature and Christian history. It was in reality a victory in which the victors were the vanquished. There was so large an absorption by the original communities of the principles of their opponents as to destroy the main reason for a separate existence. The absorption was less of speculations than of the tendency to speculate. The residuum of permanent effect was mainly a certain habit of mind. This is at once a consequence and a proof of the general argument which has been advanced above, that certain elements of education in philosophy had been so widely diffused, and in the course of centuries had become so strongly rooted, as to have caused an instinctive tendency to throw ideas into a philosophical form, and to test assertions by philosophical canons. The existence of such a tendency is shown in the first instance by the mode in which the earliest "defenders of the faith" met their opponents; and the supposition that it was instinctive is a legitimate inference from the fact that it was unconscious. For Tatian,[216] though he ridicules Greek philosophy and professes to have abandoned it, yet builds up theories of the *Logos*, of free-will, and of the nature of spirit, out of the elements of current philosophical conceptions. Tertullian, though he asks,[217] "What resemblance is there between a philosopher and a Christian, between a disciple of Greece and a disciple of heaven?" expresses Christian truths in philosophical terms, and argues against his opponents — for example, against Marcion — by methods which might serve as typical examples of the current methods of controversy

---

[216] *Orat ad Graec*. 2.

[217] *Apol*. 46.

between philosophical schools. And Hippolytus,[218] though he reproves another Christian writer for listening to Gentile teaching, and so disobeying the injunction, "Go not into the way of the Gentiles," is himself saturated with philosophical conceptions and philosophical literature.

The answer, in short, to the main question which has been before us is that Christianity came into a ground which was already prepared for it. Education was widely diffused over the Greek world, and among all classes of the community. It had not merely aroused the habit of inquiry which is the foundation of philosophy, but had also taught certain philosophical methods. Certain elements of the philosophical temper had come into existence on a large scale, penetrating all classes of society and inwrought into the general intellectual fiber of the time. They had produced a certain habit of mind. When, through the kinship of ideas, Christianity had been absorbed by the educated classes, the habit of mind which had preceded it remained and dominated. It showed itself mainly in three ways:

1. The first of these was the tendency to define. The earliest Christians had been content to believe in God and to worship Him, without endeavoring to define precisely the conception of Him which lay beneath their faith and their worship. They looked up to Him as their Father in heaven. They thought of Him as one, as beneficent, and as supreme. But they drew no fence of words round their idea of Him, and still less did they attempt to demonstrate by processes of reason that their idea of Him was true. But there is an anecdote quoted with approval by Eusebius[219] from Rhodon,

---

[218] *Refut. omn. heres.* 5.18.

a controversialist of the latter part of the second century, which furnishes a striking proof of the growing strength at that time of the philosophical temper. It relates the main points of a short controversy between Rhodon and Apelles. Apelles was in some respects in sympathy with Marcion, and in some respects followed the older Christian tradition. He refused to be drawn into the new philosophizing current; and Rhodon attacked him for his conservatism. "He was often refuted for his errors, which indeed made him say that we ought not to inquire too closely into doctrine; but that as everyone had believed, so he should remain. For he declared that those who set their hopes on the Crucified One would be saved, if only they were found in good works. But the most uncertain thing of all that he said was what he said about God. He held no doubt that there is One Principle, just as we hold too: but when I said to him, 'Tell us how you demonstrate that, or on what grounds you are able to assert that there is One Principle,'... he said that he did not know, but that that was his conviction. When I thereupon adjured him to tell the truth, he swore that he was telling the truth, that he did not know how there is one unbegotten God, but that nevertheless so he believed. Then I laughed at him and denounced him, for that, giving himself out to be a teacher, he did not know how to prove what he taught."

2. The second manifestation of the philosophical habit of mind was the tendency to speculate, that is, to draw inferences from definitions, to weave the inferences into systems, and to test assertions by their logical consistency or

---

[219] *H. E.* 5.13.

inconsistency with those systems. The earliest Christians had but little conception of a system. The inconsistency of one apparently true statement with another did not vex their souls. Their beliefs reflected the variety of the world and of men's thoughts about the world. It was one of the secrets of the first great successes of Christianity. There were different and apparently irreconcilable elements in it. It appealed to men of various mold. It furnished a basis for the construction of strangely diverse edifices. But the result of the ascendency of philosophy was, that in the fourth and fifth centuries the majority of churches insisted not only upon a unity of belief in the fundamental facts of Christianity, but also upon a uniformity of speculations in regard to those facts. The premises of those speculations were assumed; the conclusions logically followed: the propositions which were contrary or contradictory to them were measured, not by the greater or less probability of the premises, but by the logical certainty of the conclusions; and symmetry became a test of truth.

3. The new habit of mind manifested itself not less in the importance which came to be attached to it. The holding of approved opinions was elevated to a position at first co-ordinate with, and at last superior to, trust in God and the effort to live a holy life. There had been indeed from the first an element of knowledge in the conception of the means of salvation. The knowledge of the facts of the life of Jesus Christ necessarily precedes faith in him. But under the touch of Greek philosophy, knowledge had become speculation: whatever obligation attached to faith in its original sense was conceived to attach to it in its new sense: the new form of knowledge was held to be not less necessary than the old.

The Western communities not only took over the greater part of the inheritance, but also proceeded to assume in a still greater degree the correspondence of ideas with realities, and of inferences about ideas with truths about realities. It added such large groups to the sum of them, that in the dogmatic theology of Latin and Teutonic Christendom the content is more Western than Eastern. But the conception of such a theology and its underlying assumptions are Greek. They come from the Greek tendency to attach the same certainty to metaphysical as to physical ideas. They are in reality built upon a quicksand. There is no more reason to suppose that God has revealed metaphysics than that He has revealed chemistry. The Christian revelation is, at least primarily, a setting forth of certain facts. It does not in itself afford a guarantee of the certainty of the speculations which are built upon those facts. All such speculations are dogmas in the original sense of the word. They are simply personal convictions. To the statement of one man's convictions other men may assent: but they can never be quite sure that they understand its terms in the precise sense in which the original framer of the statement understood them.

The belief that metaphysical theology is more than this, is the chief bequest of Greece to religious thought, and it has been a *damnosa hereditas*. It has given to later Christianity that part of it which is doomed to perish, and which yet, while it lives, holds the key of the prison-house of many souls.

Lecture VI. GREEK AND CHRISTIAN ETHICS.

It has been common to construct pictures of the state of morals in the first centuries of the Christian era from the statements of satirists who, like all satirists, had a large element of caricature, and from the denunciations of the Christian apologists, which, like all denunciations, have a large element of exaggeration. The pictures so constructed are mosaics of singular vices, and they have led to the not unnatural impression that those centuries constituted an era of exceptional wickedness. It is no doubt difficult to gauge the average morality of any age. It is questionable whether the average morality of civilized ages has largely varied: it is possible that if the satirists of our own time were equally outspoken, the vices of ancient Rome might be found to have a parallel in modern London; and it is probable, not on merely *a priori* grounds, but from the nature of the evidence which remains, that there was in ancient Rome, as there is in modern London, a preponderating mass of those who loved their children and their homes, who were good neighbors and faithful friends, who conscientiously discharged their civil duties, and were in all the current senses of the word " moral" men.[220]

---

[220] The evidence for the above statements has not yet been fully gathered together, and is too long to be given even in outline here: the statements are in full harmony with the view of the chief modern writer on the subject, Friedlander, *Darstellungen aus der Sittengeschichte Roms*, see especially Bd. iii. p. 676, 5te aufl.

It has also been common to frame statements of the moral philosophy which dominated in those centuries, entirely from the data afforded by earlier writers, and to account for the existence of nobler elements in contemporary writers by the hypothesis that Seneca, Epictetus, and Marcus Aurelius, had come into contact with Christian teachers. In the case of Seneca, the belief in such contact went so far as to induce a writer in an imitative age to produce a series of letters which are still commonly printed at the end of his works, and which purport to be a correspondence between him and St. Paul. It is difficult, no doubt, to prove the negative proposition that such writers did not come into contact with Christianity; but a strong presumption against the idea that such contact, if it existed, influenced to any considerable extent their ethical principles, is established by the demonstrable fact that those principles form an integral part of their whole philosophical system, and that their system is in close logical and historical connection with that of their philosophical predecessors.[221]

It will be found on a closer examination that the age in which Christianity grew was in reality an age of moral reformation. There was the growth of a higher religious morality, which believed that God was pleased by moral action rather than by sacrifice.[222] There was the growth of a

---

[221] This is sufficiently shown by the fact, which is in other respects to be regretted, that in most accounts of Stoicism the earlier and later elements are viewed as constituting a homogeneous whole.

[222] "How am I to eat?" said a man to Epictetus: "So as to please God," was the reply (*Diss.* 1. 13). The idea is further developed

belief that life requires amendment.[223] There was a reaction in the popular mind against the vices of the great centers of population. This is especially seen in the large multiplication of religious guilds, in which purity of life was a condition of membership: it prepared the minds of men to receive Christian teaching, and forms not the least important among the causes which led to the rapid dissemination of that teaching: it affected the development of Christianity in that the members of the religious guilds who did so accept Christian teaching, brought over with them into the Christian communities many of the practices of their guilds and of the conceptions which lay beneath them. The philosophical phase of the reformation began on the confines of Stoicism and Cynicism. For Cynicism had revived. It had almost faded into insignificance after Zeno and Chrysippus had formed its nobler elements into a new system, and left only its "dog-bark"[224] and its squalor. But when the philosophical descendants of Zeno and Chrysippus had become fashionable *litterateurs*, and had sunk independence of thought and practice in a respectability and "worldly conformity" which the more earnest men felt to be intolerable, Cynicism revived, or rather the earlier and better Stoicism revived, to reassert the paramount importance of moral conduct, and to protest against the unnatural alliance between philosophy and the fashionable world.

It is to this moral reformation within the philosophical sphere that I wish especially to draw your attention. Its chief

---

in Porphyry, who says: "God wants nothing" (281.15).

[223] M. Aurelius, i. 7 and ii. 13.

[224] Philostr. 587.

preacher was Epictetus. He was ranked among the Stoics; but his portrait of an ideal philosopher is the portrait of a Cynic.[225] In him, whether he be called Stoic or Cynic, the ethics of the ancient world find at once their loftiest expression and their most complete realization: and it will be an advantage, instead of endeavoring to construct a composite and comprehensive picture from all the available materials, to limit our view mainly to what Epictetus says, and, as far as possible, to let his sermons speak for themselves.

The reformation affected chiefly two points: (1) the place of ethics in relation to philosophy and life; (2) the contents of ethical teaching.

1. The Stoics of the later Republic and of the age of the Caesars had come to give their chief attention to logic and literature. The study of ethics was no longer supreme; and it had changed its character. Logic, which in the systems of Zeno and Chrysippus had been only its servant, was becoming its master: it was both usurping its place and turning it into casuistry. The study of literature, of what the great masters of philosophy had taught, was superseding the moral practice which such study was intended to help and foster. The Stoics of the time could construct ingenious fallacies and compose elegant moral discourses; but they were ceasing to regard the actual "living according to nature" as the main object of their lives. The revival of Cynicism was a re-assertion of the supremacy of ethics over logic, and of conduct over literary knowledge. It was at first crude and

---

[225] *Diss*, 3.22.

repulsive. If the Stoics were "the preachers of the salon," the Cynics were "the preachers of the street."[226] They were the mendicant friars of imperial times. They were earnest, but they were squalid. The earnestness was of the essence, the squalor was accidental. The former was absorbed by Stoicism and gave it a new impulse: the latter dropped off as an excrescence when Cynicism was tested by time. Epictetus was not carried as far as the Cynics were in the reaction against Logic. The Cynics would have postponed the study of it indefinitely. Moral reformation is more pressing, they said.[227] Epictetus holds to the necessity of the study of Logic as a prophylactic against the deceitfulness of arguments and the plausibility of language. But he deprecates the exaggerated importance which had come to be attached to it. The students of his day were giving an altogether disproportionate attention to the weaving of fallacious arguments and the mere setting of traps to catch men in their speech. He would restore Logic to its original subordination. Neither it nor the whole dogmatic philosophy of which it was the instrument was of value in itself. And moreover, whatever might be the place of such knowledge in an abstract system and in an ideal world, it was impossible to disregard the actual conditions of the world as it is. The state of human nature is such, that to linger upon the threshold of philosophy is to induce a moral torpor. The student who aims at shaping his reason into harmony with nature has to begin, not with unformed and plastic material, which he can fashion to his will by systematic rules of art, but with his nature as it is shaped already, almost beyond possibility of

---

[226] H. Schiller, *Geschichte der romischen Kaiserzeit*, Bd. i. 452.

[227] *Diss.* 1.17.4.

unshaping, by pernicious habits, and beguiling associations of ideas, and false opinions about good and evil. While you are teaching him logic and physics, the very evils which it is his object to remedy will be gathering fresh strength. The old familiar names of "good" and "evil," with all the false ideas which they suggest, will be giving birth at every moment to mistaken judgments and wrong actions, to all the false pleasures and false pains which it is the very purpose of philosophy to destroy. He must begin, as he must end, with practice. He must accept precepts and act upon them before he learns the theory of them. His progress in philosophy must be measured by his progress, not in knowledge, but in moral conduct.

This view, which Epictetus preaches again and again with passionate fervor, will be best stated in his own words:[228]

> "A man who is making progress, having learnt
> from the philosophers that desire has good
> things for its object and undesire evil things, —
> having learnt moreover that in no other way
> can contentment and dispassionateness come
> to a man than by his never failing of the object
> of his desire and never encountering the object
> of undesire, — banishes the one altogether, or
> at least postpones it, while he allows the other
> to act only in regard to those things which are
> within the province of the will. For he knows
> that if he strives not to have things that are
> without the province of the will, he will some
> time or other encounter some such things and
> so be unhappy. But if what moral perfection

[228] *Diss.* 1.4.

professes is to cause happiness and dispassionateness and peace of mind, then of course progress towards moral perfection is progress towards each one of the things which moral perfection professes to secure. For in all cases progress is the approaching to that to which perfection finally brings us.

"How is it, then, that while we admit this to be the definition of moral perfection, we seek and show off progress in other things? What is the effect of moral perfection?

"'Peace of mind?'

"Who then is making progress towards it? He who has read many treatises of Chrysippus? Surely moral perfection does not consist in this — in understanding Chrysippus: if it does, then confessedly progress towards moral perfection is nothing else than understanding a good deal of Chrysippus. But as it is, while we admit that moral perfection effects one thing, we make progress — the approximation to perfection — effect another.

"'This man,' someone tells us, 'can now read Chrysippus even by himself.'

"'You are most assuredly making splendid progress, my friend,' he tells him.

"Progress indeed! why do you make game of him? Why do you lead him astray from the consciousness of his misfortunes? Will you not show him what the effect of moral perfection is, that he may learn where to look for progress towards it?

"Look for progress, my poor friend, in the direction of the effect which you have to produce. And what is the effect which you have to produce? Never to be disappointed of the object of your desire, and never to encounter the object of your undesire: never to miss the mark in your endeavors to do and not to do: never to be deceived in your assent and suspension of assent. The first of these is the primary and most necessary point: for if it is with trembling and reluctance that you seek to avoid falling into evil, how can you be said to be making progress?

"It is in these respects, then, that I ask you to show me your progress. If I were to say to an athlete, 'Show me your muscles, and he were to say, 'See here are my dumb-bells,' I should reply, 'Begone with your dumb-bells! What I want to see is, not them, but their effect.' (And yet that is just what you do:) 'Take the treatise On Effort' (you say), 'and examine me in it.' Slave! that is not what I want to know; but rather how you endeavor to do or not to do — how you desire to have and not to have — how you form your plans and purposes and preparations for action — whether you do all this in harmony with nature or not. If you do so in accordance with nature, show me that you do so, and I will say that you are making progress; but if not, begone, and do not merely interpret books, but write similar ones yourself besides. And what will you gain by it? Don't you know that the whole book costs five shillings, and do you think the man who interprets the book is worth more than the book itself costs?

"Never, then, look for the effect (of philosophy) in one place, and progress towards that effect in another.

"Where, then, is progress to be looked for? If any one of you, giving up his allegiance to things outside him, has devoted himself entirely to his will — to cultivating and elaborating it so as to make it at last in harmony with nature, lofty, free, unthwarted, unhindered, conscientious, self-respectful: if he has learned that one who longs for or shuns what is not in his power can neither be conscientious nor free, but must be carried along with the changes and gusts of things — must be at the mercy of those who can produce or prevent them: if, moreover, from the moment when he rises in the morning he keeps watch and guard over these qualities of his soul — bathes like a man of honor, eats like a man who respects himself — through all the varying incidents of each successive hour working out his one great purpose, as a runner makes all things help his running, and a singingmaster his teaching: — this man is making progress in very truth — this man is one who has not left home in vain.

"But if, on the other hand, he is wholly bent upon and labors at what is found in books, and has left home with a view to acquiring that, I tell him to go home again at once, and not neglect whatever business he may have there: for the object which has brought him away from home is a worthless one. This only (is worth anything), to study to banish from one's life sorrows and lamentations and 'Alas!' and 'Wretched me!' and misfortune and failure — and to learn what death really is, and exile and

imprisonment and the hemlock-draught, so as
to be able to say in the prison, 'My dear Crito,
if so it please the gods, so let it be.' "

This new or revived conception of philosophy as the
science of human conduct, as having for its purpose the
actual reformation of mankind, had already led to the view
that in the present state of human nature the study and
practice of it required special kinds of effort. It was not only
the science but also the art of life.[229] It formed, as such, no
exception to the rule that all arts require systematic and
habitual training. Just as the training of the muscles which is
necessary to perfect bodily development is effected by giving
them one by one an artificial and for the time an exaggerated
exercise, so the training of the moral powers was effected,
not by reading the rules and committing them to memory,
but by giving them a similarly artificial and exaggerated
exercise. A kind of moral gymnastic was necessary. The aim
of it was to bring the passions under the control of reason,
and to bring the will into harmony with the will of God.

(1) This special discipline of life was designated by the
term which was in use for bodily training, *askesis*.[230] It is
frequently used in this relation in Philo. He distinguishes
three elements in the process of attaining goodness —
nature, learning, discipline.[231] lie distinguishes those who

---

[229] Sext. Emp. iii. 239.

[230] Plutarch (Aetius), *plac. phil.* 1.2; Galen, *Hist. Phil.* 5; Diels,
Doxogr. Gr. pp. 273, 602.

[231] *De Abraham.* 11 (ii. 9); *de Joseph.* 1 (ii. 41); *de praem. ei
poen.* 8, 11 (ii. 416, 418). Philo is quoted because his writings
are in some respects as faithful a photograph of current

discipline themselves in wisdom by means of actual works, from those who have only a literary and intellectual knowledge of it.[232] He holds that the greatest and most numerous blessings that a man can have come from the gymnastic of moral efforts.[233] Its elements are "reading, meditation, reformation, the memory of noble ideals, self-restraint, the active practice of duties:"[234] in another passage he adds to these *prayer*, and the recognition of the indifference of things that are indifferent.[235] In the second century, when the idea of moral reformation had taken a stronger hold, this moral discipline was evidently carried out under systematic rules. It was not left to a student's option. He must undergo hardships, drinking water rather than wine, sleeping on the ground rather than on a bed; and sometimes even subjecting himself to austerities, being scourged and bound with, chains. There was sometimes an ostentation of endurance. Marcus Aurelius says that he owed it to Rusticus that he did not show off with a striking display either his acts of benevolence or his moral exercises.[236] "If you drink water," says Epictetus in his Student's Manual,[237] "don't take

---

scholastic methods as those of Epictetus. It is also possible that some of the writings that stand under Philo's name belong to the same period.

[232] *Quod det. potior.* 12 (i. 198, 199): *so de congr. erud. cans.* 13 (i. 529); *de mut. nom.* 13 (i. 591).

[233] *De congr. erud. cans.* 28 (i. 542).

[234] *Leg. alleg.* 3.6 (i. 91).

[235] *Quis rer. div. heres.* 51 (i. 509).

[236] M. Aurel. 1. 7. 2

[237] *Enchir.* 47: cf. *Diss.* 3.14.4. In *Diss.* 3.12.17, part of the

every opportunity of saying, I drink water And if you resolve to exercise yourself in toil and hardship, do it for yourself alone, and not for the world outside. Don't embrace statues (in public, to cool yourself); but if ever your thirst become extreme, fill your mouth with cold water and put it out again — *and tell no one*." Epictetus himself preferred that men should be disciplined, not by bodily hardships, but by the voluntary repression of desire. The true "ascetic" is he who disciplines himself against all the suggestions of evil desire:[238] "an object of desire comes into sight: wait, poor soul; do not straightway be carried off your feet by it: consider, the contest is great, the task is divine; it is for kingship, for freedom, for calm, for undisturbedness. Think of God: call Him to be your helper and to stand by your side, as sailors call upon Castor and Pollux in a storm: for yours is a storm, the greatest of all storms, the storm of strong suggestions that sweep reason away." In a similar way Lucian's friend Nigrinus condemns those who endeavor to fashion young men to virtue by great bodily hardships rather than by a mingled discipline of body and mind: and Lucian himself says that he knew of some who had died under the excessive strain.[239]

This moral gymnastic, it was thought, was often best practiced away from a man's old associations. Consequently some philosophers advised their students to leave home and study elsewhere. They went into "retreat," either in another

---

above is given as a quotation from Apollonius of Tyana.

[238] *Diss.* 2.18.27: cf. 3.2.1; 3.12.1; 4.1.81.

[239] *Nigrin.* 27.

city or in solitude. Against this also there was a reaction. In a forcible oration on the subject, Dio Chrysostom argues, as a modern Protestant might argue, against the monastic system.[240] "Coelum non animum mutant," he says, in effect, when they go from city to city. Everywhere a man will find the same hindrances both within and without: he will be only like a sick man changing from one bed to another. The true discipline is to live in a crowd and not heed its noise, to train the soul to follow reason without swerving, and not to "retreat" from that which seems to be the immediate duty before us.

The extent to which moral discipline and the system of "retreats" went on is uncertain, because they soon blended, as we shall see, with Christianity, and flowed with it in a single stream.

(2) But out of the ideas which they expressed, and the ideals which they held forth, there grew up a class of men which has never since died out, who devoted themselves "both by their preaching and living" to the moral reformation of mankind. Individual philosophers had had imitators, and Pythagoras had founded an ascetic school, but neither the one nor the other had filled a large place in contemporary society. With the revived conception of philosophy as necessarily involving practice, it was necessary that those who professed philosophy should be marked out from the perverted and degenerate world around them, in their outer as well as in their inner life. "The life of one who practices philosophy," says Dio Chrysostom, "is different from that of the mass of men: the very dress of such a one is

---

[240] *Orat.* xx. vol. i. pp. 288 sqq. (Dind.).

different from that of ordinary men, and his bed and exercise and baths and all the rest of his living. A man who in none of these respects differs from the rest must be put down as one of them, though he declare and profess that he is a philosopher before all Athens or Megara or in the presence of the Lacedaemonian kings."[241]

The distinction was marked in two chief ways:

(1) A philosopher let his beard grow, like the old Spartans. It was a protest against the elaborate attention to the person which marked the fashionable society of the time.

(2) A philosopher wore a coarse blanket, usually as his only dress. It was at once a protest against the prevalent luxury in dress and the badge of his profession. "Whenever," says Dio Chrysostom, "people see one in a philosopher's dress, they consider that he is thus equipped not as a sailor or a shepherd, but with a view to men, to warn them and rebuke them, and to give not one of them any whit of flattery nor to spare any one of them, but, on the contrary, to reform them as far as he possibly can by talking to them and to show them who they are."[242]

The frequency with which this new class of moral reformers is mentioned in the literature of the time shows the large place which it filled.

---

[241] Vol. ii. p. 240.

[242] Vol. ii. p. 246.

2. The moral reformation affected the contents of ethical teaching chiefly by raising them from the sphere of moral philosophy to that of religion. In Epictetus there are two planes of ethical teaching. The one is that of orthodox and traditional Stoicism: in the other. Stoicism is transformed by the help of religious conceptions, and the forces which led to the practice of it receive the enormous impulse which comes from the religious emotions. The one is summed up in the maxim, Follow Nature; the other in the maxim. Follow God.

On the lower plane the purpose of philosophy is stated in various ways, each of which expresses the same fact. It is the bringing of the will into harmony with nature. It consists in making the "dealing with ideas" what it should be, that is, in dealing with them according to nature.[243] It is the thorough study of the conceptions of good and evil, and the right application of them to particular objects.[244] It is the endeavor to make the will unthwarted in its action,[245] to take sorrow and disappointment out of a man's life,[246] and to change its

---

[243] *Ench.* 4, 13, 30

[244] The *chrasis phantasion* is an important element in the philosophy of Epictetus. Every object that is presented to the mind by either the senses or imagination tends to range itself in the ranks of either good pr evil, and thereby to call forth desire or undesire: in most men this association of particular objects with the ideas of good or evil, and the consequent stirring of desire, is unconscious, being the result of education and habit: it is the task of the philosopher to learn to attach the idea of good to what is really good, so that desire shall never go forth to what is either undesirable or unattainable: this is the "right dealing with ideas." *Diss.* 1.28.11; 1.30.4; 2.1.4; 2.8.4; 2.19. 32; 3.21.23; 3.22.20, 103;

[245] *Diss.* 1.2.6; 1.22.2, 7; 2.11.4, 7; 2.17.9, 12, 16; 4.1.41, 44.

disturbed torrent into a calm and steady stream. The result of the practice of philosophy is happiness.[247] The means of attaining that result are marked out by the constitution of human nature itself and the circumstances which surround it. That nature manifests itself in two forms, desires to have or not to have, efforts to do or not to do. The one is stimulated by the presentation to the mind of an object which is judged to be "good," the other by that of one which is judged to be "fitting." The one mainly concerns the individual man in himself, the other concerns him in his relations with other men. The "state according to nature" of desire is that in which it never fails of gratification, the corresponding state of effort is that in which it never fails of its mark. Both the one and the other are determined by landmarks which nature itself has set in the circumstances that surround us. The natural limits of desire are those things that are in our power: the direction of effort is determined by our natural relations.

For example:[248]

> "Bear in mind that you are a son. What is
> involved in being a son? To consider all that he
> has to be his father's property, to obey him in
> all things, never to disparage him to anyone,
> never to say or do anything to harm him, to
> stand out of his way and give place to him in all
> things, to help him by all means in his power.

---

[246] *Diss.* 1.1.31; 1.4.18; 1.17.21; and elsewhere.

[247] *Diss.* 1.4.23.

[248] *Diss.* 2.10.

> "Next remember that you are also a brother:
> the doing of what is fitting in this capacity
> involves giving way to him, yielding to his
> persuasion, speaking well of him, never setting
> up a rival claim to him in those things that are
> beyond the control of the will, but gladly letting
> them go that you may have the advantage in
> those things which the will controls.

> "Next, if you are a senator of any city,
> remember that you are a senator: if a youth,
> that you are a youth: if an old man, that you are
> an old man: if a father, that you are a father.
> For in each of these cases the consideration of
> the name you bear will suggest to you what is
> fitting to be done in relation to it."

This view of right moral conduct as being determined by the natural relations in which one man stands to another, and as constituting what is Fitting in regard to those relations, had overspread the Roman world. But in that world the philosophical theory which lay behind the conception of the Fitting was less prominent than the conception itself, and two other terms, both of which were natural and familiar to the Roman mind, came into use to express it. The one was borrowed from the idea of the functions which men have to discharge in the organization of civil government, the other from the idea of a debt. The former of these, "*officium*" has not passed in this sense outside the Latin language: the latter, "*debitum*," is familiar to us under its English form "duty."

On the higher plane of his teaching Epictetus expresses moral philosophy in terms of theology. Human life begins and ends in God. Moral conduct is a sublime religion. I will ask you to listen to a short *cento* of passages, strung loosely together, in which his teaching is expressed: —

> "'We also are His offspring.' Every one of us may call himself a son of God.[249] Just as our bodies are linked to the material universe,[250] subject while we live to the same forces, resolved when we die into the same elements,[251] so by virtue of reason our souls are linked to and continuous with Him, being in reality parts and offshoots of Him.[252] There is no movement of which He is not conscious, because we and He are part of one birth and growth;[253] to Him 'all hearts are open, all desires known;'[254] as we walk or talk or eat. He Himself is within us, so that we are His shrines, living temples and incarnations of Him.[255] By virtue of this communion with Him we are in the first rank of created things:[256] we and He together form the greatest and chiefest and most comprehensive of all organizations.[257]

---

[249] 1.9.6, 13.

[250] 1.14.6.

[251] 3.13.15.

[252] 1.14.6; 1.17.27; 2.8.11.

[253] 1.14.6.

[254] 2.14.11.

[255] 2.8.12—14.

[256] 1.9.5; 2.8.11.

[257] 1.9.4.

"If we once realize this kinship, no mean or unworthy thought of ourselves can enter our souls.[258] The sense of it forms a rule and standard for our lives. If God be faithful, we also must be faithful: if God be beneficent, we also must be beneficent. If God be high-minded, we also must be high-minded, doing and saying whatever we do and say in imitation of and union with Him.[259]

"Why did He make us?

"He made us, first of all, to complete His conception of the universe: He had need for such completion of some beings who should be intelligent.[260] He made us, secondly, to behold and understand and interpret His administration of the universe: to be His witnesses and ministers.[261] He made us, thirdly, to be happy in ourselves: like a true Father and Guardian, he has placed good and evil in those things which are within our own power.[262] What He says to each one of us is, ' If thou wilt have any good, take it from within thyself.'[263] To this end He has given us freedom of will; there is no power in heaven or earth that can bar our freedom.[264] We cry out in our sorrow,

---

[258] 1.3.1.

[259] 2.14.13.

[260] 1.6.13 : cf. 1.29.29.

[261] 1.9.4; 1.17.15; 1.29.46, 56; 2.16.33; 4.7.7.

[262] 3.24.2, 3.

[263] 3.24.3.

[264] 4.1.82, 90, 100.

'O Lord God, grant that I may not feel sorrow;' and all the time He has given us the means of not feeling it.[265] He has given us the power of bearing and turning to account whatever happens, the spirit of manliness and fortitude and high-mindedness, so that the greater the difficulty, the greater the opportunity of adorning our character by meeting it. If, for example, fever comes, it brings from Him this message, 'Give me a proof that your moral training has been real.' There is a time for learning, and a time for practicing what we have learnt: in the lecture-room we learn: and then God brings us to the difficulties of real life and says to us, 'It is time now for the real contest.' Life is in reality an Olympic festival: we are God's athletes, to whom He has given an opportunity of showing of what stuff we are made.[266]

"What is our duty to Him?

"It is simply to follow Him:[267] to be of one mind with Him:[268] to acquiesce in His administration:[269] to accept what His bounty gives, to resign ourselves to the absence of what He withholds.[270] The only thought of a

---

[265] 2.16.13.

[266] 1.24.1, 2; 1.29.33, 36, 46; 3.10.7; 4.4.32.

[267] 1.12.5, 8; 1.20.15.

[268] 2.16.42; 2.19.26.

[269] 1.12.8; 2.23.29, 42.

[270] 4.1.90, 98.

good man is, remembering who he is, and whence he came, and to Whom he owes his being, to fill the place which God has assigned to him,[271] to will things to be as they are, and to say what Socrates used to say, 'If this be God's will, so be it.'[272] Submission must be thy law: thou must dare to lift up your eyes to God and say, 'Employ me henceforth for what service Thou wilt: I am of one mind with Thee: I am Thine: I ask not that Thou shouldest keep from me one thing of all that Thou hast decreed for me.'[273]

'Lead Thou me, God, and Thou, O Fate,
Thy appointment I await:
Only lead me, I shall go
With no flagging steps nor slow:
Even though I degenerate be,
And consent reluctantly,
None the less I follow Thee.'[274]

"We can only do this when we keep our eyes fixed on Him, joined in close communion with Him, absolutely consecrated to His commandments. If we will not do it, we suffer loss. There are penalties imposed, not by a vindictive tyranny, but by a self-acting law. If we will not take what He gives under the conditions under which He gives it, we reap the fruit of wretchedness and sorrow, of

---

[271] 3.24.95.

[272] 1.29.18 ; 4.4.21.

[273] 2.16.42.

[274] Enchir. 52 : *Diss*. 4.1.131; 4.4.34 : a quotation from Cleanthes.

jealousy and fear, of thwarted effort and unsatisfied desire.[275]

"Above all, we must bide His time. He has given to every one of us a post to keep in the battle of life, and we must not leave it until He bids us.[276] His bidding is indicated by circumstances. When He does not give us what our bodies need, when He sends us where life according to nature is impossible, He, the Supreme Captain, is sounding the bugle for retreat,[277] He, the Master of the Great Household, is opening the door and saying to us, ' Come.'[278] And when He does so, instead of bewailing your misfortunes, obey and follow: come forth, not murmuring, but as God's servant who has finished His work, conscious that He has no more present need of you.[279]

"This, therefore, should take the place of every other pleasure, the consciousness of obeying God. Think what it is to be able to say, 'What others preach, I am doing: their praise of virtue is a praise of me: God has sent me into the world to be His soldier and witness, to tell men that their sorrows and fears are vain, that to a good man no evil can happen whether he live or die. He sends me at one time here, at

---

[275] 2.16.46; 3.11.1; 3.24.42; 4.4.32.

[276] 1.9.16.

[277] 1.29.29.

[278] 2.13.14.

[279] 3.24.97; cf. 3.5.8—10; 4.10.14 qq.

another time there: He disciplines me by
poverty and by prison, that I may be the better
witness to mankind. With such a ministry
committed to me, can I any longer care in what
place I am, or who my companions are, or
what they say about me: nay, rather, does not
my whole nature strain after God, His laws and
His commandments?"[280]

Between the current ethics of the Greek world and the
ethics of the earliest forms of Christianity were many points
both of difference and of contact.

The main point of difference was that Christianity rested
morality on a divine command. It took over the fundamental
idea of the Jewish theocracy. Its ultimate appeal was not to
the reasonableness of the moral law in itself, but to the fact
that God had enacted it. Greek morality, on the contrary,
was "independent." The idea that the moral laws are laws of
God is, no doubt, found in the Stoics; but they are so in
another than either the Jewish or the Christian sense: they
are laws of God, not as being expressions of His personal
will, but as being laws of nature, part of the whole
constitution of the world.

Consequent upon the conception of the moral law as a
positive enactment of God, the breach of moral law was
conceived as sin. Into the early Christian conception of sin
several elements entered. It was probably not in the popular
mind what it was in the mind of St. Paul, still less what it
became in the mind of St. Augustine. But one element was
constant. It was a trespass against God. As such, it was on

---

[280] 3.24.110—114.

the one hand something for which God must be appeased, and on the other hand something which He could forgive. To the Stoics it was shortcoming, failure, and loss: the chief sufferer was the man himself: amendment was possible for the future, but there was no forgiveness for the past.

Beyond these and other points of difference there was a wide area of agreement. The former became accentuated as time went on: it was by virtue of the latter that in the earliest ages the minds of many persons had been predisposed to accept Christianity, and that, having accepted it, they tended to fuse some elements of the new teaching with some elements of the old. The agreement is most conspicuous in those respects which were the chief aims of the contemporary moral reformation; and above all in the importance which was attached to moral conduct. This importance was overshadowed in the later Christian communities by the importance which came to be attached to doctrine: its existence in the earliest communities is shown by two classes of proofs.

1. The first of these proofs is the place which moral conduct holds in the earliest Christian writers. The documents which deal with the Christian life are almost wholly moral. They enforce the ancient code of the Ten Words. They raise those Ten Words from being the lowest and most necessary level of a legal code, to being the expression of the highest moral ideal, expanding and amplifying them so as to make them embrace thoughts and desires as well as words and actions. The most interesting of such documents is that which is known as the "Two Ways."[281]

It has recently acquired a fresh significance by having been found as part of the Teaching of the Apostles. It is there prefixed to the regulations for ceremonial and discipline which constitute the new part of that work. It proves to be a manual of instruction to be taught to those who were to be admitted as members of a Christian community. It may thus be considered to express the current ideal of Christian practice. In the "Way of Life" which it sets forth, doctrine has no place. It is summed up in the two commandments: "First, thou shalt love God who made thee; secondly, thy neighbor as thyself: whatsoever things thou wouldest not have done to thyself, do not thou to another."[282] These commandments are amplified in the spirit of the Sermon on the Mount. "Thou shalt not forswear thyself: thou shalt not bear false witness: thou shalt not speak evil: thou shalt not bear malice: thou shalt not be doubleminded nor double-tongued, for double-tonguedness is a snare of death. Thy speech shall not be false or hollow, but filled to the full with deed. Thou shalt not be covetous, nor rapacious, nor a hypocrite, nor evilly disposed, nor haughty: thou shalt not take mischievous counsel against thy neighbor. Thou shalt not hate any man, but some thou shalt rebuke, and for some thou shalt pray, and some thou shalt love more than thine own soul.[283] . . . My child, be not a murmurer, for murmuring is on the path to blasphemy: nor self-willed nor evil-minded, for from all these things blasphemies are born. But be thou meek, for the meek shall inherit the earth: be

[281] See especially Harnack, *die Apostellehre und die Jüdischen Beiden Wege*, Leipzig, 1886.

[282] *Teaching of the Apostles*, 1.1.

[283] *Teaching of the Apostles*, 2.2—7.

long-suffering, and pitiful, and guileless, and quiet, and kind, and trembling continually at the words which thou hast heard.[284] ... Thou shalt not hesitate to give, nor in giving shalt thou murmur; for thou shalt know who is the good paymaster of what thou hast earned. Thou shalt not turn away him that needeth, but thou shalt share all things with thy brother and shalt not say that they are thine own; for if ye be fellow-sharers in that which is immortal, how much more in mortal things."[285]

Another such document is the first book of the collection known as the Apostolical Constitutions: it begins at once with an exhortation to morality.

"Listen to holy teaching, ye who lay hold on His promise, in accordance with the command of the Savior, in harmony with his glorious utterances. Take heed, ye sons of God, to do all things so as to be obedient to God and to be well-pleasing in all things to the Lord our God. For if any one follow after wickedness and do things contrary to the will of God, such a one will be counted as a nation that transgresses against God. Abstain then from all covetousness and unrighteousness."[286]

2. The second proof is afforded by the place which discipline held in contemporary Christian life. The Christians

---

[284] *Ibid.* 3.6—8.

[285] *Ibid.* 4. 7, 8.

[286] *Const. Apost.* 1. 1, p. 1, ed. Lagarde. This may be supplemented by the conception of Christianity as a new law in Barnabas ii. 6, Justin *passim*, Clem. Alex. *E. T.* i. 97, 120, 470.

were drawn together into communities. Isolation was discouraged and soon passed away. To be a Christian was to be a member of a community. The basis of the community was not only a common belief, but also a common practice. It was the task of the community as an organization to keep itself pure. The offences against which it had to guard were not only the open crimes which fell within the cognizance of public law, but also and more especially sins of moral conduct and of the inner life. The qualifications which in later times were the ideal standard for church officers, were also in the earliest times the ideal standard for ordinary members. "If any man who has sinned sees the bishop and the deacons free from fault, and the flock abiding pure, first of all he will not venture to enter into the assembly of God, being smitten by his own conscience: but if, secondly, setting lightly by his sin he should venture to enter, he will forthwith be taken to task .... and either be punished, or being admonished by the pastor will be drawn to repentance. For looking round upon the assembly one by one, and finding no blemish either in the bishop or in the ranks of the people under him, with shame and many tears he will go out in peace, pricked in heart, and the flock will have been cleansed, and he will cry with tears to God and will repent of his sin, and will have hope: and the whole flock beholding his tears will be admonished that he who has sinned and repented is not lost,"[287] In other cases expulsion was a solemn and formal act: the sinful member was cast into outer darkness: re-admission was accompanied with the same rites as the original admission. In other words, the earliest communities endeavored, both in the theory which

---

[287] *Const. Apost.* 2.11, p. 22.

they embodied in their manuals of Christian life, and in the practice which they enforced by discipline, to realize what has since been known as the Puritan ideal. Each one of them was a community of saints. "Passing their days upon earth, they were in reality citizens of heaven."[288] The earthly community reflected in all but its glory and its everlastingness the life of the "new Jerusalem." Its bishop was the visible representative of Jesus Christ himself sitting on the throne of heaven, with the white-robed elders round him: its members were the "elect," the "holy ones," the "saved." "Without were the dogs, and the sorcerers, and the murderers, and the idolaters, and everyone that loveth and maketh a lie:" within were "they which were written in the Lamb's book of life." To be a member of the community was to be in reality, and not merely in conception, a child of God and heir of everlasting salvation: to be excluded from the community was to pass again into the outer darkness, the realm of Satan and eternal death.

Over these earliest communities and the theory which they embodied there passed, in the last half of the second century and the first half of the third, an enormous change. The processes of the change and its immediate causes are obscure. The interests of contemporary writers are so absorbed with the struggles for soundness of doctrine, as to leave but little room for a record of the struggles for purity of life. In the last stages of those struggles, the party which endeavored to preserve the ancient ideal was treated as schismatical. The aggregate of visible communities was no

---

[288] *Ep. ad Diogn.* 5.

longer identical with the number of those who should be saved. The dominant party framed a new theory of the Church as a *corpus permixtum*, and found support for it in the Gospels themselves. Morality became subordinated to belief in Christianity by the same inevitable drift by which practice had been superseded by theory in Stoicism.

In both the production of this change and its further developments Greece played an important part. The net result of the active forces which it brought to bear upon Christianity was, that the attention of a majority of Christian men was turned to the intellectual as distinguished from the moral element in Christian life. And when the change was effected, it operated in two further ways, which have survived in large and varied forms to the present day.

1. The idea of moral reformation had from the first seized different men with a varying tenacity of grasp.[289] There were some men who had a higher moral ideal than others: there were some whose natures were stronger: there were some to whom moral life was not the perfection of human citizenship, but the struggle of the spirit to disentangle itself from its material environment, and to rise by contemplation to fellowship with God. There are proofs of the existence in the very earliest Christian communities of those who endeavored to live on a higher plane than their fellows. Abstinence from marriage and from animal food were urged and practiced as "counsels of perfection." In some communities there was an attempt to make such counsels of perfection obligatory. In the majority of communities,

---

[289] Side by side with the average ethics were the Pauline ethics, which had found a certain lodgment in some.

though they were part of "the whole yoke of the Lord,"[290]
and were specially enjoined at certain times upon all church
members, they were not of universal or constant obligation.
Those who habitually practiced them were recognized as a
church within the Church. The practice of them was known
by a name which we have seen to be common in the Greek
philosophical schools. It was relative to the conception of
life as an athletic contest. It was that of bodily training or
gymnastic exercise (*askasis*).[291]

The secession of the Puritan party left much of this
element still within the great body of confederated
communities. At the end of the third century it became
important both within them and without. It was increased,
partly by the growing influence of the ideas which found
their highest expression outside Christianity in Neo-
Platonism; partly by the growing complexity of society itself,
the strain and the despair of an age of decadence; partly also
by the necessity of finding a new outlet, when Christianity
became a legal religion, for the passionate love of God which
had led men to a sometimes ecstatic martyrdom. It was
joined by the parallel tendency among professors of
philosophy. It soon took a new form. Hitherto those who
followed counsels of perfection lived in ordinary society,
undistinguished except by their conduct from their
fellowmen. The ideal "Gnostic" of Clement of Alexandria
takes his part in ordinary human affairs, "acting the drama of
life which God has given him to play, knowing both what is

---

[290] *Teaching of the Apostles*, 6.2.

[291] Of a type of Gnosticism, Harnack, *Dogmertgeseh*. 202.

to be done and what is to be endured."[292] But early in the fourth century the practice of the ascetic life in Christianity came to be shown in the same outward way, but with a more marked emphasis, as the similar practice in philosophy. It was indeed known as philosophy.[293] It was most akin to Cynicism, with which it had sometimes already been confused, and its badges were the badges of Cynicism, the rough blanket and the unshorn hair. To wear the blanket and to let the hair grow was to profess divine philosophy, the higher life of self-discipline and sanctity. It was to claim to stand on a higher level and to be working out a nobler ideal than average Christians. The practice soon received a further development. Just as ordinary philosophers had sometimes found life in society to be intolerable and had gone into "retreat," so the Christian philosophers began to withdraw altogether from the world, and to live their lives of self-discipline and contemplation in solitude. The retention of the old names shows the continuity of the practice. They were still practicing discipline, *askasis*, or philosophy, *pilosophia*. So far as they retired from society, they were still said "to go into retreat," *anachorein*, whence the current appellation *anachoratai*, "anchorets." The place of their retreat

---

[292] *Strom.* 7.11.

[293] Euseb. *Dem. Ev.* 3.6: " Not only old men under Jesus Christ practice this mode of philosophy, but it would be hard to say how many thousands of women throughout the whole world, priestesses, as it were, of the God of the universe, having embraced the highest wisdom, rapt with a passion for heavenly knowledge, have renounced the desire of children according to the flesh, and giving their whole care to their soul, have given themselves up wholly to the Supreme King and God of the universe, to practice perfect purity and virginity." So also id. *de Vit. Constant.* 4.26, 29; Sozom. 6.33, of the Syrian monks.

was a "school of discipline," *askatariov*, or a "place for reflection," *phrontistarion*.[294] To these were soon added the new names which were relative to the fact that moral discipline was usually practiced in solitude. Those who retired from the world were "solitaries," *monaxoi*, and the place of their retirement was a "place for solitude," *monastarion*. When the practice was once firmly rooted in Christian soil, it was largely developed in independent ways for which Greece was not primarily responsible, and which therefore cannot properly be described here; but the independence and enormous overgrowth of these later forms cannot wipe away the memory of the fact that to Greece, more than to any other factor, was due the place and earliest conception of that sublime individualism which centered all a man's efforts on the development of his spiritual life, and withdrew him from his fellow-men in order to bring him near to God.

2. It was inevitable that when the Puritan party had left the main body, and when the most spiritually-minded of those who remained detached themselves from the common life of their brethren, there should be a deterioration in the average moral conceptions of the Christian Churches. It was also inevitable that those conceptions should be largely shaped by Greek influences. The Pauline ethics vanished from the Christian world. For the average members of the churches were now the average citizens of the empire, educated by Greek methods, impregnated with the dominant ethical ideas. They accepted Christian ideas, but without the

---

[294] Socrat, i. 11.

enthusiasm which made them a transforming force. As in regard to metaphysics, so also in regard to ethics, the frame of mind which had been formed by education was stronger than the new ideas which it absorbed. The current ideals remained, slightly raised: the current rules of conduct continued, with modifications. Instead of the conceptions of righteousness and holiness, there was the old conception of virtue: instead of the code of morals which was "briefly comprehended in this saying, namely, Thou shalt love thy neighbor as thyself," there was the old enumeration of duties. At the end of the fourth century the new state of things was formally recognized by ecclesiastical writers. Love was no more "the handbook of divine philosophy:"[295] the chief contemporary theologian of the West, Ambrose of Milan, formulated the current theory in a book which is the more important because it not merely expresses the ideas of his time and seals the proof of their prevalence, but also became the basis of the moral philosophy of the Middle Ages. But the book is less Christian than Stoical. It is a *rechauffee* of the book which Cicero had compiled more than three centuries before, chiefly from Panaetius. It is Stoical, not only in conception, but also in detail. It makes virtue the highest good. It makes the hope of the life to come a subsidiary and not a primary motive. Its ideal of life is happiness: it holds that a happy life is a life according to nature, that it is realized by virtue, and that it is capable of being realized here on earth. Its virtues are the ancient virtues of wisdom and justice, courage and temperance. It tinges each of them with a Christian, or at least with a Theistic coloring; but the conception of each of them

---

[295] Clem. Alex. *Paedag.* 3.11.

remains what it had been to the Greek moralists. Wisdom, for example, is Greek wisdom, with the addition that no man can be wise who is ignorant of God: justice is Greek justice, with the addition that its subsidiary form of beneficence is helped by the Christian society.

The victory of Greek ethics was complete. While Christianity was being transformed into a system of doctrines, the Stoical jurists at the imperial court were slowly elaborating a system of personal rights. The ethics of the Sermon on the Mount, which the earliest Christian communities endeavored to carry into practice, have been transmuted by the slow alchemy of history into the ethics of Roman law. The basis of Christian society is not Christian, but Roman and Stoical. A fusion of the Roman conception of rights with the Stoical conception of relations involving reciprocal actions, is in possession of practically the whole field of civilized society. The transmutation is so complete that the modem question is not so much whether the ethics of the Sermon on the Mount are practicable, as whether, if practicable, they would be desirable. The socialistic theories which formulate in modern language and justify by modern conceptions such an exhortation as "Sell that thou hast and give to the poor," meet with no less opposition within than without the Christian societies. The conversion of the Church to Christian theory must precede the conversion of the world to Christian practice. But meanwhile there is working in Christianity the same higher morality which worked in the ancient world, and the maxim. Follow God, belongs to a plane on which Epictetus and Thomas a Kempis meet.

Lecture VII. GREEK AND CHRISTIAN THEOLOGY.

I. The Creator.

Slowly there loomed through the mists of earlier Greek thought the consciousness of one God. It came with the sense of the unity of the world.

That sense had not always been awakened. The varied phenomena of earth and sea and sky had not always been brought under a single expression. The groups into which the mind tended to arrange them were conceived as separate, belonging to different kingdoms and controlled by independent divinities. It was by the unconscious alchemy of thought, working through successive generations, that the separate groups came to be combined into a whole and conceived as forming a universe.

It came also with the sense of the order of the world. The sun which day by day rose and set, the moon which month by month waxed and waned, the stars which year by year came back to the same stations in the sky, were like a marshalled army moving in obedience to a fixed command. There was order, not only above, but also beneath. The sea, which for all its storms and murmurings, could not pass its bounds, the earth upon which seedtime and harvest never failed, but spring after spring the buds burst into blossom, and summer after summer the blossom ripened into fruit, were part of the same great system. The conception was that not merely of a universe, but of a universe moving in obedience to a law. The earliest form of the conception is probably that of Anaxagoras, which was formulated by a later writer in the expression, "The origins of matter are infinite, the origin of movement and birth is one."[296]

This conception of an ordered whole was intertwined, as it slowly elaborated itself, with one or other of two kindred conceptions, of which one had preceded it and the other grew with it.

The one was the sense of personality. By a transference of ideas which has been so universal that it may be called natural, all things that move have been invested with personality. The stars and rivers were persons. Movement meant life, and life meant everywhere something analogous to human life. It was by an inevitable application of the conception that when the sum of movements was conceived as a whole, it should be also conceived that behind the totality of the phenomena and the unity of their movements there was a single Person.

The other was the conception of mind. It was a conception which had but slowly disentangled itself from that of bodily powers. It was like the preaching of a revelation, and almost as fruitful, when Epicharmus proclaimed:[297] "It is not the eye that sees, but the mind: it is not the ear that hears, but the mind: all things except mind are blind and deaf." It was the mind that not only saw but thought, and that not only thought but willed. It alone was

---

[296] Theophrastus ap. Simplic. *in phys.* f. 6 (Diels, *Doxographi Graeci*, p. 479).

[297] Plut. *de fort.* 3, p. 98, *de Alex. magn. fort.* 3, p. 336, and elsewhere: cf Lucret. 3.36; Cic. *Tusc. Disp.* 1. 20.

the real self: and the Person who is behind nature or within it was like the personality which is behind the bodily activities of each one of us; His essence was mind.

There was one God. The gods of the old mythology were passing away, like a splendid pageantry of clouds moving across the horizon to be absorbed in the clear and infinite heaven. "But though God is one," it was said,[298] "He has many names, deriving a name from each of the spheres of His government He is called the Son of Kronos, that is of Time, because He continues from eternity to eternity; and Lightning-God, and Thunder-God, and Rain-God, from the lightnings and thunders and rains; and Fruit-God, from the fruits (which he sends); and City-God, from the cities (which he protects); and the God of births, and homesteads, and kinsmen, and families, of companions, and friends, and armies God, in short, of heaven and earth, named after all forms of nature and events as being Himself the cause of all." "There are not different gods among different peoples," says Plutarch,[299] "nor foreign gods and Greek gods, nor gods of the south and gods of the north; but just as sun and moon and sky and earth, and sea are common to all mankind, but have different names among different races, so, though there be one Reason who orders these things and one Providence who administers them ... there are different honors and appellations among different races; and men use consecrated symbols, some of them obscure and some more clear, so leading their thoughts on the path to the Divine: but it is not without risk; for some men, wholly missing their foothold,

---

[298] Pseudo-Arist. *de mundo*, 7, p. 401 a.

[299] *De Isid. et Osir.* 67, p. 378.

have slipped into superstition, and others, avoiding the slough of superstition, have in their turn fallen over the precipice of atheism."

In the conception of God as it thus uncoiled itself in Greek history, three strands of thought are constantly intertwined — the thought of a Creator, the thought of a Moral Governor, and the thought of a Supreme or Absolute Being. It is desirable to trace the history of each of these thoughts, as far as possible, separately, and to consider their separate effects upon the development of Christian theology. The present Lecture will deal mainly with the first: the two following Lectures with the other two.

It was at a comparatively late stage in its history that Greek thought came to the conception of a beginning of all things. The conception was first formulated by Anaximander, in the sixth century b.c.[300] The earlier conception was that of a chaos, out of which gods and all things alike proceeded. The first remove from that earlier conception was hylozoism, the belief that life and matter were the same. The conception of mind was not yet evolved. When it was evolved, two lines of thought began to diverge. The one, following the conception of human personality as absolutely single, conceived of both reason and force as inherent in matter: it is the theory which is known as *Monism*. The other, following the conception of human personality as a separable compound, body and soul, conceived of reason and force as external to matter: it is the

----

[300] Theophrast. ap. Simplic. *in phys*. f. 6 (Diels, p. 476): so Hippol. *Philosoph*. 1.6.

theory which is known as *Dualism*. These two theories run through all subsequent Greek philosophy.

1. The chief philosophical expression of Monism was Stoicism. The Stoics followed the Ionians in believing that the world consists of a single substance. They followed Heraclitus in believing that the movements and modifications of that substance are due neither to a blind impulse from within nor to an arbitrary impact from without. It moved, he had thought, with a kind of rhythmic motion, a fire that was kindling and being quenched with regulated limits of degree and time.[301] The substance is one, but immanent and inherent in it is a force that acts with intelligence. The antithesis between the two was expressed by the Stoics in various forms. It was sometimes the bare and neutral contrast of the Active and the Passive. For the Passive was sometimes substituted Matter, a term which, signifying, as it originally does, the timber which a carpenter uses for the purposes of his craft, properly belongs to another order of ideas; and for the Active was frequently substituted the term *Logos*, which, signifying as it does, on the one hand, partly thought and partly will, and, on the other hand, also the expression of thought in a sentence and the expression of will in a law, has no single equivalent in modern language. But the majority of Stoics used neither the colorless term the Active, nor the impersonal term the *Logos*. The *Logos* was vested with personality: the antithesis was between matter and God. This latter term was used to cover a wide range of conceptions. The two terms of the antithesis being regarded as expressing modes of a single substance,

---

[301] Heraclit. ap. Clem. Alex. *Strom.* 5.14.

separable in thought and name but not in reality, there was a natural drift of some minds towards regarding God as a mode of matter, and of others towards regarding matter as a mode of God. The former conceived of Him as the *natura naturata*: "Jupiter est quodcunque vides quodcunque moveris."[302] The latter conceived of Him as the *natura naturans*. This became the governing conception. He is the sum of an infinite number of rational forces which are continually striving to express themselves through the matter with which they are in union. He is through them and in them working to realize an end. The teleological idea controls the whole conception. He is always moving with purpose and system, and always thereby producing the world. The products are all divine, but not all equally divine. In His purest essence, He is the highest form of mind in union with the most attenuated form of matter. In the lowest form of His essence, He is the cohesive force which holds together the atoms of a stone. Between these two poles are infinite gradations of being. Nearest of all to the purest essence of God is the human soul. It is in an especial sense His offspring: it is described by the metaphors of an emanation or outflow from Him, of a sapling which is separate from and yet continues the life of its parent tree, of a colony in which some members of the mother state have settled.[303]

---

[302] Lucan, *Phars*. 9.579.

[303] M. Anton. 2. 4; Epict. *Diss*. 1.14.6; 2.8.11; M. Anton. 5. 27; Philo, *de mund. opif.* 46 (i. 32). The coordination of these and cognate terms in Philo is especially important in view of their use in Christian theology: *de mund. opif.* 51 (i. 35); *de mutat. nom.* 39 (i. 612); and he is careful to guard against an inference

If all this were expressed in modern terms, and by the help of later conceptions, it would probably be most suitably gathered into the proposition that the world is the self-evolution of God. Into such a conception the idea of a beginning does not necessarily enter: it is consistent with the idea of an eternal process of differentiation: that which is, always has been, under changed and changing forms: the theory is cosmological rather than cosmogonical: it rather explains the world as it is than gives an account of its origin.

2. The chief philosophical expression of Dualism was Platonism. Plato followed Anaxagoras in believing that mind is separate from matter and acts upon it: he went beyond him in founding upon this separation a universal distinction between the real and the phenomenal, and between God and the world. God was regarded as being outside the world. The world was in its origin only potential being (*to ma on*). The action of God upon it was that of a craftsman upon his material, shaping it as a carpenter shapes wood, or molding it as a statuary molds clay. In so acting, He acted with reason, following out thoughts in His mind. Sometimes His reason, or His mind, is spoken of as being itself the fashioner of the world.[304] Each thought shows itself in a group of material objects. Such objects, so far as they admit of being grouped, may be viewed as imitations or embodiments of a form or pattern, existing either as a thought in the mind of the Divine Workman, or as a force proceeding from His mind and acting outside it. As the conception of these forms was

---

that *apospasma* implies a breach of continuity between the divine and the human soul, *quod det, pot. insid*, 24 (i. 209).

[304] *Phileb.* 16, p. 28.

developed more and more, they tended to be regarded in the latter light rather than in the former. They were cosmic forces which had the power of impressing themselves upon matter. They were less types than causes. They came midway between God and the rude material of the universe, so that its changing phenomena were united with an unchanging element. They were themselves grouped in a vast gradation, reaching its highest point in the Form of Perfection, which was higher than the Form of Being. The highest and most perfect of types is conceived as the most powerful and most active of forces. In the elaborate cosmology of the *Timaeus*, it is further conceived as a person. The creative energy of God is spoken of as the *Demiurgus*, who himself made an ideal world, and employed subordinate agents in the construction of the actual world. The matter upon which the *Demiurgus* or his agents work is sometimes conceived as potential being,[305] the bare capacity of receiving qualities and forms, and sometimes as chaotic substance which was reduced to order.[306] The agents were gods who, having been themselves created, were bidden to create living beings, capable of growth and decay.[307] The distinction between the two spheres of

---

[305] The best account of Plato's complex, because progressive, theory of matter is that of Siebeck, *Plato's Lehre von der Materie*, in his *Untersuchungen der Philosophie der Griechen*, Freiburg im Breisg. 1888. The conception of it which was current in the Platonist schools, and which is therefore important in relation to Christian philosophy, is given in the *Placita* of Aetius, ap. Stob. *Ecl.* 1.11 (Diels, p. 308), and Hippol. *Philosoph.* 1.19.

[306] Plat. *Tim.* p. 30.

[307] Tim. p. 41, The whole theory is summed up by Professor

creation, that of a world in which nothing was imperfect since it was the work of a Perfect Being, and that of a world which was full of imperfections as being the work of created beings, came, as we shall see, to be of importance in some phases of Christian thought.

It was inevitable, in the syncretism which results when an age of philosophical reflection succeeds an age of philosophical origination, that these two great drifts of thought should tend in some points to approach each other. The elements in them which were most readily fused together were the theories of the processes by which the actual world came into being, and of the nature of the forces which lay behind those processes. In Stoicism, there was the theory of the one Law or *Logos* expressing itself in an infinite variety of material forms: in Platonism, there was the theory of the one God, shaping matter according to an infinite variety of patterns. In the one, the processes of nature were the operations of active forces, containing in themselves the law of the forms in which they exhibit themselves self-developing seeds, each of them a portion of the one *Logos* which runs through the whole. In the other, they were the operations of the infinitely various and eternally active energy of God, moving always in the direction of His thoughts, so that those thoughts might themselves be

---

Jowett in the Introduction to his translation of the *Timaeus* (Plato, vol. ii. p. 470): "The Creator is like a human artist who frames in his mind a plan which he executes by means of his servants. Thus the language of philosophy, which speaks of first and second causes, is crossed by another sort of phraseology, 'God made the world because he was good, and the demons ministered to him.'"

conceived as the causes of the operations.[308] In both the one theory and the other, the processes were sometimes regarded in their apparent multiplicity, and sometimes in their underlying unity: and in both also the unity was expressed sometimes by the impersonal term *Logos*, and sometimes by the personal term God.

But while the monism of the Stoics, by laying stress upon the antithesis between the two phases of the one substance, was tending to dualism, the dualism of the Platonists, by laying stress upon the distinction between the creative energy of God and the form in the mind of God which His energy embodied in the material universe, was tending to introduce a third factor into the conception of creation. It became common to speak, not of two principles, but of three — God, Matter, and the Form, or Pattern.[309] Hence came a new fusion of conceptions. The Platonic Forms in the mind of God, conceived, as they sometimes were, as causes operating outside Him, were more or less identified with the Stoical *Logoi*, and, being viewed as the manifold expressions of a

---

[308] Hence the definition which Aetius gives, ap. Plut. *de plac. philos.* 1.10; Euseb. *praep. evang.* 15.48; with additions and differences in Stob. *Ecl.* 1.12 (Diels, p. 308).

[309] The three *archai* are expressed by varying but identical terms: God, Matter, and the Form (*idea*), or the By Whom, From What, In view of What, in the *Placita* of Aetius, 1.3.21, ap. Plut. *de placit. phil.* 1.3, Stob. *Ecl.* 1.10 (Diels, p. 288), and in Timaeus Locrus, *de an. mundi* 2 (Mullach FPG 2.38): God, Matter, and the Pattern, Hippol. *Philosoph.* 1.19, *Herm. Irris. Gent. Phil.* 11: the Active, Matter, and the Pattern, Alexand. Aphrod. ap. Simplic. *in phys.* f. 6 (Diels, p. 485), where Simplicius contrasts this with Plato's own strict dualism.

single *Logos*, were expressed by a singular rather than a plural term, the *Logos* rather than the *Logoi* of God.

It is at this point that the writings of Philo become of special importance. They gather together, without fusing into a symmetrical system, the two dominant theories of the past, and they contain the seeds of nearly all that afterwards grew up on Christian soil. It is possible that those writings cover a much larger period of time than is commonly supposed, and that if we could find a key to their chronological arrangement, we should find in them a perfect bridge from philosophical Judaism to Christian theology. And even without such a key we are able to see in them a large representation of the processes of thought that were going on, and can better understand by the analogies which they offer both the tentative theories and those that ultimately became dominant in the sphere of Christianity. It is consequently desirable to give a brief account of the view which they present.

The ultimate cause of the world is to be found in the nature of God. As in Plato, though perhaps in a different sense, God is regarded as good. By His goodness He was impelled to make the world: He was able to make it by virtue of His power. "If any one wished to search out the reason why the universe was made, I think that he would not be far from the mark if he were, to say, what, in fact, one of the ancients said, that the Father and Maker is good, and that being good He did not grudge the best kind of nature to matter (*ousia*) which of itself had nothing excellent, though it was capable of becoming all things."[310] And again: "My soul

[310] *De mundi opif.* 5 (i. 5) : cf. Plat. *Tim.* p. 30

once told me a more serious story (than that of the Greek mythology), when seized, as it often was, with a divine ecstasy It told me that in the one really existing God there are two chief and primary faculties. Goodness and Power, and that by Goodness He begat the universe, and by Power He governs it."[311] God is thus the Creator, the Fashioner and Maker of the world, its Builder and Artificer. But when the conception of His relation to the world is more precisely examined, it is found to be based upon a recognition of a sharp distinction between the world of thought and that of sense; and to be monistic in regard to the one, dualistic in regard to the other. God is mind. From Him, as from a fountain, proceed all forms of mind and reason. Reason, whether unconscious in the form of natural law, or conscious in the form of human thought, is like a river that flows forth from Him and fills the universe.[312] In man the two worlds meet. The body is fashioned by the Artificer from the dust of the earth: "The soul came from nothing that is created, but from the Father and Leader of all things. For what He breathed into Adam was nothing else than a divine breath, a colony from that blissful and happy nature, placed here below for the benefit of our race; so that granting man to be mortal in respect of his visible part, yet in respect of that which is invisible he is the heir of immortality."[313] And again: "The mind is an offshoot from the divine and happy soul (of God), an offshoot not

---

[311] *De cherub.* 9 (i. 144) : cf. ib. 35 (i. 162).

[312] *De somn.* 2. 37 (i. 691).

[313] *De mundi opif.* 46 (i. 32) : of. *ib.* 51 (i. 35): *quod deus immut.* 10 (i. 279), and elsewhere.

separated from Him, for nothing divine is cut off and disjoined, but only extended."[314] And again, in expounding the words, "They have forsaken me, the fountain of life" (Jeremiah ii. 13), he says: "Only God is the cause of soul and life, especially of rational soul and reasonable life; but He Himself is more than life, being the ever-flowing fountain of life."[315]

This is monistic. But the theory of the origin of the sensible world is dualistic. The matter upon which He acted was outside Him. "It was in itself without order, without quality, without soul, full of difference, disproportion, and discord: it received a change and transformation into what was opposite and best, order, quality, animation, identity, proportion, harmony, all that is characteristic of a better form."[316] He himself did not touch it. "Out of it God begat all things, Himself not touching it: for it was not right that the all-knowing and blessed One should touch unlimited and confused matter: but He used the unbodied Forces whose true name is the Forms (*ideai*), that each class of things should receive its fitting shape."[317] These unbodied Forces, which are here called by the Platonic name of Forms, are elsewhere spoken of in Stoical language as Reasons (*logoi*), sometimes in Pythagorean language as Numbers or Limits, sometimes in the language of the Old Testament as Angels, and sometimes in the language of popular mythology as

---

[314] *Quod det. pot. ins.* 24 (i. 20S, 209).

[315] *Deprofug.* 36 (i. 575).

[316] *De mundi opif.* 5 (i. 5): this is the most explicit expression of his theory of the nature of matter.

[317] *De sacrif.* 13 (ii. 261).

Demons. The use of the two names Force and Form, with the synonyms which are interchanged with each of them, expresses the two sides of the conception of them. They are at once the agents or instruments by means of which God fashioned the world, and also the types or patterns after which He fashioned it.[318]

In both respects they are frequently viewed, not in the plurality of their manifestations, but in the unity of their essence. On the one hand, they collectively form the world which the Divine Architect of the great City of the Universe fashioned in His mind before His thought went outside Him to stamp with its impress the chaotic and unformed mass. The place of this world is the *Logos*, the Reason or Will or Word of God: more precisely, it constitutes that *Logos* in a special form of its activity:[319] for in the building of an ordinary city the ideal which precedes it "is no other than the mind of the architect, planning to realize in a visible city the city of his thought... The archetypal seal, which we call the ideal world, is itself the archetypal pattern, the Form of Forms, the Reason of God."[320] On the other hand, the Reason of God is sometimes viewed not as a Form but as a Force. It is His creative energy.[321] It is the instrument by

---

[318] The clearest instance of the identification is probably in *de monarch*. G (ii. 218, 219), where God tells Moses that so far from Himself being cognizable, not even the powers that minister to Him are cognizable in their essence; but that as seals are known from their impressions.

[319] *De mund. opif.* 6 (i. 5), cf. Epictet. *Diss*. 1.20.5.

[320] *De mund. opif.* 4 (i. 4).

[321] *De mund. opif.* 5 (i. 5), *de profug*. 18 (i. 560).

which He made all things.[322] It is the "river of God" that is "full of waters," and that flows forth to "make glad the city of God," the universe.[323] From it, as from a fountain, all lower Forms and Forces flow. By another and even sublimer figure, it, the eldest born of the "I am," robes itself with the world as with a vesture, the high-priest's robe, embroidered by all the Forces of the seen and unseen worlds.[324]

But in all this, Philo never loses sight of the primary truth that the world was made not by inferior or opposing beings, but by God. It is the expression of His Thought. His Thought went forth from Him, impressing itself in infinite Forms and by means of infinite Forces: but though His Thought was the charioteer, it is God Himself who gives the orders.[325] By a different conception of the genesis of the world, and one that is of singular interest in view of the similar conceptions which we shall find in some Gnostic schools, God is the Father of the world:[326] and the metaphor of Fatherhood is expanded into that of a marriage: God is conceived as the Father, His Wisdom as the Mother: "and she, receiving the seed of God, with fruitful birth-pangs brought forth this world. His visible son, only and well-beloved."[327]

---

[322] *Leg. alleg.* 1.9 (i. 47), *quod dens immut.* 12 (i. 281), *Leg. alleg.* 3. 31 (i. 106), *de cherub.* 35 (i. 162).

[323] *De somn.* 2.37 (i. 691).

[324] *De profug.* 20 (i. 562), *de migrat. Abr.* 18 (i. 452) : cf. Wisdom, 18. 24.

[325] *De profug.* 19 (i. 561).

[326] *Abrah.* 9 (i. 443), *de somn.* 1. 13 (i. 632), and elsewhere.

[327] *De ebriet.* 8 (L 361).

We have now the main elements of the current conceptions out of which the philosophers of early Christianity constructed new fabrics.

Christianity had no need to borrow from Greek philosophy either the idea of the unity of God, or the belief that He made the world. Its ultimate basis was the belief in one God. It rode in upon the wave of the reaction against polytheism. The Scriptures to which it appealed began with the sublime declaration, "In the beginning God created the heavens and the earth." It accepted that declaration as being both final and complete. It saw therein the picture of a single supreme Artificer: and it elaborated the picture by the aid of anthropomorphic conceptions: "By His almighty power He fixed firm the heavens, and by His incomprehensible wisdom He set them in order: He separated the earth from the water that encompassed it ... and last of all He formed man with His sacred and spotless hands, the impress of His own image."[328]

The belief that the one God was the Creator of heaven and earth came, though not without a struggle, to be a foremost and permanent element in the Christian creed. The various forms of ditheism which grew up with it and around it, finding their roots in its unsolved problems and their nutriment in the very love of God which it fostered, gradually withered away. But in proportion as the belief

---

[328] 1 Clem. Rom. 33. 3, 4: 33. 3,4: but it is a noteworthy instance of the contrast between this simple early belief and the developed theology which had grown up in less than a century later, that Irenaeus, *lib*. 4, *praf*. c. 4, explains the 'hands' to mean the Son and Spirit.

spread widely over the Greek world, the simple Semitic cosmogony became insufficient. The questions of the mode of creation, and of the precise relation of God to the material world, which had grown with the growth of monotheism as a philosophical doctrine, were asked not less instinctively, and with an even keener-sighted enthusiasm, when monotheism became a religious conviction. They came not from curiosity, but as the necessary outgrowth among an educated people of that which, not less now than then, is the crucial question of all theistic philosophy: How, if a good and almighty God made the world, can we account for imperfection and failure and pain?

These questions of the mode of creation and of the relation of God to the material world, and the underlying question which any answer to them must at the same time solve, fill a large place in the history of the first three centuries. The compromise which ultimately resulted has formed the basis of Christian theology to the present day.

The first answers were necessarily tentative. Thinkers of all schools, within the original communities and outside them, introduced conceptions which were afterwards discarded. One group of philosophers, treating the facts of Christianity as symbols, like the tableaux of the mysteries, framed cosmogonies which were symbolical also, and fantastic in proportion as they were symbolical. Another group of philosophers, dealing rather with the ideal than with the actual, framed cosmogonies in which abstract ideas were invested with substance and personality. The philosophers of all schools were met, not only by the common sense of the Christian communities, but also by caricature. Their opponents, after the manner of controversialists, accentuated

their weak points, and handed on to later times only those
parts of the theories which were most exposed to attack, and
which were also least intelligible except in relation to the
whole system. But so far as the underlying conceptions can
be disentangled from the details, they may be clearly seen to
have drifted in the direction of the main drifts of Greek
philosophy.

1. There was a large tendency to account for the world by
the hypothesis of evolution. In. some way it had come forth
from God. The belief expressed itself in many forms. It was
in all cases syncretist. The same writers frequently made use
of different metaphors; but all the metaphors assumed vast
grades and distances between God in Himself and the
sensible world. One metaphor was that of an outflow, as of a
stream from its source.[329] Other metaphors were taken from
the phenomena of vegetable growth, the evolution of a plant
from a seed, or the putting forth of leaves by a tree.[330] The
metaphors of other writers were taken from the phenomena
of human generation:[331] they were an elaboration of the
conception of God as the Father of the world. They were
sometimes pressed: there was not only a Father, but also a
Mother of the world, Wisdom or Silence or some other

---

[329] Derivatio: Iren. 1. 24. 3, of Basilides (or rather one of the
schools of Basilidians).

[330] e.g. Hippol. 6. 38, of Epiphanes.

[331] The conception of the double nature of God, male and
female, is found as early as Xenocrates, Aetius ap. Stob. *Ecl.*
1.2.29 and commonly among the Stoics, e.g. in the verses of
Valerius Soranus, which are quoted by Varro, and after him by
S, Augustine, *de civit.* Det, 7.9.

abstraction. In one elaborate system it was held that, though God Himself was unwedded, all the powers that came forth from Him came forth in pairs, and all existing things were the offspring of their union.[332] That which came forth was also conceived in various ways. The common expression in one group of philosophers is *aeon* a term which is of uncertain origin in this application. In other groups of philosophers the expressions are relative to the metaphor of growth and development, and repeat the Stoical term *seed*. In the syncretism of Marcus the several expressions are gathered together, and made more intelligible by the use of the synonym *logoi*;[333] the thoughts of God were conceived as active forces, embodying themselves in material forms. In the conception of one school of thinkers, the invisible forces of the world acted in the same way that the art of a craftsman acts upon his materials.[334] In the conception of another school, the distinction between intellectual and material existence tended to vanish. The powers which flowed forth from God were at once intellectual and material, corresponding to the monistic conception of God Himself. They were subtler and more active forms of matter acting upon its grosser but plastic forms. In the conception of another school, God is the unbegotten seed of which the Tree of Being is the leaves and fruit,[335] and the fruit again contains in itself infinite possibilities of renewing the original seed.[336]

---

[332] The Valentinians in, e.g., Hippol. 6.29; 10.13 : so of Simon Magus, ib. 6.12.

[333] Hippol. 6.43 (of Marcus).

[334] Hippol. 5.19 (of the Sethiani).

[335] Hippol. 8.8 (of the Docetse)

The obvious difficulty which the actual world, with, its failures and imperfections, presents to all theories of evolution which assume the existence of a good and perfect God, was bridged over by the hypothesis of a lapse. The "fall from original righteousness" was carried back from the earthly Paradise to the sphere of divinity itself. The theory was shaped in various ways, some of which are expressed by almost unintelligible symbols. That of the widely-spread school of Valentinus was, that the Divine Wisdom herself had become subject to passion, and that, having both ambition and desire, she had produced from herself a shapeless mass, in ignorance that the Unbegotten One alone can, without the aid of another, produce what is perfect. Out of this shapeless mass, and the passions that came forth from her, arose the material world and the Demiurgus who fashioned it.[337] Another theory was that of revolt and insurrection among the supernal powers.[338] Both theories simply pushed the difficulty farther back: they gave no solution of it: they were opposed as strongly by philosophers outside Christianity as they were by polemical theologians within it:[339] they helped to pave the way for the Augustinian theology of succeeding centuries, but they did not themselves win permanent acceptance either in philosophy or in theology, in either the Eastern or the Western world.

---

[336] *Ibid.* 8.8.

[337] The chief authorities for this theory, which was expressed in language that readily lent itself to caricature, are the first seven chapters of the first book of Irenaeus, and Hippolytus 6. 32 sqq.

[338] This was especially the view of the Peratae, Hippol. 5.13.

[339] Notably by Plotinus, Enn. ii. 9.2—5.

2. Side by side with these hypotheses of evolution was a tendency, which ultimately became supreme, to account for the world by the hypothesis of creation. It was the result of the action of God upon already existing matter. It was not evolved, but ordered or shaped. God was the Builder or Framer: the universe was a work of art.[340]

But this, no less than the monistic hypothesis, contained grave difficulties, arising partly from the metaphysical conception of God, and partly from the conception of moral evil. Three main questions were discussed in connection with it: (i.) "What was the ultimate relation of matter to God? (ii.) How did God come into contact with it so as to shape it? (iii.) How did a God who was almighty as well as beneficent come to create what is imperfect and evil?

(i.) The dualistic hypothesis assumed a co-existence of matter and God. The assumption was more frequently tacit than explicit. The difficulty of the assumption varied according to the degree to which matter was regarded as having positive qualities. There was a universal belief that beneath the qualities of all existing things lay a substratum or substance on which they were grafted, and which gave to each thing its unity. But the conception of the nature of this substance varied from that of gross and tangible material to that of empty and formless space. The metaphysical conception of substance tended to be confused with the physical conception of matter. Matter was sometimes conceived as a mass of atoms not coalescing according to

---

[340] The conception appears in Justin Martyr, Apol. i. 10, but Justin, though he avowedly adopts the conception from Plato, claims that Plato adopted it from Moses.

any principle or order of arrangement:[341] the action of the Creator upon them was that of a general changing a rabble of individuals into an organized army. It was sometimes conceived as a vast shapeless but plastic mass, to which the Creator gave form, partly by molding it as a potter molds clay, partly by combining various elements as a builder combines his materials in the construction of a house.[342] Both these conceptions of matter tended to regard it as more or less gross. It was plastic in the hands of the Divine Workman, but still possessed the quality of resistance. With Basilides, the conception of matter was raised to a higher plane. The distinction of subject and object was preserved, so that the action of the Transcendent God was still that of creation and not of evolution; but it was "out of that which was not" that He made things to be. That which He made was expressed by the metaphor of a seed which contained in itself possibilities, not only of growth, but of different kinds of growth. Three worlds were involved in it: the world of spirit, and the world of matter, and between the two the world of life. The metaphor is sometimes explained by the help of the Aristotelian conception of *genera* and *species*.[343] The original seed which God made is the ultimate *summum genus*. The process by which all things came into being followed in inverse order the process of our knowledge. The steps by which our ideas ascend, by an almost infinite stairway of subordinated groups, from the visible objects of

---

[341] Plutarch, *de anim. procreat.* 5. 3.

[342] Wisdom, 11. 18, Justin M. *Apol.* 1.10.59 (quoted in note, p. 194) : Athenag. *Legat.* 15.

[343] Hippol. 7. 22 (of Basilides).

sense to the highest of all abstractions, the Absolute Being and the Absolute Unity, are the steps by which that Absolute Being and Absolute Unity, who is God, evolved or made the world from that which was not. The basis of the theory was Platonic, though some of the terms were borrowed from both Aristotle and the Stoics. It became itself the basis of the theory which ultimately prevailed in the Church. The transition appears in Tatian. In him, God is the author, not only of the form or qualities, but also of the substance or underlying ground of all things.[344] "The Lord of the universe being Himself the substance of the whole, not yet having brought any creature into being, was alone: and since all power over both visible and invisible things was with Him, He Himself by the power of His word gave substance to all things with Himself." This theory is found in another form in Athenagoras:[345] he makes a point in defense of Christianity that, so far from denying the existence of God, it made Him the Author of all existence, He alone being unborn and imperishable. It is found also in Theophilus,[346] who, however, does not lay stress upon it. But its importance was soon seen. It had probably been for a long time the unreasoned belief of Hebrew monotheism: the development of the Platonic conception within the Christian sphere gave it a philosophical form: and early in the third century it had become the prevailing theory in the Christian Church. God had created matter. He was not merely the Architect of the universe, but its Source.[347]

---

[344] *Oral. ad Graec.* 5 (following the text of Schwartz).

[345] *Suppl. pro Christ.* 4.

[346] *Ad Autol.* 2. 5 and 10.

But the theory did not immediately win its way to acceptance. It rather set aside the moral difficulties than solved them. It was attacked by those who felt those difficulties strongly. There are two chief literary records of the controversy: one is the treatise of Tertullian against Hermogenes, the other is a dialogue of about the same date which is ascribed to an otherwise unknown Maximus.[348] Both treatises are interesting as examples not only of contemporary polemics, but of the insoluble difficulties which beset any attempt to explain the origin of moral evil on metaphysical grounds. The attempt was soon afterwards practically abandoned. The solution of the moral difficulties was found in the doctrine of Free-will: the solution of the metaphysical difficulties was found in the general acceptance of the belief that God created all things out of nothing.

(ii.) How, under any conception of matter, short of its having been created by God, did God come into contact with it so as to give it qualities and form? The difficulty of the question became greater as the tide of thought receded from anthropomorphism. The dominant idea was that of mediation. Sometimes, as in Philo, the mediation was regarded from the point of view of the plurality and variety of the effects, and the agents were conceived as being more than one in number. They were the angels of the Hebrews, the demons of the Greeks. Those who appealed to Scripture saw an indication of this in the use of the plural in the first

[347] The most important passage is Hermas, *Mand.* 1, which is expressed in strictly philosophical language.

[348] In Euseb. *Praep. Evang.* 7. 22, and elsewhere: reprinted in Routh, *Reliquiae Sacrae*, ii. 87.

chapter of Genesis, "Let us make man."[349] Another current of speculation flowed in the channel, which had been first formed by the Timaeus of Plato, of supposing a single Creator and Ruler of the world who, in subordination to the transcendent God, fashioned the things that exist. In some schools of thought this theory was combined with the theory of creation by the Son.[350] The uncontrolled play of imagination in the region of the unknown constructed more than one strange speculation which it is not necessary to revive.

The view into which the Christian consciousness ultimately settled down had meanwhile been building itself up out of elements which were partly Jewish and partly Greek. On the one hand, there had long been among the Jews a belief in the power of the word of God: and the belief in His wisdom had shaped itself into a conception of that wisdom as a substantive force. On the other hand, the original conception of Greek philosophy that Mind or Reason had marshalled into order the confused and warring elements of the primaeval chaos, had passed into the conception of the *Logos* as a mode of the activity of God. These several elements, which had a natural affinity for each other, had already been combined by Philo, as we have seen, into a comprehensive system: and in the second century they were entering into new combinations both outside and inside the Christian communities.[351] The vagueness of conception

---

[349] Justin M. *Tryph*. 62; Iren. 1. 24, 25; Hippol. 7. 16, 20: so Philo, *de profug*. 13 (i. 556).

[350] The Peratae in Hippol. 5.17.

[351] The Jew through whom Celsus sometimes speaks says, "If

which we have found in Philo is found also in the earliest expressions of these combinations. It is not always clear whether the *Logos* is regarded as a mode of God's activity, or as having a substantive existence. In either view, God was regarded as the Creator; His supremacy was as absolute as His unity: there was no rival, because in either view the *Logos* was God.

(iii.) How could a God who was at once beneficent and almighty create a world which contained imperfection and moral evil? The question was answered, as we have seen, on the monistic theory of creation by the hypothesis of a lapse. It was answered on the dualistic theory, sometimes by the hypothesis of evil inherent in matter, and sometimes by the hypothesis of creation by subordinate and imperfect agents.

The former of these hypotheses came rather from the East than from Greece; but it harmonized with and was supported by the Greek conception of matter as the seat of formlessness and disorder.

The latter hypothesis is an extension of the Platonic distinction between the perfect world which God created directly through the operation of His own powers, and the world of mortal and imperfect existences the creation of which He entrusted to inferior agents. In the Platonic conception, God Himself, in a certain mode of His activity, was the Creator (Demiurgus), and the inferior agents were beings whom He had created.[352] In the conception which

---

your *Logos* is the Son of God, we also assent to the same." Origen, *c Cels.* 2.31.

grew up early in the second century, and which was first formulated by Marcion, the Creator was detached from the Supreme God, and conceived as doing the work of the inferior agents. He was subordinate to the Supreme God and ultimately derived from Him:[353] but looming large in the horizon of finite thought, He seemed to be a rival and an adversary. The contradictions, the imperfections, the inequalities of both condition and ability, which meet us in both the material and the moral world, were solved by the hypothesis of two worlds in conflict, each of them moving under the impulse of a separate Power. The same solution applied also to the contrast of the Old and New Testaments. It had been already thought that the God of the Jews was different from the Father of Jesus Christ; but, with an exaggerated Paulinism, Marcion made so deep a chasm between the Law and the Gospel, the Flesh and the Spirit, that the two were regarded as inherently hostile, and the work of the Savior was regarded as bringing back into the world from which he had been shut out the God of love and grace.

The objection to all this was that, in spite of its reservations and safeguards, it tended to ditheism. The philosophical difficulties of monotheism were enormous, but the knot was not to be cut by the hypothesis of either a coexistent and resisting matter or an independent and rival God. The enormous wave of belief in the Divine Unity, which had gathered its strength from the whole sea of contemporary thought, swept away the barriers in its path.

---

[352] Cf. Origen, *c. Cels.* i. 54.

[353] Hippol. *c. Noet.* 11.

The moral difficulty was solved, as we shall see in the next Lecture, by the conception of free-will: the metaphysical difficulties of the contact of God with matter were solved, partly by the conception that God created matter, and partly by the conception that He molded it into form by His *Logos*, who is also His Son, eternally co-existent with Him.

The first patristic statement of this view is in Irenaeus; it stands in the forefront of his theology: and it seems to have been so generally accepted in the communities of which he was cognizant, that he states it as part of the recognized "rule of truth:" the following is only one of several passages in which he so states it:[354]

> "There is one Almighty God who created all things by His Word and fashioned them, and caused that out of what was not all things should be: as saith the Scripture, By the Word of the Lord were the heavens made, and all the host of them by the Breath of His mouth: and again, All things were made by Him, and without Him was not anything made that was made. There is no exception: the Father made all things by Him, whether visible or invisible, objects of sense or objects of intelligence, things temporal or things eternal. He made them not by angels or by any powers separated from His Thought: for God needs none of all these beings: but it is by His Word and His Spirit that He makes and disposes and governs and presides over all things. This God who made the world, this God who fashioned man,

---

[354] 1. 22 : cf. 4. 20.

this God of Abraham, and God of Isaac, and
God of Jacob, above whom there is no other
God, nor Beginning nor Power nor Fulness:
this God, as we shall show, is the Father of our
Lord Jesus Christ."

The same view is expressed with equal prominence and
emphasis by a disciple of Irenaeus, who shows an even
stronger impress of the philosophical speculations of his
time:[355]

"The one God, the first and sole and universal
Maker and Lord, had nothing coeval with him,
not infinite chaos, not measureless water, or
solid earth, or dense air, or warm fire, or subtle
breath, nor the azure cope of the vast heaven:
but He was one, alone by Himself, and by His
will He made the things that are, that before
were not, except so far as they existed in His
foreknowledge ... This supreme and only God
begets Reason first, having formed the thought
of him, not reason as a spoken word, but as an
internal mental process of the universe. Him
alone did He beget from existing things: for the
Father himself constituted existence, and from
it came that which was begotten. The cause of
the things that came into being was the Reason,
bearing in himself the active will of Him who
begat him, and not being without knowledge of
the Father's thought ... so that when the father
bade the world come into being, the Reason
brought each thing to perfection one by one,
thus pleasing God."

---

[355] Hippol. 10.32, 33.

This creed of Irenaeus and his school became the basis of the theology of later Christendom. It appealed, as time went on, to a widening sphere, and summed up the judgment of average Christians on the main philosophical questions of the second century. The questions were not seriously re-opened. The idealists of Alexandria, no less than the rhetoricians of Gaul, accepted, with all its difficulties, the belief that there was one God who revealed Himself to mankind by the Word by whom He had created them, and that this Word was manifested in Jesus Christ. But the Alexandrians were concerned less with the metaphysical than with the moral difficulties; and their view of those difficulties modified also their view of creation. The cosmogony of Origen was a theodicy. His aim was less to show in detail how the world came into existence, than to "justify the ways of God to man." He proceeded strictly on the lines of the older philosophies, justifying in this part of his theology even more than in other respects the criticism of Porphyry,[356] that though in his manner of life he was a Christian, in his opinions about God he was a Greek. He followed the school of Philo in believing that the original creation was of a world of ideal or "intelligible" existences, and that the cause of creation was the goodness of God.[357] He differed from, or expanded, the teaching of that school in believing that the Word or Wisdom of God, by whom He made the world, was not impersonal, but His Son, and that both the existence of the Son and the creation of the ideal world had been from all eternity.' For it is impious to think that God ever existed

---

[356] *ap. Euseb. H. E.* 6.19.

[357] *De princip.* 2.9. 1, 6.

without His Wisdom, possessing the power to create but not the will; and it is inconceivable either that Wisdom should ever have been without the conception of the world that was to be, or that there should ever have been a time at which God was not omnipotent from having no world to govern.[358] The relation of each to the world is stated in varying ways: one mode of statement is, that from the Father and the Son, thus eternally co-existent, came the actual world; the Father caused it to be, the Son caused it to be rational:[359] another is, that the whole world, visible and invisible, was made by the agency of the only begotten Son, who conveyed a share in himself to certain parts of the things so created and caused them thereby to become rational creatures.[360] This visible world, which, as also Philo and the Platonists had taught, is a copy of the ideal world, took its beginning in time: but it is not the first, nor will it be the last, of such worlds.[361] The matter of it as well as the form was created by God.[362] It was made by Him, and to Him it will return. The Stoical theory had conceived of the universe as analogous to a seed which expands to flower and fruit and withers away, but leaves behind it a similar seed which has a similar life and a similar succession: so did one universal order spring from its beginning and pass through its appointed period to the end which was like the beginning in that after it all things began anew. Origen's theory was a modification of this: it

---

[358] *Ibid.* 1.2.2, 10.

[359] *Ibid.* 1.3.5, 6, 8.

[360] *Ibid.* 2.6.3.

[361] *Ibid.* 3.5.3.

[362] *Ibid.* 2.9.4.

recognized an absolute beginning and an absolute end: both the beginning and the end were God: poised as it were between these two divine eternities were the worlds of which we are part. In them, all rational creatures were originally equal and free: they are equal no longer because they have variously used their freedom: and the hypothesis of more worlds than one is a complement, on the one hand of the hypothesis of human freedom, on the other hand of the hypothesis of the divine justice, because it accounts for the infinite diversities of condition, and gives scope for the discipline of reformation.

Large elements of this theory dominated in the theology of the Eastern Churches during the fourth century. But ultimately those parts of it which distinguished it from the theory of Irenaeus faded away. The mass of Christians were content with a simpler creed. More than one question remained unsolved; and the hypothesis of creation by a rival God was part of the creed of a Church which flourished for several centuries before it faded away, and it also left its traces in many inconsistent usages within the circle of the communities which rejected it. But the belief in the unity of God, and in the identity of the one God with the Creator of the world, was never again seriously disturbed. The close of the controversy was marked by its transference to a different, though allied, area. It was no longer Theological but Christological. The expression "Monarchy," which had been used of the sole government of the one God, in distinction from the divided government of many gods, came to be applied to the sole government of the Father, in distinction from the "economy" of the Father, the Son, and the Holy Spirit. In this new area of controversy the old conceptions reappear. The monistic and dualistic theories of the origin of the world lie beneath the two schools of Monarchianism, in one of which Christ was conceived as a mode of God, and in the other as His exalted creature. In the determination of these Christological controversies Greek philosophy had a no less important influence than it had upon the controversies which preceded them: and with some elements of that determination we shall be concerned in a future Lecture.

We may sum up the result of the influence of Greece on the conception of God in His relation to the material universe, by saying that it found a reasoned basis for Hebrew monotheism. It helped the Christian communities to believe as an intellectual conviction that which they had first accepted as a spiritual revelation. The moral difficulties of human life, and the Oriental influences which were flowing in large mass over some parts of the Christian world, tended towards ditheism. But the average opinion of thinking men, which is the ultimate solvent of all philosophical theories, had for centuries past been settling down into the belief in the unity of God. With a conviction which has been as permanent as it was of slow growth, it believed that the difficulties in the hypothesis of the existence of a Power limited by the existence of a rival Power, are greater even than the great difficulties in the belief in a God who allows evil to be. The dominant Theistic philosophy of Greece became the dominant philosophy of Christianity. It prevailed in form as well as in substance. It laid emphasis on the conception of God as the Artificer and Architect of the universe rather than as its immanent Cause. But though the substance will remain, the form may change. Platonism is not the only theory that is consistent with the fundamental thesis that "of Him, and through Him, and to Him, are all things:" and it is not impossible that, even after this long lapse of centuries, the Christian world may come back to that conception of Him which was shadowed in the far-off ages, and which has never been wholly without a witness, that He is "not far off but very nigh;" that "He is in us and we in Him;" that He is changeless and yet changing in and with His creatures; and that He who "rested from His creation," yet so " worketh hitherto" that the moving universe itself is the eternal and unfolding manifestation of Him.

Lecture VIII. GREEK AND CHRISTIAN THEOLOGY.

II. The Moral Governor.

A. The Greek Idea.

1. The idea of the unity of God had grown, as we have already seen, in a common growth with the idea of the unity of the world. But it did not absorb that idea. The dominant element in the idea of God was personality: in the idea of the world it was order. But personality implied will, and will seemed to imply the capacity to change; whereas in the world, wherever order could be traced, it was fixed and unvarying.

The order was most conspicuous in the movements of the heavenly bodies. It could be expressed by numbers. The philosopher of numbers was the first to give to the world the name Cosmos, the "order" as of a marshalled army.[363] The order being capable of being expressed by numbers, partook of the nature of numerical relations. Those relations are not only fixed, but absolutely unalterable. That a certain ratio should be otherwise than what it is, is inconceivable. Hence the same philosopher of numbers who had first conceived of the *Cosmos*, conceived of it also as being "invested with necessity," and the metaphysicians who followed him framed the formula, "All things are by necessity."[364]

---

[363] Aetius ap. Plut. *de plae. phil.* 2. 1. 1 (Diels, p. 327).

[364] Aetius, *ibid.* 1. 25 (Diels, p. 321).

This conception linked itself with an older idea of Greek religion. The length of a man's life and his measure of endowments had been spoken of as his "share" or "portion." Sometimes the assigning of this portion to a man was conceived as the work of Zeus or the other gods: sometimes the gods themselves had their portions like men; and very commonly the portion itself was viewed actively, as though it were the activity of a special being. It was sometimes personal, sometimes impersonal: it was, in any case, inevitable.[365] Through its character of inevitableness, it fused with the conception of the unalterableness of physical order. Hence the proposition, "All things are by necessity," soon came to be otherwise expressed, "All things are by destiny." [366]

Over against the personal might of Zeus there thus came to stand the dark and formless fixity of an impersonal Destiny. The conception was especially elaborated by the Stoics. In the older mythology from which it had sprung, its personifications had been spoken of sometimes as the daughters of Zeus and Themis, and sometimes as the daughters of Night.[367] The former expressed its certainty and perfect order; the other, the darkness of its working. The former element became more prominent. It was an "eternal, continuous and ordered movement."[368] It was "the linked

---

[365] For the numerous passages which prove these statements, reference may be made to Nagelsbach, *Homerische Theologie*, 2.2.3; *Nachhomerische Theologie*, 3.2.2.

[366] Aetius, *ut supra*, 1. 27 (Diels, p. 322).

[367] Hesiod, *Theog.* 218, 904.

chain of causes."[369] The idea of necessity passed into that of intelligent and inherent force: the idea of destiny was transmuted into that of law.

This sublime conception, which has become a permanent possession of the human race, was further elaborated into the picture of the world as a great city. The Greek *polis*, the state, whose equivalent in modern times is not civil but ecclesiastical, was an ideal society, the embodied type of a perfect constitution or organization (*sustama*). Its parts were all interdependent and relative to the whole; the whole was flawless and supreme, working out without friction the divine conception which was expressed in its laws. The world was such an ideal society.[370] It consisted of gods and men: the former were its rulers; the latter, its citizens. The moral law was a reason inherent in human nature, prescribing what men should do, and forbidding what they should not do: human laws were but appendages of it.[371] In this sense man was a "citizen of the world."[372] To each individual man, as to every other created being, the administrators had assigned a special task. "Thou be Sun:

---

[368] Chrysippus, ap. Theodoret. *Gr. Affect. curat.* 6.14.

[369] Aetius ap. Plut. *de placit. philos*. 1.28, Philo, *de mut. nom.* 23 (i. 598).

[370] The idea is found in almost all Stoical writers. Plutarch, *de Alex. Magn. virt.* 6, Chrysippus ap. Phaedr. Epicur. de nat. Deorum, ed. Petersen, p. 19 : Muson. Frag. 5, ed. Peerlk. p. 164 (from Stob. Flor. 40), Epict. Diss. 1. 9. 4 ; 2. 13. 6 ; 3. 22. 4 ; 3. 24. 10, most fully in Arius Didymus ap. Euseb. Proep. Evang. 15. 15. 4.

[371] Philo, *de Josepho*, 6 (ii. 46).

[372] Epict. *Diss*. 3.22.5.

thou hast the power to go on thy circuit and make the year and the seasons, to make fruits grow and ripen, to stir and lull the winds, to warm the bodies of men: go thy way, make thy circuit, and so fulfil thy ministry alike in small things and in great... Thou hast the power to lead the army to Ilium: be Agamemnon. Thou hast the power to fight in combat with Hector: be Achilles." To this function of administration the gods were limited. The constitution of the great city was unchangeable. The gods, like men, were, in the Stoical conception, bound by the conditions of things.

> "That which is best of all things and supreme," says Epictetus, "have the gods placed in our power — the faculty of rightly dealing with ideas: all other things are out of our power. Is it that they would not? I for my part think that if they had been able they would have placed the other things also in our power; but they absolutely could not ... For what says Zeus? 'Epictetus, if it had been possible, I would have made thy body and thy possessions free and unhindered. But as it is, forget not that thy body is not thine, but only clay deftly kneaded. And since I could not do this, I gave thee a part of myself, the power of making or not making effort, the power of indulging or not indulging desire; in short, the power of dealing with all the ideas of thy mind."[373]

2. Side by side with this conception of destiny were growing up new conceptions of the nature of the gods. The

---

[373] Epict. *Diss*. 1.1.10; cf. Seneca, de Provid. 5.7. But Epictetus sometimes makes it a question, not of possibility, but of will, e.g. *Diss*. 4.3.10.

gods of wrath were passing away. The awe of the forces of nature, of night and thunder, of the whirlwind and the earthquake, which had underlain the primitive religions, was fading into mist. The meaner conceptions which had resulted from a vividly realized anthropomorphism, the malice and spite and intrigue which make some parts of the earlier mythology read like the *chronique scandaleuse* of a European court, were passing into the region of ridicule and finding their expression only in burlesque. Two great conceptions, the elements of which had existed in the earliest religion, gradually asserted their supremacy. The gods were just, and they were also good. They punished wicked deeds, not by an arbitrary vengeance, but by the operation of unfailing laws. The laws were the expression of the highest conceivable morality. Their penalties were personal to the offender, and the sinner who did not pay them in this life paid them after death. The gods were also good. The idea of their kindness, which in the earlier religion had been a kindness only for favored individuals, widened out to a conception of their general benevolence.[374] The conception of their forethought, which at first had only been that of wise provision in particular cases, linked itself with the Stoical teleology.[375] The God who was the Reason of the world, and immanent in it, was working to an end. That end was the perfection of the whole, which was also the perfection of each member of the whole. In the sphere of

---

[374] The data for the long history of the moral conceptions of Greek religion which are briefly indicated above are far too numerous to be given in a note: the student is referred to Niagelsbach, *Die Nachhomerische Theologie*, i. 17—58.

[375] Epict. *Diss.* 1.6.

human life, happiness and perfection, misery and imperfection, are linked together. The forethought or "Providence" of God was thus beneficent in regard both to the universe itself and to the individual. It worked by self-acting laws. "There are," says Epictetus,[376] "punishments appointed as it were by law to those who disobey the divine administration. "Whoever thinks anything to be good that is outside the range of his will, let that man feel envy and unsatisfied longing; let him be flattered, let him be unquiet; whoever thinks anything to be evil that is outside the range of his will, let him feel pain and sorrow, let him bemoan himself and be unhappy." And again: "This is the law — divine and strong and beyond escape — which exacts the greatest punishments from those who have sinned the greatest sins. For what says it? The man who lays claim to the things that do not concern him, let him be a braggart, let him be vainglorious: the man who disobeys the divine administration, let him be mean-spirited, let him be a slave, let him feel grief, and jealousy, and pity; in short, let him bemoan himself and be unhappy."[377]

There were thus at the beginning of the Christian era two concurrent conceptions of the nature of the superhuman forces which determine the existence and control the activity of all created things, the conceptions of Destiny and of Providence. The two conceptions, though apparently antagonistic, had tended, like all conceptions which have a strong hold upon masses of men, to approach each other.

---

[376] *Diss*. 3.11.1.

[377] *Diss*. 3.24, 42, 43.

The meeting-point had been found in the conception of the fixed order of the world as being at once rational and beneficent. It was rational because it was the embodiment of the highest reason; and it was beneficent because happiness is incident to perfection, and the highest reason, which is the law of the perfection of the whole, is also the law of the perfection of the parts. There were two stages in this blending of the two conceptions into one: the identification, first of Destiny with Reason;[378] and, secondly, of Destiny or Reason with Providence.[379] The former of these is found in Heraclitus, but is absent from Plato, who distinguishes what comes into being by necessity, from what is wrought by mind: the elaboration of both the former and the latter is due to the Stoics, growing logically out of their conception of the universe as a single substance moved by an inherent law. It was probably in many cases a change rather of language than of idea when Destiny or Reason or Providence was spoken of as God;[380] and yet sometimes, whether by the

---

[378] Destiny is Reason: Heraclitus ap. Act. *Placit.* in Plut. *de placit. philos.* 1.28.1; Stob. *Ecl.* 1.5.15 (Diels, p. 323), Chrysippus, ibid.

[379] Destiny, or Reason, is Providence: Chrysippus, in the quotation given in the preceding note: Zeno ap. Aet. *Placit.* in Stob. *Ecl.* 1.5.15 (Diels, p. 322).

[380] Destiny, Reason, Providence, is God, or the Will of God: Chrysippus in Plut. *de Stoic. repug.* 34. Arius Didymus, *Epit.* ap. Euseb. *Prep. Ev.* 15.15 (Diels, p. 464): Philodemus, *de piet.* frag. ed. Gompertz, p. 83 (Diels, p. 549). The more exact statement is in the summary of Aetius ap. Plut. *de placit. philos.* 1.7.17, Stob. *Hel.* 1.2.29 (Diels, p. 306), where God is said to comprehend within Himself. The loftiest form of the conception is expressed by Lucan, Pharsal. 2.10, '*se quoque lege tenens*:' God is not the slave of Fate or Law, but voluntarily binds

lingering of an ancient belief or by an intuition which transcended logic, the sense of personality mingles with the idea of physical sequence, and all things that happen in the infinite chain of immutable causation are conceived as happening by the will of God.

3. But over against the conception of a perfect Reason or Providence administering the world, was the fact of the existence of physical pain and social inequality and moral failure. The problems which the fact suggested filled a large place in later Greek philosophy, and were solved in many ways.

The solution was sometimes found in the denial of the universality of Providence. God is the Author only of good: evil is due to other causes.[381] This view, which found its first philosophical expression in the Timaeus of Plato, was transmitted, through some of the Platonic schools, to the later syncretist writers who incorporated Platonic elements. In its Platonic form it assumed the existence of inferior agents who ultimately owed their existence to God, but whose existence as authors of evil He permitted or overlooked. In some later forms the view linked itself with Oriental conceptions of matter as inherently evil.

The solution was more commonly found in a denial of the reality of apparent evils. They were all either forms of good,

---

Himself by it,

[381] Plat. *Rep.* 2, pp. 379, 380; *Tim.* p. 41. Philo, *de mund. opif.* 24 (i. 17), so also in the (probably) post-Philonean *de Abraham.* 28 (ii. 22).

or incidental to its operation or essential to its production. This was the common solution of the Stoics. It had many phases. One view was based upon the teleological conception of nature. The world is marching on to its end: it realizes its purpose not directly but by degrees: there are necessary sequences of its march which seem to us to be evil. Another view, akin to the preceding, was based upon the conception of the world as a whole. In its vast economy there are subordinations and individual inconveniences. Such subordinations and inconveniences are necessary parts of the plan. The pain of the individual is not an evil, but his contribution to the good of the whole. "What about my leg being lamed, then?" says Epictetus,[382] "addressing himself in the character of an imaginary objector. "Slave! do you really find fault with the world on account of one bit of a leg? will you not give that up to the universe? will you not let it go? will you not gladly surrender it to the Giver?" The world, in other words, was regarded as an *economy* (*oikonomia*), like that of a city, in which there are apparent inequalities of condition, but in which such inequalities are necessary to the constitution of the whole.[383]

> "What is meant, then," asks Epictetus, "by distinguishing the things that happen to us as 'according to nature' and 'contrary to nature'? The phrases are used as if we were isolated. For example, to a foot to be 'according to nature' is to be clean; but if you consider it as a foot, a member of the body, and not as isolated, it will be its duty both to walk in mud, and to tread

[382] *Diss*, 1.12.24.

[383] Chrysippus, *de Di*is, 2, ap. Plut. *de Stoic. repug.* 35.

on thorns — nay, sometimes even to be cut off for the benefit of the whole body; if it refuse, it is no longer a foot. We have to form a similar conception about ourselves. What are you? A man. If you regard yourself as isolated, it is 'according to nature ' to live until old age, to be rich, to be in good health; but if you regard yourself as a man, a part of a certain whole, it is your duty, on account of that whole, sometimes to be ill, sometimes to take a voyage, sometimes to run into danger, sometimes to be in want, and, it may be, to die before your time. Why then are you discontented? Do you not know that, as in the example a discontented foot is no longer a foot, so neither are you a man. For what is a man? A member of a city, first the city which consists of gods and men, and next of the city which is so called in the more proximate sense, the earthly city, which is a small model of the whole. 'Am I, then, now,' you say, 'to be brought before a court: is so-and-so to fall into a fever: so-and-so to go on a voyage: so-and-so to die: so-and-so to be condemned?' Yes; for it is impossible, considering the sort of body we have, with this atmosphere round us, and with these companions of our life, that different things of this kind should not befall different men.[384]

" It is on this account that the philosophers rightly tell us that if a perfectly good man had foreknown what was going to happen to him, he would co-operate with nature in both falling

---

[384] *Diss.* 2.5.24.

> sick and dying and being maimed, being
> conscious that this is the particular portion that
> is assigned to him in the arrangement of the
> universe, and that the whole is supreme over
> the part, and the city over the citizen."[385]

This Stoical solution, if the teleological conception which underlies it be assumed, may have been adequate as an explanation both of physical pain and of social inequality. But it was clearly inadequate as an explanation of misery and moral evil. And the sense of misery and moral evil was growing. The increased complexity of social life revealed the distress which it helped to create, and the intensified consciousness of individual life quickened also the sense of disappointment and moral shortcoming. The solution of the difficulties which these facts of life presented, was found in a belief which was correlative to the growing belief in the goodness of God, though logically inconsistent with the belief in the universality of His Providence. It was, that men were the authors of their own misery. Their sorrows, so far as they were not punitive or remedial, came from their own folly or perversity. They belonged to a margin of life which was outside the will of the gods or the ordinances of fate. The belief was repeatedly expressed by Homer, but does not appear in philosophy until the time of the Stoics: it is found in both Cleanthes and Chrysippus, and the latter also quotes it as a belief of the Pythagoreans.[386] Out of it came the solution of a problem not less important than that from which it had itself sprung. The conception that men were free to bring ruin upon themselves, led to the wider

---

[385] *Diss*, 2.10.5.

[386] Aul. Gell. 7 (6). 2.12—15.

conception that they were altogether free. There emerged for the first time into prominence the idea which has filled a large place in all later theology and ethics, that of the freedom of the will. The freedom which was denied to external nature was asserted of human nature. It was within a man's own power to do right or wrong, to be happy or miserable.

> "Of all things that are," says Epictetus,[387] "one part is in our control, the other out of it; in our control are opinion, impulse to do, effort to obtain, effort to avoid — in a word, our own proper activities; out of our control are our bodies, property, reputation, office — in a word, all things except our proper activities. Things in our control are in their nature free, not liable to hindrance in the doing or to frustration of the attainment; things out of our control are weak, dependent, liable to hindrance, belonging to others. Bear in mind, then, that if you mistake what is dependent for what is free, and what belongs to others for what is your own, you will meet with obstacles in your way, you will be regretful and disquieted, you will find fault with both gods and men. If, on the contrary, you think that only to be your own which is really your own, and that which is another's to be, as it really is, another's, no one will thwart you, you will find fault with no one, you will reproach no one, you will do no single thing against your will, no one will harm you, you will not have an enemy."

---

[387] *Euch.* 1.

The incompatibility of this doctrine with that of the universality of Destiny or Reason or Providence — the "antinomy of the practical understanding" — was not always observed[388]. The two doctrines marched on parallel lines, and each of them was sometimes stated as though it had no limitations. The harmony of them, which is indicated by both Cleanthes and Chrysippus, and which underlies a large part of both the theology and the ethics of Epictetus, is in effect this: The world marches on to its end, realizing its own perfection, with absolute certainty. The majority of its parts move in that march unconsciously, with no sense of pleasure or pain, no idea of good or evil. To man is given the consciousness of action, the sense of pleasure and pain, the idea of good and evil, and freedom of choice between them. If he chooses that which is against the movement of nature, he chooses for himself misery; if he chooses that which is in accordance with that movement, he finds happiness. In either case the movement of nature goes on, and the man fulfils his destiny: "*Ducunt volentem fata, nolentem trahunt.*"[389] It is a man's true function and high privilege so to educate his mind and discipline his will, as to think that to be best which is really best, and that to be avoided which nature has not willed: in other words, to acquiesce in the will of God, not as submitting in passive resignation to the power of one who is stronger, but as having made that will his own.[390]

---

[388] Eg. Sext. Empir. *Pyrr*. 3.9.

[389] Seneca, *Ep*. 107. 11: a free Latin rendering of one of the verses of Cleanthes quoted from Epictetus in Lecture VI. p. 157.

[390] Seneca, *Dial*. 1.5.8:

If a man realizes this, instead of bemoaning the difficulties of life, he will not only ask God to send them, but thank Him for them. This is the Stoical theodicy. The life and teaching of Epictetus are for the most part a commentary upon it.

> "Look at the powers you have; and when you have looked at them, say, 'Bring me, God, what difficulty Thou wilt; for I have the equipment which Thou hast given me, and the means: for making all things that happen contribute to my adornment.' 'Nay, but that is not what you do: you sit sometimes shuddering at the thought of what may happen, sometimes bewailing and grieving and groaning over what does happen. Then you find fault with the gods! For what but impiety is the consequence of such degeneracy? And yet God has not merely given you these powers by which we may bear whatever happens without being lowered or crushed by it, but also, like the good King and true Father that He is, has given to this part of you the capacity of not being thwarted, or forced, or hindered, and has made it absolutely your own, not even reserving to Himself the power of thwarting or hindering it."[391]

> "What words are sufficient to praise or worthily describe the gifts of Providence to us? If we were really wise, what should we have been doing in public or in private but sing hymns to God, and bless Him and recount His gifts (*tas charitas*)? Digging or ploughing or

---

[391] Epict. *Diss.* 1.6.37—40.

eating, ought we not to be singing this hymn to God, 'Great is God for having given us these tools for tilling the ground; great is God for having given us hands to work with and throat to swallow with, for that we grow unconsciously and breathe while we sleep '? This ought to be our hymn for everything: but the chiefest and divinest hymn should be for His having given us the power of understanding and of dealing rationally with ideas. Nay — since most of you are utterly blind to this — ought there not to be someone to make this his special function, and to sing the hymn to God for all the rest? What else can a lame old man like me do but sing hymns to God? If I were a nightingale, I should do the work of a nightingale; if a swan, the work of a swan; but being as I am a rational being, I must sing hymns to God. This is my work: this I do: this rank — as far as I can — I will not leave; and I invite you to join with me in this same song."[392]

B. The Christian Idea.

In primitive Christianity we find ourselves in another sphere of ideas: we seem to be breathing the air of Syria, with Syrian forms moving round us, and speaking a language which is not familiar to us. For the Greek city, with its orderly government, we have to substitute the picture of an Eastern sheik, at once the paymaster of his dependents and their judge. Two conceptions are dominant, that of wages for work done, and that of positive law.

---

[392] *Ibid.* 1.16.15—21.

1. The idea of moral conduct as work done for a master who will in due time pay wages for it, was a natural growth on Semitic soil. It grew up among the *fellahin*, to whom the day's work brought the day's wages, and whose work was scrutinized before the wages were paid. It is found in many passages of the New Testament, and not least of all in the discourses of our Lord. The ethical problems which had vexed the souls of the writers of Job and the Psalms, are solved by the teaching that the wages are not all paid now, but that some of them are in the keeping of the Father in heaven. The persecuted are consoled by the thought, "Great are your wages in heaven."[393] Those who do their alms before men receive their wages in present reputation, and have no wages stored up for them in heaven.[394] The smallest act of casual charity, the giving of a cup of cold water, will not go without its wages.[395] The payment will be made at the return of the Son of Man, whose "wages are with him to give to every man according as his work is."[396] So fundamental is the conception that "he that cometh to God must believe," not only "that He is," but also that He "pays their due to them that seek after Him."[397] So also in the early Christian literature which moved still within the sphere of Syrian ideas. In the " Two Ways," what is given in charity should be given without murmuring, for God will repay it:[398] in the Epistle of

---

[393] S. Matthew, 5.12; S. Luke, 6.23,

[394] *Ibid.* 6.1.

[395] *Ibid.* 10.42; S. Mark, 9.41.

[396] Revelation, 22.12: so Barnab. 21.3:

[397] Hebrews, 11.6.

Barnabas, the conception of the paymaster is blended with that of the judge.[399] "The Lord judges without respect of persons: every one shall receive according as he has done: if he be good, his righteousness shall go before him: if he be wicked, the wages of his wickedness are before his face."

2. God is at once the Lawgiver and the Judge. The underlying conception is that of an Oriental sovereign who issues definite commands, who is gratified by obedience and made angry by disobedience, who gives presents to those who please him and punishes those with whom he is angry. The punishments which he inflicts, are vindictive and not remedial. They are the manifestation of his vengeance against unrighteousness. They are external to the offender. They follow on the offence by the sentence of the judge, and not by a self-acting law. He sends men *into* punishment.

The introduction into this primitive Christianity of the ethical conceptions of Greek philosophy, raised difficulties which were long in being solved, if indeed they can be said to have been solved even now. The chief of these difficulties were, (i.) the relation of the idea of forgiveness to that of law; (ii.) the relation of the conception of a Moral Governor to that of free-will.

(i.) The Christian conception of God on its ethical side was dominated by the idea of the forgiveness of sins. God was a Sovereign who had issued commands: He was a Householder who had entrusted His servants with powers to be used in His service. As Sovereign, He could, at His

---

[398] Didache, 4.7.

[399] Barnab. 4.12.

pleasure, forgive a breach of His orders: as Householder, He could remit a debt which was due to Him from His servants. The special message of the Gospel was, that God was willing to forgive men their If transgressions, and to remit their debts, for the sake of Jesus Christ. The corresponding Greek conception had come to be dominated by the idea of order. The order (was rational and beneficent, but it was universal. It could not be violated with impunity. The punishment of its violation came by a self-acting law. There was a possibility of amendment, but there was none of remission. Each of these conceptions is consistent with itself: each by itself furnishes the basis of a rational theology. But the two conceptions are apparently irreconcilable with each other; and the history of a large part of early Christian theology is the history of endeavors to reconcile them. The one conception belonged to a moral world, controlled by a Personality who set forces in motion; the other to a physical world, controlled by a force which was also conceived as a Personality. Stated in Christian terms, the one resolved itself into the proposition, God is good; the other into the proposition, God is just. The two propositions seemed at first to be inconsistent with each other: on the one hand, the infinite love of God excluding the idea of punishment; on the other hand. His immutable righteousness excluding the idea of forgiveness.[400] The difficulty seemed insoluble, except upon the hypothesis of the existence of two Gods. The ditheism was sometimes veiled by the conception that the second God had been created by the first, and was

---

[400] These conceptions of the earliest Christian philosophers are stated, in order to be modified, by Origen, *de prince.* 2. 5.1.

ultimately subordinate to Him. In the theology of Marcion, which filled a large place in the Christianity of both the second and the third centuries, ditheism was presented as the only solution of this and all the other contrasts of which the world is full, and of which that of Law and Grace is the most typical example.[401] The New Testament was the revelation of the good God, the God of love; the Old Testament was that of the just God, the God of wrath. Redemption was the victory of forgiveness over punishment, of the God who was revealed by Jesus Christ over the God who was manifested in the Law.

The ditheistic hypothesis was itself more difficult than the difficulties which it explained. The writers who opposed it were helped, not only by the whole current of evangelical tradition, but also by the dominant tendencies of both philosophy and popular religion. They insisted that justice and goodness were not only compatible but necessarily coexistent in the Divine nature. 'Goodness meant not indiscriminating beneficence; justice meant not inexorable wrath: goodness and justice were combined in the power of

---

[401] The title of Marcion's chief work was 'Contrasts': the extent to which his opinions prevailed is shown both by contemporary testimony, e.g. Justin M. *Apol.* 1.26, Iren, 3.3.4, and also by the fact that the Churches into which his adherents were organized flourished side by side with the Catholic Churches for many centuries (there is an inscription of one of them, dated A.D, 318, in Le Bas et Waddington, vol. iii. No. 2558, and they had not died out at the time of the Trullan Council in A.D. 692: the importance which was attached to him is shown by the large place which he occupies in early controversies, Justin Martyr, Irenaeus, the Clementines, Origen, Tertullian, being at pains to refute him.

God to deal with every man according to his deserts, including in the idea of deserts. that of repentance.

The solution is found in Irenaeus, who argues that in the absence of either of the two attributes, God would cease to be God:

> "If the God who judges be not also good, so as to bestow favors on those on whom He ought, and to reprove those whom He should, He will be as a Judge neither wise nor just. On the other hand, if the good God be only good, and not also able to test those on whom He shall bestow His goodness, He will be outside goodness as well as outside justice, and His goodness will seem imperfect, inasmuch as it does not save all, as it should do if it be not accompanied with judgment. Marcion, therefore, by dividing God into two, the one a God who judges, and the other a God who is good, on both sides puts an end to God."[402]

It is found in Tertullian, who, after arguing on *a priori* grounds that the one attribute implies the other, passes by an almost unconscious transition from physical to moral law: just as the "justice" of God in its physical operation controlled His goodness in the making of an orderly world, so in its moral operation it has, since the Fall, regulated His dealings with mankind.

> "Nothing is good which is unjust; all that is just is good … The good is where the just is. From the beginning of the world the Creator has

---

[402] Iren. 3.25.2.

been at once good and just. The two qualities came forth together. His goodness formed the world, His justice harmonized it. It is the work of justice that there is a separation between light and darkness, between day and night, between heaven and earth, between the greater and the lesser lights … As goodness brought all things into being, so did justice distinguish them. The whole universe has been disposed and ordered by the decision of His justice. Every position and mode of the elements, the movement and the rest, the rising and the setting of each one of them, are judicial decisions of the Creator … When evil broke out, and the goodness of God came henceforward to have an opponent to contend with, the justice also of God acquired another function, that of regulating the operation of His goodness according to the opposition to it: the result is that His goodness, instead of being absolutely free, is dispensed according to men's deserts; it is offered to the worthy, it is denied to the unworthy, it is taken away from the unthankful, it is avenged on all its adversaries. In this way this whole function of justice is an agency for goodness: in condemning, in punishing, in raging with wrath, as you Marcionites express it, it does good and not evil."[403]

It is found in the Clementines,[404] the "Recognitions" going so far as to make the acceptance of it an element in "saving knowledge:" " it is not enough for salvation to know that

---

[403] Tert. *c. Marc.* 2.11, 12.

[404] *Homil.* 4.13; 9. 19; 18.2, 3.

God is good; we must know also that He is just."[405] It is elaborated by both Clement of Alexandria[406] and Origen; but in the latter it is linked closely with other problems, and his view will be best considered in relation to them. The Christian world in his time was settling down into a general acceptance of the belief that goodness and justice coexisted, each limiting the other in the mind of God: the general effect of the controversy was to emphasize in Christianity the conception of God as a Moral Governor, administering the world by laws which were at once beneficent and just.

(ii.) But this problem of the relation of goodness to justice passed, as the corresponding problem in Greek philosophy passed, into the problem of the relation of a good God to moral evil. The difficulties of the problem were increased in its Christian form by the conception of moral evil as guilt rather than as misery, and by the emphasis which was laid on the idea of the Divine foreknowledge.

The problem was stated in its plainest form by Marcion:

"If God is good, and prescient of the future, and able to avert evil, why did He allow man, that is to say His own image and likeness, nay more, His own substance, to be tricked by the devil and fall from obedience to the law into death? For if He had been good, and thereby unwilling that such an event should happen, and prescient, and thereby not ignorant that it would happen, and powerful, and thereby able

---

[405] *Recogn.* 3.37.

[406] Especially *Paedag.* 1.8, 9.

> to prevent its happening, it would certainly not
> have happened, being impossible under these
> three conditions of divine greatness. But since
> it did happen, the inference is certain that God
> must be believed to be neither good nor
> prescient nor powerful."[407]

The hypothesis of the existence of two Gods, by which Marcion solved this and other problems of theology, was consistently opposed by the great mass of the Christian communities. The solution which they found was almost uniformly that of the Stoics: evil is necessary for the production of moral virtue: there is no virtue where there is no choice: and man was created free to choose. It was found, in short, in the doctrine of free-will.

This solution is found in Justin Martyr:

> "The nature of every created being is to be
> capable of vice and virtue: for no one of them
> would be an object of praise if it had not also
> the power of turning in the one direction or the
> other."[408]

It is found in Tatian:

> "Each of the two classes of created things
> (men and angels) is born with a power of self-
> determination, not absolutely good by nature,
> for that is an attribute of God alone, but
> brought to perfection through freedom of
> voluntary choice, in order that the bad man
> may be justly punished, being himself the cause

---

[407] ap. Tert. *c. Marc*. 2.5.

[408] *Apol*. 2.7.

of his being wicked, and that the righteous man
may be worthily praised for his good actions,
not having in his exercise of moral freedom
transgressed the will of God."[409]

It is found in Irenaeus:

"In man as in angels, for angels also are
rational beings, God has placed the power of
choosing, so that those who have obeyed might
justly be in possession of what is good; and
that those who have not obeyed may justly not
be in possession of what is good, and may
receive the punishment which they deserve …
But if it had been by nature that some were bad
and others good, neither would the latter be
deserving of praise for being good, inasmuch
as they were so constituted; nor the others of
blame for being bad, inasmuch as they were
born so. But since in fact all men are of the
same nature, able on the one hand to hold fast
and to do what is good, and again on the other
hand to reject it and not do it, it is right for
them to be in the one case praised for their
choice of the good and their adherence to it,
and in the other case blamed and punished for
their rejection of it, both among well-governed
men and much more in the sight of God."[410]

It is found in Theophilus[411] and Athenagoras,[412] and, as a
more elaborate theory, in Tertullian and the philosophers of

---

[409] Tatian, *Orat. ad Grac.* 7.

[410] Iren. 4. 37,

[411] *Ad Autol.* 2.27.

Alexandria. Just as Epictetus and the later Stoics had made freedom of will to be the specially divine part of human nature, so Tertullian[413] answers Marcion's objection, that if God foreknew that Adam would fall He should not have made him free, by the argument that the goodness of God in making man necessarily gave him the highest form of existence, that such highest form was "the image and likeness of God," and that such image and likeness was freedom of will. And just as Epictetus and the later Stoics had conceived of life as a moral discipline, and of its apparent evils as necessary means of testing character, so the Christian philosophers of Alexandria conceive of God as the Teacher and Trainer and Physician of men, of the pains of life as being disciplinary, and of the punishments of sin as being not vindictive but remedial.[414]

There was still a large margin of unsolved difficulties. The hypothesis of the freedom of the will, as it had hitherto been stated, assumed that all beings who possessed it were equal in both their circumstances and their natural aptitudes. It took no account of the enormous difference between one man and another in respect of either the external advantages or disadvantages of their lives, or the strength and weakness of their characters. The difficulty was strongly felt by more than one school of Christian philosophers, the more so because it applied, not only to the diversities among mankind, but also to the larger differences between mankind

[412] *Legat.* 51.

[413] *c. Marc*, 2. 5.

[414] E.g. Clem. Alex. *Paedag.* 1.1; Origen, *de princ*. 2.10.6; *c. Cele* 6.56: so also Tert. *Scorp.* 5.

as a whole and the celestial beings who rose in their sublime gradations above it.

> "Very many persons, especially those who come from the school of Marcion and Valentinus and Basilides, object to us that it is inconsistent with the justice of God in making the world to assign to some creatures an abode in the heavens, and not merely a better abode, but also a loftier and more honorable position; to grant to some principality, to others powers, to others dominations; to confer upon some the noblest seats of the heavenly tribunals, to cause others to shine out with brighter rays, and to flash forth the brilliance of a star; to give to some the glory of the sun, and to others the glory of the moon, and to others the glory of the stars; to make one star differ from another star in glory In the second place, they object to us about terrestrial beings that a happier lot of birth has come to some men than to others; one man, for example, is begotten by Abraham and born according to promise; another is the son of Isaac and Rebekah, and, supplanting his brother even in the womb, is said even before he is born to be beloved of God. One man is born among the Hebrews, among whom he finds the learning of the divine law; another among the Greeks, themselves also wise and men of no small learning; another among the Ethiopians, who are cannibals; another among the Scythians, with whom parricide is legal; another among the Taurians, who offer their guests in sacrifice.

> "They consequently argue thus: If this great diversity of circumstances, this varied and

different condition of birth — a matter in
which free-will has no place — is not caused by
a diversity in the nature of the souls
themselves, a soul of an evil nature being
destined for an evil nation, and a soul of a good
nature for a good one, what other conclusion
can be drawn than that all this is the result of
chance and accident? And if that conclusion be
admitted, it will no longer be credible either
that the world was made by God or that it is
governed by His providence: and consequently
neither will the judgment of God upon every
man's doings seem a thing to be looked for."[415]

It is to this phase of the controversy that the ethical
theology of Origen is relative. In that theology, Stoicism and
Neo-Platonism are blended into a complete theodicy: nor
has a more logical superstructure ever been reared on the
basis of philosophical theism.

It is necessary to show the coherence of his view as a
whole, and it is advisable, in doing so, to use chiefly his own
words:[416]

"There was but one beginning of all things, as
there will be but a single end. The diversities of
existence which have sprung from a single
beginning will be absorbed in a single end.[417]
The causes of those diversities lie in the diverse

---

[415] Origen, *de prince*. 2.9.5.

[416] The passage which follows is, with the exception of one
extract from the *contra Celsum*, a catera of extracts from the *de
principiis*.

[417] *De princ*. 1.6.2.

things themselves.[418] They were created absolutely equal; for, on the one hand, God had no reason in Himself for causing inequalities;[419] and, on the other hand, being absolutely impartial, He could not give to one being an advantage which He did not give to another.[420] They were also, by a similar necessity, created with the capacity of being diverse; for spotless purity is of the essence of none save God; in all created beings it must be accidental, and consequently liable to lapse.[421] The lapse, when it takes place, is voluntary; for every being endowed with reason has the power of exercising it, and this power is free;[422] it is excited by external causes, but not coerced by them.[423] For to lay the fault on external causes and put it away from ourselves by declaring that we are like logs or stones, dragged by forces that act upon them from without, is neither true nor reasonable. Every created rational being is thus capable of both good and evil; consequently of praise and blame; consequently also of happiness and misery; of the former if it chooses holiness and clings to it, of the latter if by sloth and negligence it swerves into wickedness and ruin.[424]

---

[418] 1.8.2; 2.9.7.

[419] 2.9.6.

[420] 1.8.4

[421] 1.5.5; 1.6.2.

[422] 3.1.4.

[423] 3.1.5.

The lapse, when it has taken place, is not only voluntary but also various in degree. Some beings, though possessed of freewill, never lapsed: they form the order of angels. Some lapsed but slightly, and form in their varying degrees the orders of 'thrones, dominations, princedoms, virtues, powers.' Some lapsed lower, but not irrecoverably, and form the race of men.[425] Some lapsed to such a depth of unworthiness and wickedness as to be opposing powers; they are the devil and his angels.[426] In the temporal world which is seen, as well as in the eternal worlds which are unseen, all beings are arranged according to their merits; their place has been determined by their own conduct.'[427]

"The present inequalities of circumstance and character are thus not wholly explicable within the sphere of the present life. But this world is not the only world. Every soul has existed from the beginning; it has therefore passed through some worlds already, and will pass through others before it reaches the final consummation. It comes into this world strengthened by the victories or weakened by the defeats of its previous life. Its place in this world as a vessel appointed to honor or to dishonor is determined by its previous merits or demerits. Its work in this world determines its place in the world which is to follow this.[428]

---

[424] 1.5.2, 5.

[425] 1.6.2.

[426] 1.6.3.

[427] 3.3.5; 3.5.3.

"All this takes place with the knowledge and under the oversight of God. It is an indication of His ineffable wisdom that the diversities of natures for which created beings are themselves responsible are wrought together into the harmony of the world.[429] It is an indication not only of His wisdom but of His goodness that, while no creature is coerced into acting rightly, yet when it lapses it meets with evils and punishments. All punishments are remedial. God calls what are termed evils into existence to convert and purify those whom reason and admonition fail to change. He is thus the great Physician of souls.[430] The process of cure, acting as it does simply through free-will, takes in some cases an almost illimitable time. For God is longsuffering, and to some souls, as to some bodies, a rapid cure is not beneficial. But in the end all souls will be thoroughly purged.[431] All that any reasonable soul, cleansed of the dregs of all vices, and with every cloud of wickedness completely wiped away, can either feel or understand or think, will be wholly God: it will no longer either see or contain anything else but God: God will be the mode and measure of its every movement:

---

[428] 3.1.20, 21: but sometimes beings of higher merit are assigned to a lower grade, that they may benefit those who properly belong to that grade, and that they themselves may be partakers of the patience of the Creator, 2.9.7.

[429] 1.2.1.

[430] c. Cels. 6.56; de prince, 2.10.

[431] De prince. 3.1.14,17.

and so God will be 'all.' Nor will there be any
longer any distinction between good and evil,
because evil will nowhere exist; for God is all
things, and in Him no evil inheres. So, then,
when the end has been brought back to the
beginning, that state of things will be restored
which the rational creation had when it had no
need to eat of the tree of the knowledge of
good and evil; all sense of wickedness will have
been taken away; He who alone is the one
good God becomes to the soul 'all,' and that
not in some souls but 'in all.' There will be no
longer death, nor the sting of death, nor any
evil anywhere, but God will be 'all in all'"[432]

Of this great theodicy, only part has been generally
accepted. The Greek conceptions which underlie it, and
which preceded it, have survived, but in other forms. Free-
will, final causes, probation, have had a later history in which
Greece has had no share. The doctrine of free-will has
remained in name, but it has been so mingled on the one
hand with theories of human depravity, and on the other
with theories of divine grace, that the original current of
thought is lost in the marshes into which it has descended.
The doctrine of final causes has been pressed to an almost
excessive degree as proving the existence and the providence
of God; but His government of the human race has been
often viewed rather as the blundering towards an ultimate
failure than as a complete vindication of His purpose of
creation. The Christian world has acquiesced in the
conception of life as a probation; but while some of its
sections have conceived of this life as the only probation,

---

[432] 3.6.3.

and others have admitted a probation in a life to come, none
have admitted into the recognized body of their teaching
Origen's sublime conception of an infinite stairway of
worlds, with its perpetual ascent and descent of souls, ending
at last in the union of all souls with God.

Lecture IX. GREEK AND CHRISTIAN THEOLOGY.

III. God as the Supreme Being.

It was in the Gentile rather than in the Jewish world that the theology of Christianity was shaped. It was built upon a Jewish basis. The Jewish communities of the great cities and along the commercial routes of the empire had paved the way for Christianity by their active propaganda of monotheism. Christianity won its way among the educated classes by virtue of its satisfying not only their moral ideals, but also their highest intellectual conceptions. On its ethical side it had, as we have seen, large elements in common with reformed Stoicism; on its theological side it moved in harmony with the new movements of Platonism.[433] And those movements reacted upon it. They gave a philosophical form to the simpler Jewish faith, and especially to those elements of it in which the teaching of St. Paul had already given a foothold for speculation. The earlier conceptions remained; but blending readily with the philosophical conceptions that were akin to them, they were expanded into large theories in which metaphysics and dialectics had an ample field. The conception, for example, of the one God whose kingdom was a universal kingdom and endured throughout all ages, blended with, and passed into, the philosophical conception of a Being who was beyond time and space. The conception that "clouds and darkness were round about Him," blended with, and passed into, the philosophical conception of a Being who was beyond not

---

[433] Cf. Justin, *Dial. c. Tryph.* 2.

only human sight but human thought. The conception of
His transcendence obtained the stronger hold because it
confirmed the prior conception of His unity; and that of His
incommunicability, and of the consequent need of a
mediator, gave a philosophical explanation of the truth that
Jesus Christ was His Son.

A. The Idea and its Development in Greek Philosophy.

But the theories which in the fourth century came to
prevail, and which have formed the main part of speculative
theology ever since, were the result of at least two centuries
of conflict. At every stage of the conflict the conceptions of
one or other of the forms of Greek philosophy played a
decisive part; and the changing phases of the conflict find a
remarkable parallel in some of the philosophical schools.

The conflict may be said to have had three leading stages,
which are marked respectively by the dominance of
speculations as to (1) the transcendence of God, (2) His
revelation of Himself, (3) the distinctions in His nature.

(1) *The Transcendence of God.* — Nearly seven hundred years
before the time when Christianity first came into large
contact with Greek philosophy, the mind of a Greek thinker,
outstripping the slow inferences of popular thought, had
leapt to the conception of God as the Absolute Unity. He
was the ultimate generalization of all things, expressed as the
ultimate abstraction of number:[434] He was not limited by
parts or by bodily form: "all of Him is sight, all of Him is

---

[434] Aetius ap. Stob *Ecl. Phys.* 2.29.

understanding, all of Him is hearing." But it is probable that the conception in its first form was rather of a material than of an ideal unity:[435] the basis of later metaphysics was first securely laid by a second form of the conception which succeeded the first half-a-century afterwards. The conception was that of Absolute Being. Only the One really *is*: it was not nor will be: it *is* now, and is everywhere entire, a continuous unity, a perfect sphere which fills all space, undying and immovable. Over against it are the Many, the innumerable objects of sense: they are not, but only seem to be: the knowledge that we seem to have of them is not truth, but illusion. But the conception, even in this second form, was more consistent with Pantheism than with Theism. It was lifted to the higher plane on which it has ever since rested by the Platonic distinction between the world of sense and the world of thought. God belonged to the latter, and not to the former. Absolute Unity, Absolute Being, and all the other terms which expressed His unique supremacy, were gathered up in the conception of Mind; for mind in the highest phase of its existence is self-contemplative: the modes of its expression are numerous, and perhaps infinite: but it can itself go behind its modes, and so retire, as it were, a step farther back from the material objects about which its modes employ themselves. In this sense God is transcendent (*epekeina tas ousias*) beyond the world of sense and matter. "God therefore is Mind, a form separate from all matter, that is to say, out of contact with it, and not involved with anything that is capable of being acted on."[436]

---

[435] The form in which it is given by Sextus Empiricus, in whose time the distinction was clearly understood, implies this: *Pyrrh. Hypotyp.* 225,

This great conception of the transcendence of God filled a large place in later Greek philosophy, even outside the Platonic schools.[437] The history of it is beyond our present purpose; but we shall better understand the relation of Christian theology to current thought if we take three expressions of the conception at the time when that theology was being formed — in Plutarch, in Maximus of Tyre, and in Plotinus.

Plutarch says:

> "What, then, is that which really exists? It is the Eternal, the Uncreated, the Undying, to whom time brings no change, For time is always flowing and never stays: it is a vessel charged with birth and death: it has a before and after, a 'will be' and a 'has been:' it belongs to the 'is not' rather than to the 'is.' But God is: and that not in time but in eternity, motionless, timeless, changeless eternity, that has no before or after: and being One, He fills eternity with one Now, and so really 'is' not 'has been,' or 'will be,' without beginning and without ceasing."[438]

---

[436] This is a post-Platonic summary of Plato's conception; into the inner development, and consequently varying expressions, of it in Plato's own writings it is not necessary to enter here. It is more important in relation to the history of later Greek thought to know what he was supposed to mean than what he meant. The above is taken from the summary of Aetius in Plut. *de plac. philos*. 1.7, Euseb. *Prep. evang*. 14.16 (Diels, *Doxographt Greci*, p. 304).

[437] It was a struggle between this and Stoicism.

[438] Plutarch, *de Ei ap. Delph*. 18.

Maxinius of Tyre says:

> "God, the Father and Fashioner of all things
> that are, He who is older than the sun, older
> than the sky, greater than time and lapse of
> time and the whole stream of nature, is
> unnamed by legislators, and unspoken by the
> voice and unseen by the eyes: and since we
> cannot apprehend His essence, we lean upon
> words and names and animals, and forms of
> gold and ivory and silver, and plants and rivers
> and mountain-peaks and springs of waters,
> longing for an intuition of Him, and in our
> inability naming by His name all things that are
> beautiful in this world of ours."[439]

And again:

> "It is of this Father and Begetter of the
> universe that Plato tells us: His name he does
> not tell us, for he knew it not: nor does he tell
> us His color, for he saw Him not; nor His size,
> for he touched Him not. Color and size are felt
> by the touch and seen by the sight: but the
> Deity Himself is unseen by the sight, unspoken
> by the voice, untouched by fleshly touch,
> unheard by the hearing, seen only — through
> its likeness to Him, and heard only — through
> its kinship with Him, by the noblest and purest
> and clearest-sighted and swiftest and oldest
> element of the soul."[440]

Plotinus similarly, in answer to the old problem, "how
from the One, being such as we have described Him?

---

[439] Max. Tyr. *Diss*. 8.9.

[440] Max. Tyr. 17.9.

anything whatever has substance, instead of the One abiding by Himself," replies:

> "Let us call upon God Himself before we thus answer — not with uttered words, but stretching forth our souls in prayer to Him, for this is the only way in which we can pray, alone to Him who is alone. We must, then, gaze upon Him in the inner part of us, as in a temple, being as He is by Himself, abiding still and beyond all things (*epekeina apantōn*). Everything that moves must have an object towards which it moves. But the One has no such object; consequently we must not assert movement of Him ... Let us not think of production in time, when we speak of things eternal ... What then was produced was produced without His moving: ... it had its being without His assenting or willing or being moved in anywise. It was like the light that surrounds the sun and shines forth from it, though the sun is itself at rest: it is reflected like an image. So with what is greatest. That which is next greatest comes forth from Him, and the next greatest is *nous*; for *nous* sees Him and needs Him alone."[441]

But the conception of transcendence is capable of taking two forms. It may be that of a God who passes beyond all the classes into which sensible phenomena are divisible, by virtue of His being pure Mind, cognizable only by mind; or it may be that of a God who exists *extra flammantia moenia mundi*, filling the infinite space which surrounds and contains

---

all the spheres of material existence. The one God is transcendent in the proper sense of the term; the other is supra-cosmic. In either case He is said to be unborn, undying, uncontained; and I since the same terms are thus used to express the elements of both forms of the conception, it is natural that these forms should readily pass into each other, and that the distinction between them should not always be present to a writer's mind or perceptible in his writings. But the conception in one or other of its forms fills a large place in later Greek philosophy. It blended in a common stream with the new currents of religious feeling. [The process is well illustrated by Philo.]

> The words "I am thy God" are used not in a proper but in a secondary sense. For Being, *qua* Being, is out of relation: itself is full of itself and sufficient for itself, both before the birth of the world and equally so after it.[442] He transcends all quality, being better than virtue, better than knowledge, and better even than the good itself and the beautiful itself.[443] He is not in space, but beyond it; for He contains it. He is not in time, for He is the Father of the universe, which is itself the father of time, since from its movement time proceeds.[444] He is "without body, parts or passions": without feet, for whither should He walk who fills all things: without hands, for from whom should He receive anything who possesses all thing?:

---

[442] *De mut. nom.* 4; i. 582, ed. Mangey.

[443] *De mund. op.* 2; i.2.

[444] *De post. Cain*, 5; i. 228, 229.

without eyes, for how should He need eyes
who made the light.[445] He is invisible, for how
can eyes that are too weak to gaze upon the
sun be strong enough to gaze upon its Maker.[446]
He is incomprehensible: not even the whole
universe, much less the human mind, can
contain the conception of Him:[447] we know
that He is, we cannot know what He is:[448] we
may see the manifestations of Him in His
works, but it were monstrous folly to go
behind His works and inquire into His essence.[449]
He is hence unnamed: for names are the
symbols of created things, whereas His only
attribute is *to be*.[450]

(2) The Revelation of the Transcendent. — Side by side
with this conception of the transcendence of God, and
intimately connected with it, was the idea of beings or forces
coming between God and men. A transcendent God was in
Himself incommunicable: the more the conception of His
transcendence was developed, the stronger was the necessity
for conceiving of the existence of intermediate links.

   i. A basis for such a conception was afforded in the
popular mythology by the belief in demons — spirits inferior

---

[445] *Quod deus immut.* 12; i, 281.

[446] *De Abrah.* 16; ii. 12.

[447] i, 224, 281, 566; ii. 12, 654; *Frag. ap Joan. Dam.* ii. 654.

[448] *De prem. et paen.* 7; ii. 415.

[449] *De post. Cain*, 48; i. 258.

[450] *De mut. nom.* 2; 1. 580; cf. 630, 648, 655; ii. 8-9, 19, 92-93, 597.

to the gods, but superior to men. The belief was probably "a survival of the primitive psychism which peopled the whole universe with life and animation."[451] There was an enormous contemporary development of the idea of demons or genii. They are found in Epictetus, Dio Chrysostom, Maximus, and Celsus. In the latter some are good, some bad, most of them of mixed nature; to them is due the creation of all things except the human soul; they are the rulers of day and night, of the sunlight and the cold.[452]

ii. A philosophical basis for the theory was afforded by the Platonic *Ideai* or Forms, and the Stoical *Logoi* or Reasons. We have already seen the place which those Forms, viewed also as Forces, and those Reasons, viewed also as productive Seeds, filled in the later Greek cosmologies and cosmogonies. They were not less important in relation to the theory of the transcendence of God. The Forms according to which He shaped the world, the Forces by which He made and sustains it, the Reasons which inhere in it and, like laws, control its movements, are outflows from and reflections of His nature, and communicate a knowledge of it to His intelligent creatures. In the philosophy of Philo, these philosophical conceptions are combined with both the Greek conception of Demons and the Hebrew conception of Angels. The four conceptions, Forms, *Logoi*, Demons, and Angels, pass into one another, and the expressions which are

---

[451] Benn, *Greek Philosophers*, 2.252.

[452] Cf. Hesiod in Sext. Emp. ix. 86. Similarly, Thales, (Diels, 301); Pythagoras, Empedocles in Hippolytus, Plato and the Stoics (Diels, 307), e.g. Plutarch, Epictetus, 1. 14. 12; 3.13.15 (Diels, 1307); Athenagoras, 23; Philo, ii. 635; Frag. ap. Eus. Prep. Evan, 8.13; see references in Keim's Celsus, p. 120.

relative to them are interchangeable. The most common expression for them is *Logoi*, and it is more commonly found in the singular. *Logos*.

(3) The Distinctions in the Nature of God. — The *Logos* is able to reveal the nature of God because it is itself the reflection of that nature. It is able to reveal that nature to intelligent creatures because the human intelligence is itself an offshoot of the Divine. As the eye of sense sees the sensible world, which also is a revelation of God,[453] since it is His thought impressed upon matter, so the reason sees the intelligible world, the world of His thoughts conceived as intelligible realities, existing separate from Him.

> "The wise man, longing to apprehend God, and travelling along the path of wisdom and knowledge, first of all meets with the divine Reasons, and with them abides as a guest; hut when he resolves to pursue the further journey, he is compelled to abstain, for the eyes of his understanding being opened, he sees that the object of his quest is afar off and always receding, an infinite distance in advance of him."[454] "Wisdom leads him first into the antechamber of the Divine Reason, and when he is there he does not at once enter into the Divine Presence; but sees Him afar off, or rather not even afar off can he behold Him, but only he sees that the place where he stands is still infinitely far from the unnamed, unspeakable, and incomprehensible God."[455]

[453] Philo, *de confus. ling.* 20 (i. 419).

[454] *De post. Cain.* 6 (i. 229).

What he sees is not God Himself but the likeness of Him, "just as those who cannot gaze upon the sun may yet gaze upon a reflection of it."[456] The *Logos* reflecting not only the Divine nature, but also the Divine will and the Divine goodness, becomes to men a messenger of help; like the angel to Hagar, it brings advice and encouragement;[457] like the angel who redeemed Jacob (Gen. xlviii. 16), it rescues men from all kinds of evil;[458] like the angel who delivered Lot from Sodom, it succors the kinsmen of virtue and provides for them a refuge.[459]

> "Like a king, it announces by decree what men ought to do; like a teacher, it instructs its disciples in what will benefit them; like a counsellor, it suggests the wisest plans, and so greatly benefits those who do not of themselves know what is best; like a friend, it tells many secrets which it is not lawful for the uninitiated to hear."[460]

And standing midway between God and man, it not only reflects God downwards to man, but also reflects man upwards to God.

> "It stands on the border-line between the Creator and the creation, not unbegotten like

---

[455] *De somn.* 1.11 (i. 630).

[456] *Ibid.* 1. 41 (i. 656).

[457] *De profug.* 1 (i. 547); *so de Cherub.* 1 (i. 139).

[458] *Leg. Alleg.* 3.62 (1. 122),

[459] *De somn.* 1.15 (i. 633).

[460] *Ibid.* 1. 33 (i. 649).

God, not begotten like ourselves, and so
becomes not only an ambassador from the
Euler to His subjects, but also a suppliant from
mortal man yearning after the immortal."[461]

The relation of the *Logos* to God, as distinguished from its
functions, is expressed by several metaphors, all of which are
important in view of later theology. They may be gathered
into two classes, corresponding to the two great conceptions
of the relation of the universe to God which were held
respectively by the two great sources of Philo's philosophy,
the Stoics and the Platonists. The one class of metaphors
belongs to the monistic, the other to the dualistic,
conception of the universe. In the former, the *Logos* is
evolved from God; in the other, created by Him.[462] The
chief metaphors of the former class are those of a phantom,
or image, or outflow: the *Logos* is projected by God as a
man's shadow or phantom was sometimes conceived as
thrown off by his body,[463] expressing its every feature, and
abiding as a separate existence after the body was dead; it is a
reflection cast by God upon the space which He contains, as
a parhelion is cast by the sun;[464] it is an outflow as from a

---

[461] *Quis rer. div. her.* 42 (i. 501).

[462] *De sacrif. Abel. et Cain.* 18 (1.175),

[463] The word *skia* seems to be used, in relation to the *Logos*, not
of the shadow cast by a solid object in the sunlight, but rather, as
in Homer, *Odyss.* 10.495, and frequently in classical writers, of
a ghost or phantom: hence God is the *paradeigma*, the substance
of which the *Logos* is the unsubstantial form, *Leg. Alleg.* 3.31 (i.
106): hence also *skux* is used as convertible with *eikov* (*ibid.*), in
its sense of either a portrait-statue or a reflection in a mirror: *in
de confus. ling.* 28 (i. 427), the *Logos* is the eternal *eikov* of God.

spring.[465] The chief metaphor of the second class is that of a son; the *Logos* is the first-begotten of God;[466] and by an elaboration of the metaphor which reappears in later theology, God is in one passage spoken of as its Father, Wisdom as its Mother.[467] It hence tends sometimes to be viewed as separate from God, neither God nor man, but "inferior to God though greater than man."[468] The earlier conception had already passed through several forms: it had begun with that which was itself the greatest leap that any one thinker had yet made, the conception that Reason made the world: the conception of Reason led to the conception of God as Personal Reason: out of that grew the thought of God as greater than Reason and using it as His instrument: and at last had come the conception of the Reason of God as in some way detached from Him, working in the world as a subordinate but self-acting law. It was natural that this should lead to the further conception of Reason as the offspring of God and Wisdom, the metaphor of a human birth being transferred to the highest sphere of heaven.

B. The Idea and its Development in Christian Theology.

(1) *The Transcendence of God.* — All the conceptions which we have seen to exist in the sphere of philosophy were reproduced in the sphere of Christianity. They are sometimes relative to God, in contrast to the world of sensible

---

[464] *De somn.* 1.41 (i. 656).

[465] *Quod det. pot. ins*, 23 (i. 207).

[466] *De agric.* 12 (i. 308): *de confus. ling.* 28 (i. 427).

[467] *De profug.* 20 (i. 562).

[468] *Quod a Deo mit. somn.* i. 683.

phenomena: phenomena come into being, God is unbegotten and without beginning: phenomena are visible and tangible, God is unseen and untouched. They are sometimes relative to the idea of perfection: God is unchangeable, indivisible, unending. He has no name: for a name implies the existence of something prior to that to which a name is given, whereas He is prior to all things. These conceptions are all negative: the positive conceptions are that He is the infinite depth (*buthos*) which contains and embosoms all things, that He is self-existent, and that He is light. "The Father of all," said one school of philosophers,[469] "is a primal light, blessed, incorruptible, and infinite." "The essence of the unbegotten Father of the universe is incorruptibility and self-existing light, simple and uniform."[470]

From the earliest Christian teaching, indeed, the conception of the transcendence of God is absent. God is near to men and speaks to them: He is angry with them and punishes them: He is merciful to them and pardons them. He does all this through His angels and prophets, and last of all through His Son. But he needs such mediators rather because a heavenly Being is invisible, than because He is transcendent. The conception which underlies the earliest expression of the belief of a Christian community is the simple conception of children:

> "We give Thee thanks, Holy Father, for Thy
> holy name which Thou hast caused to dwell in
> our hearts, and for the knowledge and faith and

---

[469] i.E. Sethiani ap. Iren. 1.30.1.

[470] Ptolemeus, *ad Flor.* 7.

immortality which Thou hast made known to
us through Jesus Christ, Thy servant. To Thee
be glory forever. Thou, Almighty Master, hast
created all things for Thy name's sake, hast
given food and drink to men for their
enjoyment, that they may give thanks to Thee:
and upon us hast Thou bestowed spiritual food
and drink and eternal life through Thy servant.
Before all things we give Thee thanks for that
Thou art mighty: to Thee be glory forever."[471]

In the original sphere of Christianity there does not appear
to have been any great advance upon these simple
conceptions. The doctrine upon which stress was laid was,
that God is, that He is one, that He is almighty and
everlasting, that He made the world, that His mercy is over
all His works.[472] There was no taste for metaphysical
discussion: there was possibly no appreciation of
metaphysical conceptions. It is quite possible that some
Christians laid themselves open to the accusation which
Celsus brings, of believing that God is only cognizable
through the senses.[473] They were influenced by Stoicism,
which denied all intellectual existences, and regarded spirit
itself as material.[474] This tendency resulted in Adoptian
Christology.[475]

---

[471] Teaching of the Twelve Apostles, 10. 2—4.

[472] Cf. the Ebionites, Alogi, and the *Clementines*.

[473] Origen, *c. Cels*. 7.36; cf. *de prince*. 1.1.7.

[474] *Con. Cels*. 7.37. See also Orig. *in Gen*. vol. ii. p. 25
(Delarue), and Eus. P. E. iv. 26, for a view ascribed to Melito.

[475] Harnack, *Doqmengesch* p. 160.

But most of the philosophical conceptions above described were adopted by the Apologists, and through such adoption found acceptance in the associated Christian communities. They are for the most part stated, not as in a dogmatic system, but incidentally. For example, Justin thus protests against a literal interpretation of the anthropomorphic expressions of the Old Testament:

> "You are not to think that the unbegotten God 'came down' from anywhere or ' went up.' For the unutterable Father and Lord of all things neither comes to any place nor walks nor sleeps nor rises, but abides in His own place wherever that place may be, seeing keenly and hearing keenly, not with eyes or ears, but with His unspeakable power, so that He sees all things and knows all things, nor is any one of us hid from Him: nor does He move, He who is uncontained by space and by the whole world, seeing that He was before the world was born."[476]

And Athenagoras thus sums up his defense of Christianity against the charge of atheism:

> "I have sufficiently demonstrated that they are not atheists who believe in One who is unbegotten, eternal, unseen, impassible, incomprehensible and uncontained: comprehended by mind and reason only, invested with ineffable light and beauty and spirit and power, by whom the universe is brought into being and set in order and held firm, through the agency of his own *Logos*."[477]

---

[476] *Dial. c. Tryph.* C. 127.

Theophilus replies thus to his heathen interlocutor who asked him to describe the form of the Christian God:

> "Listen, my friend: the form of God is unutterable and indescribable, nor can it be seen with fleshly eyes: for His glory is uncontained. His size is incomprehensible, His loftiness is inconceivable. His strength is incomparable, His wisdom is unrivalled. His goodness beyond imitation. His beneficence beyond description. If I speak of Him as light, I mention His handiwork: if I speak of Him as reason, I mention His government: if I speak of Him as spirit, I mention His breath: if I speak of Him as wisdom, I mention His offspring: if I speak of Him as strength, I mention His might: if I speak of Him as providence, I mention His goodness: if I speak of His kingdom, I mention His glory."[478]

It is not easy to determine in regard to many of these expressions whether they are relative in the writer's mind to a supra-cosmic or to a transcendental conception of God. The case of Tertullian clearly shows that they are compatible with the former conception no less than with the latter; for though he speaks of God as "the great Supreme, existing in eternity, unborn, unmade, without beginning, and without end,"[479] yet he argues that He is material; for "how could one who is empty have made things that are solid, and one who is void have made things that are full, and one who is

---

[477] *Legatio*, 10.

[478] *Ad Autolycum*. 1.3; cf, Minuc. Felix, *Octavius*, 18, and Novatian, *de Trin*. 1. 2.

[479] *Adv. Marc*. 1.3.

incorporeal have made things that have body?"[480] But there were some schools of philosophers in which the transcendental character of the conception is clearly apparent. The earliest of such schools, and the most remarkable, is that of Basilides. It anticipated, and perhaps helped to form, the later developments of Neo-Platonism. It conceived of God as transcending being. He was absolutely beyond all predication. Not even negative predicates are predicable of Him. The language of the school becomes paradoxical and almost unmeaning in the extremity of its effort to express the transcendence of God, and at the same time to reconcile the belief in His transcendence with the belief that He is the Creator of the world. "When there was nothing, neither material, nor essential, nor non-essential, nor simple, nor compound, nor unthought, nor unperceived, nor man, nor angel, nor god, nor absolutely any of the things that are named or perceived or thought, ... God who was not (*ouk on theos*), without thought, without perception, without will, without purpose, without passion, without desire, willed to make a world. In saying 'willed,' I use the word only because some word is necessary, but I mean without volition, without thought, and without perception; and in saying 'world,' I do not mean the extended and divisible world which afterwards came into being, with its capacity of division, but the seed of the world."[481] This was said more briefly, but probably with the same meaning, by Marcus: There is no conception and no essence of God.[482]

---

[480] *Adv. Prax.* 7.

[481] ap. Hippol. 7.21, p. 358.

[482] ibid. 6.42, p. 302; cf. 12 ff, pp. 424 ff, for Monoimus, and

These exalted ideas of His transcendence, which had especially thriven on Alexandrian soil, were further elaborated at the end of the second century by the Christian philosophers of the Alexandrian schools, who inherited the wealth at once of regenerated Platonism, of Gnosticism, and of theosophic Judaism. Clement anticipated Plotinus in conceiving of God as being "beyond the One and higher than the Monad itself,"[483] which was the highest abstraction of current philosophy.[484] There is no name that can properly be named of Him: "neither the One, nor the Good, nor Mind, nor Absolute Being, nor Father, nor Creator, nor Lord." No science can attain unto Him; "for all science depends on antecedent principles; but there is nothing antecedent to the Unbegotten."[485] Origen expressly protests against the conceptions of God which regarded Him as supra-cosmic rather than transcendent,[486] and as having a material substance though not a human form.[487] His own conception is that of a nature which is absolutely simple and intelligent, or which transcends both intelligence and existence. Being absolutely simple. He has no more or less, no before or after, and consequently has no need of either space or time. Being absolutely intelligent. His only attribute is to know and to be known. But only "like knows like." He is to be apprehended through the intelligence which is made

---

also Ptolemeus, *ad Floram*, 7.

[483] *Paedag.* 1.8.

[484] Moller, *Kosmologie*, p. 26, cf. 124 129, 130.

[485] *Strom.* 5.12.

[486] *c. Cels.* 6.19 sqq.

[487] *De prince* 1.1.2, 5, 7.

in His image: the human mind is capable of knowing the Divine by virtue of its participation in it. But in the strict sense of the word He is beyond our knowledge: our knowledge is like the vision of a spark as compared with the splendor of the sun.[488]

(2) *Revelation or Mediation of the Transcendent.* — But as in Greek philosophy, so also in Christian theology, the doctrine whether of a supra-cosmic or of a transcendent God necessitated the further question, How could He pass into the sphere of the phenomenal? The rougher sort of objectors ridiculed a God who was "solitary and destitute" in his unapproachable uniqueness:[489] the more serious heathen philosophers asked. If like knows like, how can your God know the world? and the mass of Christian philosophers,[490] both within and without the associated communities, felt this question, or one of the questions that are cognate to it, to be the cardinal point of their theology.[491]

The tentative answers were innumerable. One early group of them maintained the existence of a capacity in the Supreme Being to manifest Himself in different forms. The conception had some elements of Stoical and some of popular Greek theology, in both of which

---

[488] *Ibid.* 1.1, *passim*; cf. 4.1.36.

[489] eg, Min. Felix, c. 10; cf. Keim, *Celsus*, 158.

[490] The older sort, who clung to tradition pure and simple, were dubious of the introduction of dialectic methods into Christianity: see Eus. v. 28; cf. v. 13. Tert. *adv. Prax.* 3. Cf. Weingarten, p. 25.

[491] Cf. Julius Africanus (Routh, Rel. Sac. i. p. 379).

anthropomorphism had been possible.[492] It came to an especial prominence in the earlier stages of the Christological controversies, as an explanation of the nature of Jesus Christ. It lay beneath what is known as Modal Monarchianism, the theory that Christ was a temporary mode of the existence of the one God. It was simply His will to exist in one mode rather than in another.[493]

> "One and the same God," said Noetus, "is the Creator and Father of all things, and, because it was His good pleasure, He appeared to righteous men of old. For when He is not seen He is invisible, and when He is seen He is visible: He is uncontained when He wills not to be contained, and contained when He is contained … When the Father had not been born, He was rightly styled Father: when it was His good pleasure to undergo birth, He became on being born His own son, not another's."[494]

But the dominant conception was in a line with that of both Greek philosophy and Greek religion. From the Supreme God came forth, or in Him existed, special forms and modifications by which He both made the world and revealed Himself to it.

(i.) The speculations as to the nature of these forms varied partly with the large underlying variations in the conception of God as supra-cosmic or as transcendental, and partly with the greater or less development of the tendency to give a

---

[492] ap. Hipp. 5.7.

[493] Cf. Harnack, art. in *Encycl. Brit.* "Sabellius."

[494] Hipp. 9.10; Schmid, *Dogmeng.* 47, *n.*

concrete shape to abstract ideas. They varied also according as the forms were viewed in relation to the universe, as its types and formative forces; or in relation to the Supreme Being and His rational creatures, as manifestations of the one and means of knowledge to the other. The variations are found to exist, not only between one school of philosophers and another, but also in the same school. For example, Tertullian distinguishes between two schools of Valentinians, that of Valentinus himself and that of his great, though independent, follower Ptolemy.[495] The former regarded the Aeons as simply modes of God's existence, abiding within His essence: the latter, in common with the great majority of the school, looked upon them as "personal substances" which had come forth from God and remained outside Him. And again, most philosophers of the same school made a genealogy of Aeons, and furnished their opponents thereby with one of their chief handles for ridicule: but Colorbasus regarded the production of the Aeons as a single momentary act.[496] Sometimes, however, the expressions, which came from different sources, were blended.

Almost all these conceptions of the means by which God communicated Himself to the world were relative to the conception of Him as Mind. It is as inherent a necessity for thought to reveal itself as it is for light to shine. Following the tendency of current psychology to regard the different manifestations of mind as relative to different elements in mind itself, some schools of philosophers gave a separate

---

[495] Tert, *c. Valent.* 4 ;cf. Ptol. ap, Iven. 1.12.3.

[496] ap. Iren. 1.12.3.

personality to each supposed element in the mind of God. There came forth thought and reflection, voice and name, reasoning and intention:[497] or from the original Will and Thought came forth Mind and Truth (Reality) as visible forms and images of the invisible qualities (*diatheseov*) of the Father.[498]

(ii.) But side by side with this tendency to individualize and hypostatize the separate elements or modes of the Divine Mind, there was a tendency to regard the mind of God as a unity existing either as a distinct element in His essence or objective to Him. On one theory, mind is the only-begotten of God.'[499] He alone knows God and wishes to reveal Him. On another theory, mind is born from the unborn Father, and from Mind are born *Logos* and Prudence, Wisdom and Force, and thence in their order all the long series of Powers by whom the universe was formed.[500] Another theory, that of Marcus, probably contains the key to some of the others; the meaning of the conception of Mind as the only-begotten of God, is that Mind is the revelation of God to Himself: His self-consciousness is, so to speak, projected out of Him. It is at once a revelation and a creation — the only immediate revelation and the only immediate creation. The Father, "resolving to bring forth that which is ineffable in Him, and to endow with form that which is invisible, opened His mouth and sent forth the *Logos*" which is the image of Him, and revealed Him to Himself.[501] The *Logos*. or Word,

---

[497] Hipp. 6.12.

[498] Ptolemy ap. Iren. 1.12.1; cf. Hipp. c. *Noet.* 10.

[499] ap. Iren. 1.2.1, 5 (Valentinians).

[500] ap. Iren. 1.24.3 (Basilides): cf, Clem. Al. *Protrep.* 10,

which was so sent forth was made up of distinct utterances: each utterance was an *aeon*, a *Logos*, a root and seed of being: in other words, each was a part and phase of God's nature which expressed and reflected itself in a part and phase of the world, so that collectively the *logoi* are equivalent to the *Logos*, who is the image and reflection of God.

The theory is not far distant from that which is found in the earlier Apologists, and which passed through more than one phase before it won its way to general acceptance. The leading point in both is the relation of the individual *logoi* to the *Logos*. We have already become acquainted with the syncretism which had blended the Platonic *ideas* with the Stoical *logoi*, the former being regarded as forces as well as forms, and the latter being not only productive forces, but also the laws of those forces; and which had viewed them both in their unity, rather than in their plurality, as expressions of a single *Logos*. We have also seen that the solution of the problem, How could God create? was found in the doctrine that He created by means of His *Logos*, who impressed himself in the innumerable forms of created things. The solution of the metaphysical difficulty, How can a transcendent God know and be known? was found to lie in the solution which had already been given to the cosmogonical difficulty. How could God come into contact with matter?[502] The Forces were also Reasons: they were activities and also thoughts: in men they woke to

---

[501] Iren. 1.14.1.

[502] As compared with Philo, who emphasizes the Logos in relation to the work of creation, Justin lays stress on the Logos as Revealer, making known to us the will of God: cf. *Tryph.* 61.

consciousness: and the mind of man knew the mind of God, as like knows like, by virtue of containing within it "a seed of the *Logos*," a particle of the divine *Logos* itself. That divine *Logos* "of which the whole human race is partaker," "which had at one time appeared in the form of fire, and at another in the form of angels, now by the will of God, on behalf of the human race, had become a man, and endured to suffer all that the daemons effected that he should suffer at the hands of the foolish Jews."[503] The difference between Christ and other men was thought to be, that other men have only a "seed of the *Logos*," whereas in him the whole *Logos* was manifest: and the difference between Christians and philosophers was, that the latter lived by the light of a part only of the divine *Logos*, whereas the former lived by the knowledge and contemplation of the whole *Logos*.[504]

Within half a century after these tentative efforts,[505] and largely helped by the dissemination of the Fourth Gospel, which had probably at first only a local influence, the mass of Christians were tending to acquiesce not only in the belief of the transcendental nature of God, but also in the belief that, in some way which was not yet closely defined, Jesus Christ was the *Logos* by whom the world had been made, and who revealed the unknown Father to men.

---

[503] Justin, *Apol.* i. 63.

[504] *Apol.* ii. 8.

[505] It would be beyond our present purpose to go into Christology. It will be sufficient to indicate three theories: (1) Modal Monarchianism; (2) Dynamical Monarchianism; (3) Logos theory. Cf. Harnack, Dogmeng. 1. 161, 220, for Gnostic Christology.

The form in which the belief is stated by Irenaeus is the following:

> "No one can know the Father except by the Word of God, that is by the Son revealing Him: nor can anyone know the Son except by the good pleasure of the Father. But the Son performs the good pleasure of the Father: for the Father sends, and the Son is sent and comes. And His Word knows that the Father is, as far as concerns us, invisible and unlimited: and since He is ineffable, He himself declares Him to us: and, on the other hand, it is the Father alone who knows His own Word: both these truths has the Lord made known to us. Wherefore the Son reveals the knowledge of the Father by manifesting Himself: for the manifestation of the Son is the knowledge of the Father: for all things are manifested by the Word ... The Father therefore has revealed Himself to all by making His Word visible to all: and conversely the Word showed to all the Father and the Son, since He was seen by all. And therefore the righteous judgment of God comes upon all who, though they have seen as others, have not believed as others. For by means of the creation itself the Word reveals God the Creator; by means of the world, the Lord who is the Fashioner of the world; and by means of His handiwork (man), the Workman who formed it; and by the Son, that Father who begat the Son."[506]

---

[506] Iren. 4.6.3, 5, 6; cf. Clem. Alex. *Strom.* 7. 2.

(3) *The Distinctions in the Nature of God, or the Mediation and Mediator.* — It was by a natural process of development that Christian philosophers, while acquiescing in the general proposition that Jesus Christ was the *Logos* in human form, should go on to frame large theories as to the nature of the *Logos*. It was an age of definition and dialectic. It was no more possible for the mass of educated men to leave a metaphysical problem untouched, than it is possible in our own days for chemists to leave a natural product unanalyzed. Two main questions engaged attention: (i.) what was the genesis, (ii.) what was the nature, of the *Logos*. In the speculations which rose out of each of these questions, the influence of Greek thought is even more conspicuous than before.

(i.) The question of the genesis of the *Logos* was mainly answered by theories which were separated from one another by the same broad line of distinction which separated theories as to the genesis of the world.

The philosophers of the school of Basilides, who, as we have seen, had been the first to formulate the doctrine of an absolute creation, that is, of a creation of all things out of nothing, conceived that whatever in their theory corresponded to the *Logos* was equally included with all other things in the original seed. Hence came the definite proposition, which played a large part in the controversies of the fourth century, that the *Logos* was made "out of the things that were not."[507]

---

[507] Cf. Hipp. 7. 21, 22; Schmid, *Dogm.* 52,

But the majority of theories expressed under various metaphors the idea, which was relative to the other theory of creation, that in some way the *Logos* had come forth from God. The rival hypotheses as to the nature of creation were reconciled by the hypothesis that, though the world was created out of nothing, it was so created by the *Logos*, who was not created by God, but came forth from Him. The metaphors were chiefly those of the "putting forth" (*probola*, *prolatio*), as of the leaves or fruit of a plant, and of the begetting of a son. They were in use before the doctrine of the *Logos* had established itself, and some of them were originally relative, not to the *Logos*, but to other conceptions of mediation between God and the world. They were supplemented by the metaphors, which also were in earlier use, of the flowing of water from a spring, and of the radiation of light.[508] That there was not originally any important distinction between them, is shown both by the express disclaimer of Irenaeus and by the fact of their use in combination in the same passages of the same writers. The combination was important. The metaphors supplemented each other. Each of them contained an element in the theory which ultimately expressed the settled judgment of the Christian world.

The main difficulty which they presented was that of an apparent inconsistency with the belief in the unity of God. The doctrine of the "sole monarchy" of God, which had been strongly maintained against those who explained the difficulties of the world by the hypothesis of two Gods in

---

[508] Tert. *Apol.* 51; Hipp. *c. Noet.* p. 62.

conflict, seemed to be running another kind of danger in the very ranks of its defenders. The *Logos* who reflected God and revealed Him to rational creatures, who also contained in himself the form and forces of the material world, must be in some sense God. In Athenagoras there is a pure monism: "God is Himself all things to Himself, unapproachable light, a perfect universe, spirit, force, *Logos?*"[509] But in other writers the idea of development or generation, however lightly the metaphor might be pressed, seemed to involve an existence of the *Logos* both outside God and posterior to Him.[510] He was the "first-born," the "first offspring of God," the "first force after the Father of all and the Lord God;" for "as the beginning, before all created things, God begat from Himself a kind of rational Force, which is called by the Holy Spirit (i.e. the Old Testament) sometimes 'the Glory of the Lord,' sometimes 'Son,' sometimes 'Wisdom,' sometimes 'Angel,' sometimes 'God,' sometimes 'Lord and *Logos*,' sometimes he speaks of himself as 'Captain of the Lord's host:' for he has all these appellations, both from his ministering to the Father's purpose and from his having been begotten by the Father's pleasure."[511] It follows that "there is, and is spoken of, another God and Lord beneath the Maker of the universe."[512] The theory thus formulated tended to ditheism and was openly accused of it.[513] It was saved from the charge

---

[509] *Leg.* 16; cf. Clem. Al. *Strom.* 5.1.

[510] Philo applied the phrase "Son of God" to the world: cf. Keim, *Celsus*, 95.

[511] Justin, Dial. *c. Tryph.* 61 A, cf. 62 E, and Hipp. *c. Noet.* 8, 10, 16; Tatian, c. 5; Irenaeus ap. Schmid, p. 31.

[512] Justin, Dial. *C. Tryph.* 56 C; p. 180.

by the gradual formulating of two distinctions, both of which came from external philosophy, one of them being an inheritance from Stoicism, the other from Neo-Platonism.[514] The one was that the generation or development had taken place within the sphere of Deity itself: the generation had not taken place by the severing of a part from the whole, as though the Divine nature admitted of a division,[515] but by distinction o function or by multiplication, as many torches may be lit from one without diminishing the light of that one.[516] The other was that the generation had been eternal. In an early statement of the theory it was held that it had taken place in time: it was argued that "God could not have been a Father before there was a Son, but there was a time when there was not a Son."[517] But the influence of the other metaphors in which the relation was expressed overpowered the influences which came from pressing the conception of paternity. Light, it was argued, could never have been without its capacity to shine.[518] The Supreme Mind could

---

[513] Hipp. 9. 12; Callistus, while excommunicating the Sabellians (cf. Schmid, 48 ; Weing. 31), also called Hippolytus and his party ditheists. For Callistus' own view, cf. ibid. 9.11. See Schmid, p. 50; also p. 45 for Praxeas ap. Tert.

[514] The Gnostic controversies in regard to the relation to God of the Powers who were intermediate between Him and the world, had helped to forge such intellectual instruments.

[515] Justin, *c. Tryph.* 128: cf. Plotinus ap. *Harn. Dogm.* 493.

[516] Justin, *Dial. c. Tryph.* 61 C, where the metaphor of "speech" is also employed.

[517] ap. Tert. *c. Hermog.* 3.

[518] For metaphor of light, cf. Monoimus ap. Hipp. 8.12; also

never have been without His Thought. The Father Eternal was always a Father, the Son was always a Son.[519]

(ii.) The question of the nature of the eternally-begotten *Logos* was answered variously, according as the supra-cosmic or the transcendental idea of God was dominant in a writer's mind.[520] To Justin Martyr, God is conceived as supra-cosmic. He abides "in the places that are above the heavens:" the "first-begotten," the *Logos*, is the "first force after the Father:" he is "a second God, second numerically but not in 'will,'" doing only the Father's pleasure.[521] It is uncertain how far the idea of personality entered into this view. There is a similar uncertainty in the view of Theophilus, who introduced the Stoical distinction between the two aspects of the *Logos*, thought and speech — "ratio" and "oratio"[522] while Tertullian still speaks of "virtus" side by side with these.

Tatian, c. 5.

[519] There is uncertainty as to eternal generation in Justin; see Engelhardt, p. 118. It is not in Hippolytus, *c. Moet.* 10. Though implied in Irenaeus (Harn. p. 495), it is in Origen that this solution attains clear expression, e.g. *de princ.* 1.2 ff., though his view is not throughout steady and uniform. Emanation seemed to him to imply division into parts. But he hovers between the Logos as thought and as substance. For Clement and Origen in this connection, see Harnack, pp. 579, 581.

[520] God unchangeable in Himself comes into contact with human affairs: *c. Cels.* 4.14. His Word changes according to the nature of the individuals into whom he comes, *c. Cels.* 4.18.

[521] Justin, *Apol.* i. 22. 23. 32, *c. Try.* 56.

[522] *ad Autolye.* ii. 22.

It was only gradually that the subject was raised to the higher plane, from which it never afterwards descended, by the spread and dominance of the transcendental as distinguished from the supra-cosmic conception of God. It came, as we have already seen, mainly from the schools of Alexandria. It is in Basilides, in whom thought advanced to the belief that God transcended not merely phenomena but being, that the conception of a quasi-physical influence emanating from Him is seen to be first expressly abandoned.[523] But the place of the later doctrine in the Christian Church is mainly due to Origen. He uses many of the same expressions as Tertullian, but with another meaning. The Savior is God, not by partaking, but by essence.[524] He is begotten of the very essence of the Father. The generation is an outflow as of light from light.

But the controversies did not so much end with Origen as begin with him. From that time they were mostly internal to Christianity. But their elements were Greek in origin. The conceptions which were introduced into the sphere of Christian thought were the current ones of philosophy. In Christian theology that philosophy has survived.

But although it would be beyond our present purpose to describe the Christological controversies which followed the final dominance in the Church of the transcendental idea of God, it is within that purpose to point out the Greek elements, confining ourselves as far as possible to the later Greek uses of the terms.

---

[523] see Clem. Alex. *Strom.* 5.1.

[524] Cf. Harnack, *Dogmeng.* p. 580,

Ousia is used in at least three distinct senses: the distinction is clearly phrased by Aristotle.[525]

(a) It is used as a synonym of *hlye*, to designate the material part of a thing. The use is most common among the Stoics. In their monistic conception of the universe, the visible world was regarded as the *ousia* of God.[526] In the same way Philo speaks of the blood as the material vehicle, *to ousiodes*, of the vital force.[527] Hence in both philosophical and Christian cosmologies, *ousia* was sometimes used as interchangeable with *hlye*, to denote the matter out of which the world was made.

(b) It is used of matter embodied in a certain form: this has since been distinguished as the *substantia conereta*. In Aristotle, a sensible material thing, a particular man or a particular horse, which in a predication must always be the subject and cannot be a predicate, is an *ousia* in the strictest sense.[528]

(c) It is used of the common element in the classes into which sensible material things may be grouped: this has since been distinguished as the *substantia abstracta*: in the language of Aristotle, it was the form (*eidos*), or ideal essence (*to ti an einai*).[529] This sense branched out into other senses,

---

[525] *Metaph.* 6.10, p. 1095 a, "*ousia* is matter, form, and the compound of matter and form."

[526] Diog. L. 7. 148: so in M. Anton. e.g. 4, 40,

[527] *Quod det. pot. insid*, 25, i. 209.

[528] *Categ.* 5, p. 2a: but in the Metaphysics a different point of view is taken, and the term is used in the following sense, i.e. of the form, e.g. 6, 11, p. 1037.

according as the term was used by a realist or a nominalist: to the former it was the common essence which exists in the individual members of a class (*to eidos to enon*),[530] and not outside them (since *adunaton choris einai tan ousian kai ou a ousia*);[531] or which exists outside them, and by participation in which they are what they are: this latter is Plato's conception of *eidos*,[532] and of its equivalent *ousia*.

To a nominalist, on the other hand, *ousia* is only the common name which is predicable in the same sense to a number of individual existences.[533]

The Platonic form of realism grew out of a distinction between the real and the phenomenal, which in its turn it tended to accentuate. The visible world of concrete individuals was regarded as phenomenal and transitory: the invisible world of intelligible essences was real and permanent: the one was *genesis*, or "becoming;" the other, *ousia*, or "being."[534] The distinction played a large part in the later history of Platonism:[535] and whereas in the view of Aristotle the species, or smaller class, as being nearer to the

---

[529] Frequently in the *Metaphysics*, e.g. 6.7, p. 1032 b, 7. 1, p. 1042 a.

[530] Arist. *Metaph.* 6. 11, p. 1037a.

[531] *Ibid.* 12.5, p. 1079 b.

[532] eg. *Parmen.* p. 132e.

[533] Suidas, 8. v.

[534] Plat. *Sophist.* p. 246.

[535] e.g. it is stated by Celsus and adopted by Origen: Origen, *c. Cels.* 7.45 sq.

concrete individuals, was more *ousia* than the genus, or wider class, in the later philosophy, on the contrary, that was *ousia* in its highest sense which was at the farthest remove from the concrete, and filled the widest sphere, and contained the largest number of other classes in itself: it was the *summum genus*.[536] Hence Plotinus says that in respect of the body we are farthest from *ousia*, but that we partake of it in respect of our soul; and our soul is itself a compound, not pure *ousia*, but *ousia* with an added difference, and hence not absolutely under our control.[537]

Of these two meanings of *ousia*, namely "species " and "genus," the former expressing the whole essence of a class-name or concept, the latter part of the essence, the former tended to prevail in earlier, the latter in later Greek philosophy. In the one, the knowledge of the *ousia* was completely unfolded in the definition, so that a definition was itself defined as "a proposition which expresses the *ousia*."[538] in the latter, it was only in part so unfolded, so that it is necessary for us to know not only the *ousia* of objects of thought, for example, whether they fall within or without the class "body," but also the species (*eida*).[539]

But in the one meaning as in the other, the members of the same class, or the sub-classes of the same wider class, were spoken of as *homoousioi*: for example, there was an

---

[536] Porphyr. *Eisag*. 2.24.

[537] Plotin. *Enn*. 6.8.12.

[538] Arist. *Anal. post*. 2.3, p. 90 ; *Top*. 5.2, p. 130b; *Metaph*. 6.4, p. 1030 b.

[539] Sext. Empir. *Pyrrh. Hypotyp*. 3.1.2.

argument that animals should not be killed for food, on the ground that they belong to the same class as men, their souls being *homoousioi* with our own:[540] so men are *homoousioi* with one another, and Abraham washed the feet of the three strangers who came to him, thinking them to be men "of like substance" with himself.[541]

The difficulty of the whole conception in its application to God was felt and expressed. Some philosophers, as we have already seen, denied that such an application was possible. The tide of which Neo-Platonism was the most prominent wave placed God beyond *ousia*, Origen meets Celsus' statement of that view by a recognition of the uncertainty which flowed from the uncertain meaning of the term.[542] The Christological controversies of the fourth century were complicated to no small extent from the existence of a neutral and conservative party, who met the dogmatists on both sides with the assertion that neither *ousia* nor *hypostasis* was predicable of God.[543] And, in spite of the acceptance of the Nicene formula, the great Christian mystic who most fully represents Neo-Platonism within the Christian Church, ventured more than a century later on to recur to the position that God has no *ousia*, but is *hyperousios*.[544] Even those who maintained the applicability of the term to God, denied the possibility of defining it when so applied to Him.

[540] Porphyr. *de Abstin*. 1.19.

[541] *Clement. Hom*, 20.7, p. 192,

[542] *c. Cels*. 6.64.

[543] eg.in S. Athanas. *ad Afr. episc*. 4, vol. i. 714.

[544] Dionys. Areop. *de div. num*. 5.

In this they followed Philo: "Those who do not know the *ousia* of their own soul, how shall they give an accurate account of the soul of the universe?"[545] But in spite of these difficulties, the conservative feeling against the introduction of metaphysical terms into theology, and the philosophical doctrine of absolute transcendence, were overborne by the practical necessity of declaring that He is, and by the corollary that since He is, there must be an *ousia* of Him.

But when the conception of the one God as transcending numerical unity became dominant in the Christian Church, the term *homoousios* was not unnaturally adopted to express the relation of God the Father to God the Son. It accentuated the doctrine that the Son was not a creature (*ktisma*); and so of the term as applied to the Holy Spirit. Those who maintained that the Holy Spirit was a creature, thereby maintained that He was severed from the essence of the Father.[546] The term occurs first in the sphere of Gnosticism, and expresses part of one of the two great conceptions as to the origin of the world.[547] It was rejected in its application to the world, but accepted within the

[545] Philo, Leg. *Alleg*. 1.30, vol. i. 62; cf. *de post. Cain*. 8, vol. i. 229: there is a remarkable Christian application of this in a dialogue between a Christian and a Jew who was curious as to the Trinity, *Hieronymi Theologi Greeci, Dialogus de sancta Trinitate*, in Gallandi, *Vet. Patr. Bibl*. vol. vii., reprinted in Migne, *Patrol. Gr*. vol. xl. 845.

[546] Athan. *ad Antioch*, 3, vol. i. 616.

[547] Cf. Harnack, i. 191, 219, 476 sqq., 580. In the Valentinian system, the spiritual existence which Achamoth brought forth was of the same essence as herself, Iren. 1.5.1. Cf. Hippolytus, 7.22: Iren. 1.11.3 (Hipp. 6. 38), Cf. Clem. *Hom*. 20.7; Iren. *ap. Harn*. 481, Tert. *Apol*. 21, Harn. 488, 491.

sphere of Deity as an account of the origin of His plurality.
But *homoousios*, though true, was insufficient. It expressed the
unity, but did not give sufficient definition to the conception
of the plurality. It was capable of being used by those who
held the plurality to be merely modal or phenomenal.[548] It
thus led to the use of another term, of which it is necessary
to trace the history.

The term *ousia* in most of its senses had come to be
convertible with two other terms, hypostasis and *hyparsis*.
The latter of these played but a small part in Christian
theology, and may be disregarded here.[549] The term *hypostasis*
is the conjugate of the verb *uphistanai*, which had come into
use as a more emphatic form than *einai*. It followed almost
all the senses of *ousia*. Thus it was contrasted with
phenomenal existence not merely in the Platonic but in the
conventional sense; e. g. of things that take place in the sky,
some are appearances, some have a substantial existence,
kath upostasiv.[550] It also, like *ousia*, is used of that which has an
actual as compared with a potential existence;[551] also of that
which has an objective existence in the world, and not
merely exists in the thinking subject.[552] Hence when things

---

[548] It was expressly rejected at the Council of Antioch in
connection with Paul of Samosata ; and Basil, *Ep*. 9, says that
Dionysius of Alexandria gave it up because of its use by the
Sabellians: cf. Ep. 52 (300).

[549] It is found, e.g., in Athan. *ad Afr. epise*. 4, vol. i. 714. The
distinction is found in Stoical writers, e.g. Chrysippus, Diels,
Doxogr. Graeci. 462.1.

[550] Diels, *ibid*. 372 ; cf. 363.

[551] Sext. Empir. p. 192, 226.

came into being, *ousia* was said *uphistamai*.[553] Moreover, in one of its chief uses, namely that in which it designated the permanent element in objects of thought, the term *ousia* had sometimes been replaced by the term *upistasis*.[554] "When, therefore, the use of *ousia* in its Neo-Platonic sense prevailed, there arose a tendency to differentiate the two terms, and to designate that which in Aristotle had been *prota ousia* by the term *upostasis*. This is expressed by Athanasius when he says: "Ousia signifies community," while "hypostasis has property which is not common to the hypostases of the same ousia;"[555] and even more clearly by Basil.[556]

There was the more reason for the growth of the distinction, because the term *homoousios* lent itself more readily to a Sabellian Christology. This was anticipated by Irenaeus in his polemic against the Valentinian heresy of the emission of Aeons. *Ousiai*, in the sense of genera and species, might be merely conceptions in the mind: the alternative was that of their having an existence of their own.[557] So that hypostasis came in certain schools of thought to be the term for the *substantia concreta*, the individual, the *ousia atomos* of Galen.[558] The distinction, however, was far from being

---

[552] Diels, 318.

[553] Ib. 469. 20. p. 462, 26.

[554] Epict. 1.14.2.

[555] Ath. *Dial. de Trin.* 2. Still the identity of the two terms was allowed even after they were tending to be differentiated: cf. Athan. *ad Afr. Ep.* 4, vol. i. 714.

[556] Cf. Harn. *Dogm.* 693.

[557] Sext. Empir. *de Pyrrh.* 2.219.

universally recognized. The clearest and most elaborate exposition of it is contained in a letter of Basil to his brother Gregory, who was evidently not quite clear upon the point.[559] The result was, that just as *upostasis* had been used to express one of the senses of *ousia*, so a new term came into use to define more precisely the sense of *upostasis*. Its origin is probably to be traced to the interchange of documents between East and West, which leading to a difficulty in regard to this use of *upostasis*, ended in the introduction of a third term.

So long as *ousia* and *upostasis* had been convertible terms, the one Latin word *substantia*, the etymological equivalent of *upostasis,* had sufficed for both. When the two words became differentiated in Greek, it became advisable to mark the difference. However, the word *essentia*, the natural equivalent for *ousia*, jarred upon a Latin ear.[560] Consequently *substantia* was claimed for *ousia*, while for *upostasis* a fresh equivalent had to be sought. This was found in *persona*, whose antecedents may be those of "a character in a play," or of "person" in the juristic sense, a possible party to a contract, in which case Tertullian may have originated this usage.[561] Such Western practice would tend to stimulate the

---

[558] Ed. Kuhn, 5. 662.

[559] *Ep.* 210; Harn. *Dogm.* 693.

[560] Cf. Quintilian, who ascribes it in turn to Plautus and to Sergius Flavius, 2.14.2; 3.6. 23; 8.3.33: Seneca, *Ep.* 58.6, to Cicero, and more recently Fabianus.

[561] Cf. Harnack, 489, 543 ; forits use by Sabellius, &c, ib. 679 ; also Orig. *de prince*. 1.2.8.

employment of the corresponding Greek term *prosopon* whose use hitherto seems to have been subordinate to that of *upostasis*.[562] And, finally, the philosophic terms *phusis* and *natura* came into use. In the second century *phusis* had been distinct from *ousia* and identical with Reason.[563] But in the fourth century it came to be identified with *ousia*,[564] and afterwards again distinguished from it, whereas the Monophysites identified it with *upostasis*.

To sum up, then. We have in Greek four terms, *ousia, upostasis, prosopon, phusis* , and in Latin three, *substantia, persona, natura*, the two series not being actually parallel even to the extent to which they are so in appearance. Times have changed since Tertullian's[565] loose and vague usage caused no remark; when Jerome, thinking as a Latin, hesitates to speak of *treis upostasises*, by which he understood *tres substantias*, and complains that he is looked upon as a heretic in the East in consequence. There is a remarkable saying of Athanasius which is capable of a wider application than he gave it: it runs as follows:[566] "They seemed to be ignorant of the fact that when we deal with words that require some

---

[562] Eg. *Ath. et Cyr. in Expos. orth. fid.*; In Epictetus, 1.2.7, 14, 28, it denotes individuality of character, that which distinguishes one man from another.

[563] In Ath. ad. Ant. 7.25. So *Leg. All.* 3.80 (i. 106).

[564] Leontius of Byzantium, *Pat. Graec.* lxxxvi. 1193.

[565] E.g. *adv. Prax.* 2 (E.T. ii. 337), where he makes the distinctions within the *aeconomia* of the Godhead to be *gradu, forma, specie*, with a unity of *substantia, status, potestas*; cf. Bp. Kaye, in E. T. ii. p- 407.

[566] *De Sententia Dionys*. 18.

training to understand them, different people may take them in senses not only differing but absolutely opposed to each other." Thus there was an indisposition to accept *ousia*. The phrase was not understood of the people.[567] A reaction took place against the multiplicity of terms; but the simple and unstudied language of the childhood of Christianity, with its awe-struck sense of the ineffable nature of God, was but a fading memory, and on the other hand the tendency to trust in and insist upon the results of speculation was strong. Once indeed the Catholic doctrine was formulated, then, though not till then, the majority began to deprecate investigations as to the nature of God.

But I do not propose to dwell upon the sad and weary history of the way in which for more than a century these metaphysical distinctions formed the watchwords of political as well as of ecclesiastical parties — of the strife and murder, the devastation of fair fields, the flame and sword, therewith connected. For all this, Greek philosophy was not responsible. These evils mostly came from that which has been a permanently disastrous fact in Christian history, the interference of the State, which gave the decrees of Councils that sanction which elevated the resolutions of the majority upon the deepest subjects of human speculation to the factitious rank of laws which must be accepted on pain of forfeiture, banishment or death.

Philosophy branched off from theology. It became its handmaid and its rival. It postulated doctrines instead of investigating them. It had to show their reasonableness or to

---

[567] Athan. *de Synod.* 8 (i. 577).

find reasons for them. And for ages afterwards philosophy was dead. I feel as strongly as you can feel the weariness of the discussions to which I have tried to direct your attention. But it is only by seeing how minute and how purely speculative they are, that we can properly estimate their place in Christian theology. Whether we do or do not accept the conclusions in which the greater part of the Christian world ultimately acquiesced, we must at least recognize that they rest upon large assumptions. Three may be indicated which are all due to the influence of Greek philosophy.[568]

(1) It is assumed that metaphysical distinctions are <u>important.</u>

[568] [As this summing up never underwent the author's final revision, and the notes which follow stand in his MS. parallel with the corresponding portion of the Lecture as originally delivered, it has been thought well to place them here. — Ed.]

(1) The tendency to abstract has combined with the tendency to regard matter as evil or impure, in the production of a tendency to form rather a negative than a positive conception of God. The majority of formularies define God by negative terms, and yet they have claimed for conceptions which are negative a positive value.

(2) We owe to Greek philosophy — to the hypothesis of the chasm between spirit and matter — the tendency to interpose powers between the Creator and His creation. It may be held that the attempt to solve the insoluble problem, how God, who is pure spirit, made and sustains us, has darkened the relations which it has attempted to explain by introducing abstract metaphysical conceptions.

I am far from saying that they are not: but it is not less important to recognize that much of what we believe rests upon this assumption that they are. There is otherwise no justification whatever for drawing men's thoughts away from the positive knowledge which we may gain both of ourselves and of the world around us, to contemplate, even at far distance, the conception of Essence.

(2) The second is the assumption that these metaphysical distinctions which we make in our minds correspond to realities in the world around us, or in God who is beyond the world and within it.

Again, I am far from saying that they do not; but it is at least important for us to recognize the fact that, in speaking of the essence of either the world or God, we are assuming the existence of something corresponding to our conception of essence in the one or the other.[569]

(3) The third assumption is that the idea of perfection which we transfer from ourselves to God, really corresponds to the nature of His being.

It is assumed that rest is better than motion, that passionlessness is better than feeling, that changelessness is better than change. We know these things of ourselves: we cannot know them of One who is unlike ourselves, who has no body that can be tired, who has no imperfection that can

---

[569] It may be noted that even in the later Greek philosophy there was a view, apparently identical with that of Bishop Berkeley, that matter or substance merely represented the sum of the qualities, Origen, *de Princ.* 4.1.84.

miss its aim, with whom unhindered movement may conceivably be perfect life.

I have spoken of these assumptions because, although it would be difficult to overestimate the importance of the conceptions by which Greek thought lifted men from the conception of God as a Being with human form and human passions, to the lofty height on which they can feel around them an awful and infinite Presence, the time may have come when — in face of the large knowledge of His ways which has come to us through both thought and research — we may be destined to transcend the assumptions of Greek speculation by new assumptions, which will lead us at once to a diviner knowledge and the sense of a diviner life.[570]

---

[570] These Lectures are the history of a genesis: it would otherwise have been interesting to show in how many points theories which have been thought out in modern times revive theories of the remote past of Christian antiquity.

Lecture X. THE INFLUENCE OF THE MYSTERIES UPON CHRISTIAN USAGES.

A. The Greek Mysteries and related Cults.

Side by side in Greece with the religion which was openly professed and with the religious rites which were practiced in the temples, not in antagonism to them, but intensifying their better elements and elaborating their ritual, were the splendid rites which were known as the Mysteries. Side by side also with the great political communities, and sheltered within them by the common law and drawn together by a stronger than political brotherhood, were innumerable associations for the practice of the new forms of worship which came in with foreign commerce, and for the expression in a common worship of the religious feelings which the public religion did not satisfy. These associations were known as *thiasoi, eranoi*, or *orgeones*.

I will speak first of the mysteries, and then of the associations for the practice of other cults.

1. The mysteries were probably the survival of the oldest religions of the Greek races and of the races which preceded them. They were the worship not of the gods of the sky, Zeus and Apollo and Athene, but of the gods of the earth and the under-world, the gods of the productive forces of nature and of death.[571]

---

[571] For what follows, reference in general may be made to Keil,

The most important of them were celebrated at Eleusis, near Athens, and the scattered information which exists about them has been made more impressive and more intelligible to us by excavations, which have brought to light large remains of the great temple — the largest in Greece — in which they were celebrated. It had been a cult common to the Ionian tribes, probably borrowed from the earlier races among whom they had settled. It was originally the cult of the powers which produce the harvest, conceived as a triad of divinities — a god and two goddesses, Pluto, Demeter and Kore, of whom the latter became so dominant in the worship, that the god almost disappeared from view, and was replaced by a divinity, Iacchus, who had no place in the original myth.[572] Its chief elements were the initiation, the sacrifice, and the scenic representation of the great facts of natural life and human life, of which the histories of the gods were themselves symbols.[573]

(i.) The main underlying conception of initiation was, that there were elements in human life from which the candidate must purify himself before he could be fit to approach God.

Attische Culte aus Inschriften, Philologus, Bd. xxiii. 212—259, 592— 622: and Weingarten, *Histor. Zeitschrift*, Bd. xlv. 1881, p. 441 sqq., as well as to the authorities cited in the notes.

[572] Foucart, *Le culte de Pluton dans la religion éleusinienne, Bulletin de Correspondance Hellénique*, 1883, pp. 401 sqq.

[573] The successive stages or acts of initiation are variously described and enumerated, but there were at least four: the preparatory purification ; the initiatory rites and sacrifices ; the prior initiation; and the higher or greater initiation, which admitted to the holiest act of the ritual. Cf. Lobeck, *Aglaoph.* pp. 39 ff.

There was a distinction between those who were not purified, and those who, in consequence of being purified, were admitted to a diviner life and to the hope of a resurrection. The creation of this distinction is itself remarkable. The race of mankind was lifted on to a higher plane when it came to be taught that only the pure in heart can see God. The rites of Eleusis were originally confined to the inhabitants of Attica: but they came in time to be open to all Greeks, later to all Romans, and were open to women as well as to men.[574] The bar at the entrance came to be only a moral bar.

The whole ceremonial began with a solemn proclamation: "Let no one enter whose hands are not clean and whose tongue is not prudent." In other mysteries it was: "He only may enter who is pure from all defilement, and whose soul is conscious of no wrong, and who has lived well and justly."[575]

The proclamation was probably accompanied by some words or sights of terror. When Nero went to Eleusis and thought at first of being initiated, he was deterred by it. Here is another instance of exclusion, which is not less important in its bearing upon Christian rites. Apollonius of Tyana was excluded because he was a magician and not pure in respect of *ta daimonia* — he had intercourse with other divinities than those of the mysteries, and practiced magical rites.[576]

---

[574] An interesting inscription has recently come to light, which shows that the public slaves of the city were initiated at the public expense. Foucart, l.c. p. 394.

[575] Cf. Origen, *c. Cels*. 3. 59.

[576] Philostratus, *Vita Apoll*. 4.18, p. 138.

We learn something from the parody of the mysteries in Lucian's romance of the pseudo-prophet Alexander. In it Alexander institutes a celebration of mysteries and torchlights and sacred shows, which go on for three successive days. On the first there is a proclamation of a similar kind to that at Athens. "If any Atheist or Christian or Epicurean has come as a spy upon the festival, let him flee; let the initiation of those who believe in the god go on successfully." Then forthwith at the very beginning a chasing away takes place. The prophet himself sets the example, saying, "Christians, away!" and the whole crowd responds, "Epicureans, away!" Then the show begins — the birth of Apollo, the marriage of Coronis, the coming of Aesculapius, are represented; the ceremonies proceed through several days in imitation of the mysteries and in glorification of Alexander.[577]

The proclamation was thus intended to exclude notorious sinners from the first or initial ceremonial.[578] The rest was

---

[577] *Alex*, 38.

[578] Cf. Lobeck, *Aglaoph*. pp. 39 ff. and 89 ff.; Welcker, *Griech. Gotterl.* ii, 580—532. "The first and most important condition required of those who would enter the temple at Lindus is that they be pure in heart and not conscious of any crime."— Professor W. M. Ramsay in *Ency. Brit*. s.v. "Mysteries." For purification before admission to the worship of a temple, see, in *C.I.A*. iii. Pt. i. 73.74, instances of regulation prescribed at the temple of Men Tyrannus at Laurium in Attica, 6.5., various periods of purification being specified. Cf. Reinach, *Zraité d'Epigr. Grecque*, p. 133, on the inser. of Andania in Messenia, B.C. 91; the mysteries of the Cabiri in Le Bas and Foucart, *Inscr. du Peloponnese*, ii. § 5, p. 161; and *Sauppe, die Mysterieninschr. von Andania*.

thrown upon a man's own conscience. He was asked to confess his sins, or at least to confess the greatest crime that he had ever committed. "To whom am I to confess it?" said Lysander to the mystagogoi who were conducting him. "To the gods." "Then if you will go away," said he, "I will tell them."

Confession was followed by a kind of baptism.[579] The candidates for initiation bathed in the pure waters of the sea. The manner of bathing and the number of immersions varied with the degree of guilt which they had confessed. They came from the bath new men. It was a *katharsis*, a *loutron* a laver of regeneration. They had to practice certain forms of abstinence: they had to fast; and when they ate they had to abstain from certain kinds of food.[580]

(ii.) The purification was followed by a sacrifice — which was known as *sotaria* — a sacrifice of salvation: and in addition to the great public sacrifice, each of the candidates for initiation sacrificed a pig for himself.[581] Then there was

---

[579] Tertullian, *de Baptismo*, 5; Clem. Alex. *Strom.* Bk. 5. 4: "The mysteries are not exhibited incontinently to all, but only after certain purifications and previous instructions." Ibid. 5.11: "It is not without reason that in the mysteries that obtain among the Greeks, lustrations hold the first place, as also the laver among the Barbarians. After these are the minor mysteries, which have some foundation of instruction and of preliminary preparation for what is to come after; and the great mysteries, in which nothing remains to be learned of the universe, but only to contemplate and comprehend nature and things." We have thus a sort of baptism and catechumenate.

[580] The fast lasted nine days, and during it certain kinds of food were wholly forbidden. Cf. Lobeck, *Aglaoph.* pp. 189—197.

an interval of two days before the more solemn sacrifices and shows began. They began with a great procession — each of those who were to be initiated carrying a long lighted torch, and singing loud paeans in honor of the god.[582] It set out from Athens at sunrise and reached Eleusis at night. The next day there was another great sacrifice. Then followed three days and nights in which the initiated shared the mourning of Demeter for her daughter, and broke their fast only by drinking the mystic *kukeon* — a drink of flour and water and pounded mint, and by eating the sacred cakes.[583]

(iii.) And at night there were the mystic plays: the scenic representation, the drama in symbol and for sight. Their torches were extinguished: they stood outside the temple in the silence and the darkness. The doors opened — there was a blaze of light — and before them was acted the drama of Demeter and Kore — the loss of the daughter, the wanderings of the mother, the birth of the child. It was a symbol of the earth passing through its yearly periods. It was

---

[581] There was a lesser and a greater initiation: "It is a regulation of law that those who have been admitted to the lesser should again be initiated into the greater mysteries." Hippol. 5, 8: see the whole chapter, as also cc. 9, 20.

[582] Cf. Clem. Alex. Protrept. 12: "O truly sacred mysteries! O stainless light! My way is lighted with torches and I survey the heavens and God: I am become holy whilst I am initiated. The Lord is the hierophant, and seals while illuminating him who is initiated," &e. Ib. 2: "Their (Demeter's and Proserpine's) wanderings, and seizure, and grief, Eleusis celebrates by torchlight processions;" and again p. 32. So Aelius Aristid. i. p. 454 (ed. Canter).

[583] "I have fasted, I have drunk the cup," &c. Clem, *Alex. Protrept.* 2.

the poetry of Nature. It was the drama which is acted every year, of summer and winter and spring. Winter by winter the fruits and flowers and grain die down into the darkness, and spring after spring they come forth again to new life. Winter after winter the sorrowing earth is seeking for her lost child; the hopes of men look forward to the new blossoming of spring.

It was a drama also of human life. It was the poetry of the hope of a world to come. Death gave place to life. It was a *purgatio animae*, by which the soul might be fit for the presence of God. Those who had been baptized and initiated were lifted into a new life. Death had no terrors for them. The blaze of light after darkness, the symbolic scenery of the life of the gods, were a foreshadowing of the life to come.[584]

There is a passage in Plutarch which so clearly shows this, that I will quote it.[585]

> "When a man dies, he is like those who are being initiated into the mysteries. The one expression, *teleutan* — the other, *teleisthai*, correspond ... Our whole life is but a succession of wanderings, of painful courses, of long journeys by tortuous ways without outlet. At the moment of quitting it, fears,

---

[584] Cf. Aelius Aristid. 1, 454, *on the burning of the temple at Eleusis. The gain of the festival was not for this life only, but that hereafter they would not lie in darkness and mire like the uninitiated.*

[585] Fragm. ap. Stob, *Florileg.* 120. *Lenormant, Cont. Rev.* Sept. 1880, p. 430.

terrors, quiverings, mortal sweats, and a
lethargic stupor, come over us and overwhelm
us; but as soon as we are out of it, pure spots
and meadows receive us, with voices and
dances and the solemnities of sacred words and
holy sights. It is there that man, having become
perfect and initiated — restored to liberty,
really master of himself — celebrates, crowned
with myrtle, the most august mysteries, holds
converse with just and pure souls, looking
down upon the impure multitude of the
profane or uninitiated, sinking in the mire and
mist beneath him — through fear of death and
through disbelief in the life to come, abiding in
its miseries."

There was probably no dogmatic teaching — there were
possibly no words spoken — it was all an acted parable.[586]
But it was all kept in silence. There was an awful individuality
about it. They saw the sight in common, but they saw it each
man for himself. It was his personal communion with the
divine life. The glamor and the glory of it were gone when it
was published to all the world.[587] The effect of it was
conceived to be a change both of character and of relation to
the gods. The initiated were by virtue of their initiation made
partakers of a life to come. "Thrice happy they who go to
the world below having seen these mysteries: to them alone
is life there, to all others is misery."[588]

---

[586] Synes. *Orat.* p. 48 (ed. Petav.).

[587] Cf. Lenormant, *Cont. Rev.* Sept. 1880, p. 414 sq.

[588] Soph. *frag.* 719, ed. Dind.: so in effect Pindar, *frag. thren*, 8 ;
Cic. *Legg.* 2.14. 36; Plato, *Gorg.* p. 493 B, *Phedo.* 69 C (the lot
of the uninitiated), They were bound to make their life on earth
correspond to their initiation; see Lenormant, *ut sup.* p. 429 sqq.

2. In time, however, new myths and new forms of worship were added. It is not easy to draw a definite line between the mysteries, strictly so called, and the forms of worship which went on side by side with them. Not only are they sometimes spoken of in common as mysteries, but there is a remarkable syncretist painting in a non-Christian catacomb at Rome, in which the elements of the Greek mysteries of Demeter are blended with those of Sabazius and Mithra, in a way which shows that the worship was blended also.[589] These forms of worship also had an initiation: they also aimed at a pure religion. The condition of entrance was: "Let no one enter the most venerable assembly of the association unless he be pure and pious and good." Nor was it left to the individual conscience: a man had to be tested and examined by the officers.[590] But the main element in the association was not so much the initiation as the sacrifice and the common meal which followed it. The offerings were brought by individuals and offered in common: they were offered upon what is sometimes spoken of as the "holy table." They were distributed by the servants (the deacons), and the offeror shared with the rest in the distribution. In one association, at Xanthos in Lycia, of which the rules remain on an inscription, the offeror had the right to half of what he had

---

In later times it was supposed actually to make them better; Sopatros in Walz, *Rhet. Gr.* viii, 114.

[589] See Garrucci, *Les Mystéres du Syncretisme Phrygien dans les Cutacombles Romaines de Pretextat*, Paris, 1854.

[590] There was a further and larger process before a man was *teleios*. Tert. *adv. Valent.* c. 1, says that it took five years to become *teleios*.

brought. The feast which followed was an effort after real fellowship.[591] There was in it, as there is in Christian times, a sense of communion with one another in a communion with God.

During the earliest centuries of Christianity, the mysteries, and the religious societies which were akin to the mysteries, existed on an enormous scale throughout the eastern part of the Empire. There were elements in some of them from which Christianity recoiled, and against which the Christian Apologists use the language of strong invective.[592] But, on the other hand, the majority of them had the same aims as Christianity itself — the aim of worshipping a pure God, the aim of living a pure life, and the aim of cultivating the spirit of brotherhood.[593] They were part of a great religious revival which distinguishes the age.[594]

B. The Mysteries and the Church.

It was inevitable when a new group of associations came to exist side by side with a large existing body of associations, from which it was continually detaching

---

[591] The most elaborate account is that of the Arval feast at Rome: cf. Henzen, *Acta fratrum Arvalium.*

[592] Clem. Alex. *Protrep.* 2; Hippol. 1, *proaem.* Cf. Philo, *de sacrif.* 12 (ii. 260).

[593] They also had the same sanction—the fear of future punishments, cf. Celsus in Orig. 8. 48. Origen does not controvert this statement, but appeals to the greater moral effect of Christianity as an argument for its truth. They possibly also communicated divine knowledge. cf. Porphyry in Eusebius, *Prep. Ev.* 5.14.

[594] This revival had many forms, cf. Harnack, *Dogm.* p. 101.

members, introducing them into its own midst with the
practices of their original societies impressed upon their
minds, that this new group should tend to assimilate, with
the assimilation of their members, some of the elements of
these existing groups.[595] This is what we find to have been in
fact the case. It is possible that they made the Christian
associations more secret than before. Up to a certain time
there is no evidence that Christianity had any secrets. It was
preached openly to the world. It guarded worship by
imposing a moral bar to admission. But its rites were simple
and its teaching was public. After a certain time all is
changed: mysteries have arisen in the once open and easily
accessible faith, and there are doctrines which must not be
declared in the hearing of the uninitiated.[596] But the

---

[595] Similar practices existed in the Church and in the new
religions which were growing up. Justin Martyr speaks of the
way in which, under the inspiration of demons, the supper had
been imitated in the Mithraic mysteries: *Apol.* 1.66. Tertullian
points to the fact as an instance of the power of the devil (*de
presse. her.* 40); cf. Orig. *c. Cels.* 6.22.

[596] The objection which Celsus makes (*c. Cels.* 1.1; Keim, p. 3)
to the secrecy of the Christian associations would hardly have
held good in the apostolic age. Origen admits (*c. Cels.* 1.7) that
there are exoteric and esoteric doctrines in Christianity, and
justifies it by (1) the philosophies, (2) the mysteries. On the rise
of this conception of Christian teaching as something to be
hidden from the mass, cf. the Valentinians in Tert. *c. Valent.* 1,
where there is a direct parallel drawn between them and the
mysteries: also the distinction of men into two classes among
the Guostics Harn. Dogm. 222, cf. Hipp. 1, *proaem*, p. 4. Yet
this very secrecy was naturalized in the Church. Cf. Cyril Hier.
Catech. vi. 30; Aug. in *Psalm* ciii., *Hom. xevi.* in *Joan*;
Theodoret, *Quaest.* xv.in Num., and *Dial.* ii. (*Inconfusus*); Chry.

influence of the mysteries, and of the religious cults which were analogous to the mysteries, was not simply general; they modified in some important respects the Christian sacraments of Baptism and the Eucharist — the practice, that is, of admission to the society by a symbolical purification, and the practice of expressing membership of the society by a common meal. I will ask you to consider first Baptism, and secondly the Lord's Supper, each in its simplest form, and then I will attempt to show how the elements which are found in the later and not in the earlier form, are elements which are found outside Christianity in the institutions of which I have spoken.

1. Baptism. In the earliest times, (1) baptism followed at once upon conversion; (2) the ritual was of the simplest kind, nor does it appear that it needed any special minister.

The first point is shown by the Acts of the Apostles; the men who repented at Pentecost, those who believed when Philip preached in Samaria, the Ethiopian eunuch, Cornelius, Lydia, the jailor at Philippi, the converts at Corinth and Ephesus, were baptized as soon as they were known to recognize Jesus Christ as the Messiah.[597] The second point is also shown by the Acts. It was a baptism of water.

A later, though still very early stage, with significant modifications, is seen in the "Teaching of the Apostles:"[598]

Hom. xix. *in Matt.* Sozomen's (1. 20. 3) reason for not giving the Nicene Creed is significant alike as regards motive and language.

[597] Acts ii. 38, 41; viii 12, 13, 36, 38; x. 47, 48; xvi 15, 33; xvill, 8; xix. 3.

(1) no special minister of baptism is specified, the vague "he that baptizeth" seeming to exclude a limitation of it to an officer; (2) the only element that is specified is water; (3) previous instruction is implied, hut there is no period of catechumenate defined; (4) a fast is enjoined before baptism.

These were the simple elements of early Christian baptism. When it emerges after a period of obscurity — like a river which flows under the sand — the enormous changes of later times have already begun.

(i.) The first point of change is the change of name.

(a) So early as the time of Justin Martyr we find a name given to baptism which comes straight from the Greek mysteries — the name "enlightenment".[599] It Came to be the constant technical term.[600]

(b) The name "seal", which also came both from the mysteries[601] and from some forms of foreign cult, was used partly of those who had passed the tests and who were "consignati," as Tertullian calls them,[602] partly of those who were actually sealed upon the forehead in sign of a new ownership.[603]

---

[598] c. 7.

[599] *Apol.* 1.61; cf. Otto, vol. 1. p. 146, n. 14; Engelhardt, p. 102.

[600] Clem. Alex. *Pedag.* 1.6; Can. Laod. 47, Bruns, p. 78; Greg. Naz. *Orat.* xl. pp. 638, 639. Cf. Cyr. Hier. *Catech.* 13.21, p. 193.

[601] Lobeck, *Aglaoph.* p. 36, cf. 31 ff.

[602] *Apol.* 8. See Otto, vol. 1. p. 141; cf. *ad Valent.* 1.

(c) The term *mustaroin* is applied to baptism,[604] and with it comes a whole series of technical terms unknown to the Apostolic Church, but well known to the mysteries, and explicable only through ideas and usages peculiar to them. Thus we have words expressive either of the rite or act of initiation, like *muasis*,[605] *teleta*,[606] *teleiosis*,[607] *mustagogia*;[608] of the agent or minister, like *mustagogos*[609] of the subject, like *mustagogoumenos*,[610] *memuamenos*, *muatheis*, or, with reference to the unbaptized, *amuatos*.[611] In this terminology we can more

---

[603] For the seal in baptism, cf. Clem. Al. *Strom.* 2.3; *Quis dives*, 42, ap. Euseb. *Hist.* 3.23; Euseb. *Vita Const.* 1.4.62; Cyr. Hier. *Catech.* 5; Greg. Naz. *Orat.* 40, p. 639; Orig. *c. Cels.* 6.27. For the use of imagery and the terms relating to sealing—illumination—initiation—from the mysteries, Clem. *Al. Protrep.* 12. The effect of baptism is illumination, perfection, *Paedag.* 1.6; hence sins before and after baptism, i.e. enlightenment, are different, *Strom.* 2.13.

[604] Greg. Naz. *Orat.* 39, p. 632; Chrys. *Hom.* 85 *in Joan.* xix. 84: Sozomen, ii. 8, 6.

[605] Sozomen, i. 3 5.

[606] Dion. Areop. *Eccles, Hierar.* 3, p. 242.

[607] Clem. Alex. *Pedag.* 1.6, p. 93; Athan. *Cont. Ar.* 3, p. 413C.; Greg. Naz. *Orat.* 40, p. 648; Dion. Areop. *Eccles. Hier.* 3, 242.

[608] Chrys. *Hom.* 99, vol. v.; Theod. *in Cantic.* 1.

[609] Dion. Areop. *Eccles. Hier.* 1.1; *Mys. Theol.* 1. 1.

[610] Chrys. *Hom.* 1 *in Act.* p. 615; *Hom.* 21 *ad popul. Antioch*; Sozomen, ii. 17.9.

[611] Sozomen, i. 3.5; ii. 7.8; iv. 20.3; vi. 38.15; vii. 8. 7. These examples do not by any means exhaust or even adequately represent the obligations in the sphere of language, and of the ideas it at once denotes and connotes, which the ecclesiastical theory and practice of baptism lies under to the mysteries; but

easily trace the influence of the mysteries than of the New Testament.[612]

(ii.) The second point is the change of *time*, which involves a change of *conception*. (a) Instead of baptism being given immediately upon conversion, it came to be in all cases postponed by a long period of preparation, and in some cases deferred until the end of life.[613] (b) The Christians were separated into two classes, those who had and those who had not been baptized. Tertullian regards it as a mark of heretics that they have not this distinction: who among them is a catechumen, who a believer, is uncertain: they are no sooner hearers than they "join in the prayers;" and "their catechumens are perfect before they are fully instructed."[614] And Basil gives the custom of the mysteries as a reason for the absence of the catechumens from the service.[615] (c) As if to show conclusively that the change was due to the influence of the mysteries, baptized persons were, as we have

---

they may help to indicate the degree and nature of the obligation.

[612] For the sphere of the influence of the mysteries on the language and imagery of the New Testament, see 1 Cor. ii. 6 ff.; cf. Heb. vi 4.

[613] *Apost. Const*. 8.32. Cf. passages quoted from Clem. Alex. and others, *supra*, p. 287, note 1; p. 295, notes 2 and 5. See Bingham, vol, iii. pp. 443—446.

[614] *De presc. haer*. 41. Cf. Epiphan. 41.3; *Apost. Const*. 8.12.

[615] *de Spir. Sanct*. 27; cf. Orig. *c. Cels*. 3.59 *ad f*in. and 60, e.g. "then and not before do we invite them to participation in our mysteries," and "initiating those already purified into the sacred mysteries."

seen, distinguished from unbaptized by the very term which was in use for the similar distinction in regard to the mysteries — initiated and uninitiated, and the minister is *mustagogos,* and the persons being baptized are *mustagogoumenoi.* I dwell upon these broad features, and especially on the transference of names, because it is necessary to show that the relation of the mysteries to the sacrament was not merely a curious coincidence; and what I have said as to the change of name and the change of conception, might be largely supplemented by evidence of parallelism in the benefits which were conceived to attach to the one and the other. There are many slighter indications serving to supplement what has been already adduced.

(A) As those who were admitted to the inner sights of the mysteries had a formula or password, so the catechumens had a formula which was only entrusted to them in the last days of their catechumenate — the baptismal formula itself and the Lord's Prayer.[616] In the Western rites the *traditio symboli* occupies an important place in the whole ceremony. There was a special rite for it. It took place a week or ten days before the great office of Baptism on Easter-eve. Otherwise the Lord's Prayer and the Creed were kept secret and kept so as mysteries; and to the present day the technical name for a creed is *sumbolon* or password.

(B) Sometimes the baptized received the communion at once after baptism, just as those who had been initiated at Eleusis proceeded at once — after a day's fast — to drink of the mystic *kukeon* and to eat of the sacred cakes.

---

[616] See p. 293, note 1; also *Dict. Christian Antiquities*, s.vv. *Baptism, Catechumens*, especially p. 318, and *Creed*.

(C) The baptized were sometimes crowned with a garland, as the initiated wore a mystic crown at Eleusis. The usage was local, but lasted at Alexandria until modern times. It is mentioned by Vansleb.[617]

(D) Just as the divinities watched the initiation from out of the blaze of light, so Chrysostom pictures Christian baptism in the blaze of Easter-eve;[618] and Cyril describes the white-robed band of the baptized approaching the doors of the church where the lights turned darkness into day.

(E) Baptism was administered, not at any place or time, but only in the great churches, and only as a rule once a year — on Easter-eve, though Pentecost was also a recognized season. The primitive "See here is water, what doth hinder me to be baptized?" passed into a ritual which at every turn recalls the ritual of the mysteries. I will abridge the account which is given of the practice at Rome so late as the ninth century.[619] Preparation went on through the greater part of Lent. The candidates were examined and tested: they fasted: they received the secret symbols, the Creed and the Lord's Prayer. On Easter-eve, as the day declined towards afternoon, they assembled in the church of St. John Lateran. The rites of exorcism and renunciation were gone through in solemn form, and the rituals survive. The Pope and his priests come forth in their sacred vestments, with lights carried in front of them, which the Pope then blesses: there

---

[617] *Histoire de l'église d' Alexandrie*, p. 12: Paris, 1677.

[618] *De baptismo Christi*, 4. ii. 374. Cyril, *Prefatio ad Catech*, 15.

[619] Mabillon, *Com. prev. ad. ord. Rom.; Museum Ital.* 11. Xcix.

is a reading of lessons and a singing of psalms. And then, while they chant a litany, there is a procession to the great bath of baptism, and the water is blessed. The baptized come forth from the water, are signed with the cross, and are presented to the Pope one by one, who vests them in a white robe and signs their foreheads again with the cross. They are arranged in a great circle, and each of them carries a light. Then a vast array of lights is kindled; the blaze of them, says a Greek Father, makes night continuous with dawn. It is the beginning of a new life. The mass is celebrated — the mystic offering on the Cross is represented in figure; but for the newly baptized the chalice is filled, not with wine, but with milk and honey, that they may understand, says an old writer, that they have entered already upon the promised land. And there was one more symbolical rite in that early Easter sacrament, the mention of which is often suppressed — a lamb was offered on the altar — afterwards cakes in the shape of a lamb.[620] It was simply the ritual which we have seen already in the mysteries. The purified crowd at Eleusis saw a blaze of light, and in the light were represented in symbol life and death and resurrection.

2. Baptism had felt the spell of the Greek ritual: not less so had the Lord's Supper. Its elements in the earliest times may be gathered altogether apart from the passages of the New Testament, upon which, however clearly we may feel, no sensible man will found an argument, and which, taken by themselves, possibly admit of more than one meaning.

The extra-biblical accounts are:

---

[620] It was one of the points to which the Greeks objected in the discussions of the ninth century.

(1) "The Teaching of the Apostles;"[621] which implies:

(a) Thanksgiving for the wine. "We thank Thee, our Father, for the holy vine of David Thy servant, which Thou hast made known to us through Jesus Christ Thy Servant. To Thee be glory forever."

(b) Thanksgiving for the broken bread. "We thank Thee, our Father, for the life which Thou hast made known to us through Jesus Thy Servant. To Thee be glory forever."

After the thanksgiving they ate and drank: none could eat or drink until he had been baptized into the name of the Lord. After the partaking there was another thanksgiving and a prayer of supplication.

(2) There is a fragmentary account which has been singularly overlooked, in the Apostolical Constitutions,[622] which carries us one stage further. After the reading and the teaching, the deacon made a proclamation which vividly recalls the proclamation at the beginning of the Mysteries. "Is there anyone who has a quarrel with any? Is there any one with bad feeling?"

(3) The next stage is found in the same book of the Apostolical Constitutions.[623] The advance consists in the fact that the catechumens and penitents go out, just as those who

---

[621] c. 9.

[622] Bk. ii. 57, p. 87; cf. viii. 5, p. 239, lines 18, 19.

[623] viii. 11. 12, p. 248.

were not yet initiated and those who were impure were excluded from the Greek Mysteries.

This marked separation of the catechumens and the baptized, which was possibly strengthened by the philosophic distinction between *oi prokoptontes* and *oi teleioi* lasted until, under influences which it would be beyond our present purpose to discuss, the prevalence of infant baptism caused the distinction no longer to exist.[624]

(4) In a later stage there is a mention of the holy table as an altar, and of the offerings placed upon the table of which the faithful partook, as mysteries.[625]

(a) The conception of the table as an altar is later than the middle of the second century.[626] It is used in the Apostolic Fathers of the Jewish altar. It is used by Ignatius in a Christian sense, but always metaphorically.[627] It may be noted that though the Apostolic Constitutions (Bk. ii.) speak of a *thusia* they do not speak of a *thusuastarion*.[628] This use of *thusuastarion* is probably not earlier than Eusebius.[629]

---

[624] Origen, *c. Cels.* 3.59. Degrees and distinctions came to be recognized within the circle of the very initiated themselves, *Apost. Const.* vii. 44, viii. 13.

[625] The earlier offerings were those of Irenaeus, 4. 17. 5.

[626] Found in Chrys. e.g. *Hom. in Ep.* ii. *ad Corinth.* v. c. 3, vol. x. 470.

[627] *Ad Ephes.* 5; see Lightfoot's note. Cf. *Trall.* 7; *Philad.* 4; *Mag.* 7; *Rom.* 2.

[628] *Ap. Const.* ii. 57, p. 88.

[629] *H. E.* x. 4, 44.

(b) The conception of the elements as *mustaria* is even later;[630] but once established, it became permanent, like the Latin term "sacramentum."

(5) The conception of a priest — into which I will not now enter — was certainly strengthened by the mysteries and associations.

The full development or translation of the idea is found in the great mystical writer of the end of the fifth century, in whom every Christian ordinance is expressed in terms which are applicable only to the mysteries. The extreme tendency which he shows is perhaps personal to him; but he was in sympathy with his time, and his influence on the Church of the after-time must count for a large factor in the history of Christian thought. There are few Catholic treatises on the Eucharist and few Catholic manuals of devotion into which his conceptions do not enter.[631]

I will here quote his description of the Communion itself: "All the other initiations are incomplete without this. The consummation and crown of all the rest is the participation of him who is initiated in the thearchic mysteries. For though it be the common characteristic of all the hierarchic acts to make the initiated partakers of the divine light, yet this alone imparted to me the vision through whose mystic light, as it were, I am guided to the contemplation of the

---

[630] Isid. Pelus, *Epist.* 3.340, p. 390. Cf. Chrys. *de comp. ad Demet.* 1.6, vol. i.

[631] In Dionysius Areop. (5. N., ed. Corderius, i. 839), (c. 4), (c. 5, 3, p. 233).

other sacred things." The ritual is then described. The sacred bread and the cup of blessing are placed upon the altar. "Then the sacred hierarch initiates the sacred prayer and announces to all the holy peace: and after all have saluted each other, the mystic recital of the sacred lists is completed. The hierarch and the priests wash their hands in water; he stands in the midst of the divine altar, and around him stand the priests and the chosen ministers. The hierarch sings the praises of the divine working and consecrates the most divine mysteries, and by means of the symbols which are sacredly set forth, he brings into open vision the things of which he sings the praises. And when he has shown the gifts of the divine working, he himself comes into a sacred communion with them, and then invites the rest. And having both partaken and given to the others a share in the thearchic communion, he ends with a sacred thanksgiving; and while the people bend over what are divine symbols only, he himself, always by the thearchic spirit, is led in a priestly manner, in purity of his godlike frame of mind, through blessed and spiritual contemplation, to the holy realities of the mysteries."[632]

Once again I must point out that the elements — the conceptions which he has added to the primitive practices — are identical with those in the mysteries. The tendency which he represented grew: the Eucharistic sacrifice came in the East to be celebrated behind closed doors: the breaking of bread from house to house was changed into so awful a mystery that none but the hierophant himself might see it.

---

[632] Dion. Arcop. *Eccles. Hier.* c. 3, par. 1, 1, 2, pp. 187, 188.

The idea of prayer and thought as offerings was preserved by the Neo-Platonists.

There are two minor points which, though interesting, are less certain and also less important, (a) It seems likely that the use of *diptucha* — tablets commemorating benefactors or departed saints — was a continuation of a similar usage of the religious associations. (b) The blaze of lights at mysteries may have suggested the use of lights at the Lord's Supper.[633]

It seems fair to infer that, since there were great changes in the ritual of the sacraments, and since the new elements of these changes were identical with elements that already existed in cognate and largely diffused forms of worship, the one should be due to the other.

This inference is strengthened when we find that the Christian communities which were nearest in form and spirit to the Hellenic culture, were the first in which these elements appear, and also those in which they assumed the strongest form. Such were the Valentinians, of whom Tertullian expressly speaks in this connection.[634] We read of Simon

---

[633] Cf. for the use of lights in worship, the money accounts, from a Berlin papyrus, of the temple of Jupiter Capitolinus at Arsinoe, A.L. 215, in Hermes, Bd. xx. p. 430.

[634] *Adv. Valent.* 1. Hippolytus (1, *proaem*, 5.23, 24) says the heretics had mysteries which they disclosed to the initiated only after long preparation, and with an oath not to divulge them: so the Naassenes, 5.8, and the Peratae, 5.17 (ad fin.), whose mysteries "are delivered in silence." The Justinians had an oath of secrecy before proceeding to behold "what eye hath not seen" and " drinking from the living water," 5. 27.

Magus that he taught that baptism had so supreme an efficacy as to give by itself eternal life to all who were baptized. The *loutron zoas* was expanded to its full extent, and it was even thought that to the water of baptism was added a fire which came from heaven upon all who entered into it. Some even introduced a second baptism.[635]

So also the Marcosians and some Valentinian schools believed in a baptism that was an absolute sundering of the baptized from the corruptible world and an emancipation into a perfect and eternal life. Similarly, some other schools added to the simple initiation rites of a less noble and more sensuous order.[636]

It was but the old belief in the effect of the mysteries thrown into a Christian form. So also another Gnostic school is said to have not only treated the truths of Christianity as sacred, but also to have felt about them what the initiated were supposed to feel about the mysteries — "I swear by Him who is above all, by the Good One, to keep these mysteries and to reveal them to no one;" and after that oath each seemed to feel the power of God to be upon him, as it were the password of entrance into the highest mysteries.[637] As soon as the oath had been taken, he sees what no eye has seen, and hears what no ear has heard, and drinks of the living water — which is their baptism, as they

---

[635] E.g. Mareus, in connection with initiation into the higher mysteries, Hipp. 6. 41, and the Elkasaites as cleansing from gross sin, 9, 15.

[636] Eus. *H.E.* iv. 7.

[637] Hipp. 5. 27, of the Justinians, Cf. Hilgenfeld, *Ketzergesch.* p. 270.

think, a spring of water springing up within them to everlasting life.

Again, it is probably through the Gnostics that the period of preparation for baptism was prolonged. Tertullian says of the Valentinians that their period of probation is longer than their period of baptized life, which is precisely what happened in the Greek practice of the fourth century.

The general inference of the large influence of the Gnostics on baptism, is confirmed by the fact that another element, which certainly came through them, though its source is not certain and is more likely to have been Oriental than Greek, has maintained a permanent place in most rituals — the element of anointing. There were two customs in this matter, one more characteristic of the East, the other of the West — the anointing with (1) the oil of exorcism before baptism and after the renunciation of the devil, and (2) the oil of thanksgiving, which was used immediately after baptism, first by the presbyter and then by the bishop, who then sealed the candidate on the forehead. The very variety of the custom shows how deep and yet natural the action of the Gnostic systems, with the mystic and magic customs of the Gnostic societies or associations, had been on the practices and ceremonies of the Church.[638]

---

[638] For the Eastern custom, see Cyril Hier. *Catech. Myst.* ii. 3, 4, p. 312: the candidate is anointed all over before baptism with exorcised oil, which, by invocation of God and prayer, purifies from the burning traces of sin, but also puts to flight the invisible powers of the evil one. Cf. *Apost. Const.* vii. 22, 41, iii. 15, 16; *the Coptic Constitutions*, c. 46 (ed. Tattam), cf. Boetticher's Gr. translation in Bunsen's *Anal. Ante-Nic.* ii. 467;

But beyond matters of practice, it is among the Gnostics that there appears for the first time an attempt to realize the change of the elements to the material body and blood of Christ. The fact that they were so regarded is found in Justin Martyr.[639] But at the same time, that the change was not vividly realized, is proved by the fact that, instead of being regarded as too awful for men to touch, the elements were taken by the communicants to their homes and carried about with them on their travels. But we read of Marcus that in his realistic conception of the Eucharistic service the white wine actually turned to the color of blood before the eyes of the communicants.[640]

Thus the whole conception of Christian worship was changed.[641] But it was changed by the influence upon

---

Clem. *Recog.* 3. 67; Chrys. *Hom.* 6. 4, *in Ep. ad Col.* xi. 342; Dionys. Areop. *Eccles. Hier.* 2.7; Basil, *de Spir. Sanct.* 66, vol. iv. 55. For earlier Western as distinct from Eastern thought on the subject, cf. Tert. *de bapt.* 6 and 7; *de resurr. carnis.* 8; *adv. Mare.* i. 14; Cyprian, *Ep.* 70. For the later Western usage, introduced from the East, see *Conc. Rom.* 402, c. 8, ed. Bruns. pt. ii. 278; *Ordo* 6, *ad fac. Catech.* in Marténe, *de ant. ecel. rit.* i. p. 17; Theodulfus Aurel. *de ord. bapt.* 10 ; unction of the region of the heart before and behind, symbolizing the Holy Spirit's unction with a view to both prosperity and adversity (Sirmond, vol. ii. 686); Isid. Hisp. *de off eccl.* 2.21; Catechumens *exorcizantur, sales aecipiunt et unguntur, the salt being made ut eorum gustu condimentum sapientice percipiant, neque desipiant a sapore Christi* (Migne, Ixxxiii. col. 814, 815); Cus, Arelat. *serm.* 22.

[639] Apol. 1.66.

[640] ap. Hipp. 6.39.

[641] Tert. *ad Scap.* 2, holds that sacrifice may consist of simple

Christian worship of the contemporary worship of the mysteries and the concurrent cults. The tendency to an elaborate ceremonial which had produced the magnificence of those mysteries and cults, and which had combined with the love of a purer faith and the tendency towards fellowship, was based upon a tendency of human nature which was not crushed by Christianity. It rose to a new life, and though it lives only by a survival, it lives that new life still. In the splendid ceremonial of Eastern and "Western worship, in the blaze of lights, in the separation of the central point of the rite from common view, in the procession of torch-bearers chanting their sacred hymns — there is the survival, and in some cases the galvanized survival, of what I cannot find it in my heart to call a pagan ceremonial; because though it was the expression of a less enlightened faith, yet it was offered to God from a heart that was not less earnest in its search for God and in its effort after holiness than our own.

prayer.

Lecture XI. THE INCORPORATION OF CHRISTIAN IDEAS, AS MODIFIED BY GREEK, INTO A BODY OF DOCTRINE.

The object which I have in view in this Lecture is to show the transition by which, under the influence of contemporary Greek thought, the word Faith came to be transferred from simple trust in God to mean the acceptance of a series of propositions, and these propositions, propositions in abstract metaphysics.

The Greek words which designate belief or faith are used in the Old Testament chiefly in the sense of trust, and primarily trust in a person. They expressed confidence in his goodness, his veracity, his uprightness. They are as much moral as intellectual. They implied an estimate of character. Their use in application to God was not different from their use in application to men. Abraham trusted God. The Israelites also trusted God when they saw the Egyptians dead upon the seashore. In the first instance there was just so much of intellectual assent involved in belief, that to believe God. involved an assent to the proposition that God exists. But this element was latent and implied rather than conscious and expressed. It is not difficult to see how, when this proposition came to be conscious and expressed, it should lead to other propositions. The analysis of belief led to the construction of other propositions besides the bare original proposition that God is. Why do I trust God? The answer was: Because He is wise, or good, or just. The propositions followed: I believe that God is wise, that He is good, that He is just. Belief in God came to mean the assent to certain propositions about God.[642]

In Greek philosophy the words were used rather of intellectual conviction than of moral trust, and of the higher rather than of the lower forms of conviction. Aristotle distinguishes faith from impression — for a man, he says, may have an impression and not be sure of it. He uses it both of the convictions that come through the senses and of those that come through reason.

There is in Philo a special application of this philosophical use, which led to even more important results. He blends the sense in which it is found in the Old Testament with that which is found in Greek philosophy. The mass of men, he says, trust their senses or their reason. The good man trusts God. Just as the mass of men believe that their senses and their reason do not deceive them, so the latter believes that God does not deceive him. To trust God was to trust His veracity. But the occasions on which God spoke directly to a man were rare, and what He said when He so spoke commanded an unquestioning acceptance. He more commonly spoke to men through the agency of messengers. His angels spoke to men, sometimes in visions of the night, sometimes in open manifestation by day. His prophets spoke to men. To believe God, implied a belief in what He said indirectly as well as directly. It implied the acceptance of what His prophets said, that is to say, of what they were recorded to have said in the Holy Writings. Belief in this sense is not a vague and mystical sentiment, the hazy state of

---

[642] Cf. Celsus' idea of faith: Orig. *c. Cels.* 3.39; Keim, p. 39.

mind which precedes knowledge, but the highest form of conviction. It transcends reason in certainty. It is the full assurance that certain things are so, because God has said that they are so.[643]

In this connection we may note the way in which the Christian communities were helped by the current reaction against pure speculation — the longing for certainty. The mass of men were sick of theories. They wanted certainty. The current teaching of the Christian teachers gave them certainty. It appealed to definite facts of which their predecessors were eye-witnesses. Its simple tradition of the life and death and resurrection of Jesus Christ was a necessary basis for the satisfaction of men's needs. Philosophy and poetry might be built upon that tradition; but if the tradition were shown to be only cloudland, Christian philosophy was no more than Stoicism.

We have thus to see how, under the new conditions, faith passed beyond the moral stage, or simple trust in a person, to the metaphysical stage, or belief in certain propositions or technical definitions concerning Him, His nature, relations and actions. In this latter we may distinguish two correlated and interdependent phases or forms of belief, the one more intellectual and logical, the other more historical and concrete, namely, (1) the conviction that God being of a certain nature has certain attributes; (2) the conviction that, God being true, the statements which He makes through His prophets and ministers are also true.[644] The one of these

---

[643] Philo's view of faith is well expressed in two striking passages, *Quis rer. div. Heres*, 18, i. 485; and *de Abrah*. 46, ii. 39.

forms of belief was elaborated into what we know as the Creed; the other, into the Canon of the New Testament.

We shall first deal with these phases or forms of belief, and then with the process by which the metaphysical definitions became authoritative.

1. In the first instance the intellectual element of belief was subordinated to the ethical purpose of the religion. Belief was not insisted upon in itself and for itself, but as the ground of moral reformation. The main content of the belief was "that men are punished for their sins and honored for their good deeds:"[645] the ground of this conviction was the underlying belief that God is, and that He rewards and punishes. The feature which differentiated Christianity from philosophy was, that this belief as to the nature of God had been made certain by a revelation. The purpose of the revelation was salvation — regeneration and amendment of life. By degrees stress came to be laid on this underlying element. The revelation had not only made some propositions certain which hitherto had been only

---

[644] Cf "He that cometh to God must believe that He is, and that He is a rewarder of them that seek Him," Heb. xi. 6; and "He that is of God heareth God's words," John viii. 47.

[645] It was one of Celsus' objections to Christianity that its preachers laid more stress on belief than on the intellectual grounds of belief: Orig. *c. Cels*. 1.9. Origen's answer, which is characteristic rather of his own time than expressive of the belief of the apostolic age, is that this was necessary for the mass of men, who have no leisure or inclination for deep investigation (1.10), and in order not to leave men altogether without help (1.12).

speculative, it had also added new propositions, assertions of its distinctive or differentiating belief. But it is uncertain, except within the narrowest limits, what those assertions were. There are several phrases in the New Testament and in subapostolic writings which read like references to some elementary statements or rule.[646] But none of them contain or express a recognized standard. Yet the standard may be gathered partly from the formula of admission into the Christian community, partly from the formulae in which praise was ascribed to God. The most important of these, in view of its subsequent history, is the former. But the formula is itself uncertain; it existed at least in two main forms. There is evidence to show that the injunction to baptize in the name of the three Persons of the Trinity, which is found in the last chapter of St. Matthew, was observed.[647] It is the formula in the Teaching of the Apostles.[648] But there is also evidence, side by side with this evidence as to the use of the Trinitarian formula, of baptism into the name of Christ, or into the death of Christ.[649]

---

[646] E.g. Rom. vi. 17; 2 John, 9; 2 Tim. i, 13; 1 Tim. vi. 12; Jude 3. Polycrates, ap. Eus. H. E. 5.24: see passages collected in Gebhardt and Harnack's *Patres Apost.* Bd. i. th. 2 (Barnabas), p. 133.

[647] Cf. Schmid, *Dogmeng.* p. 14, Das Taufsymbol.

[648] c. 7.4.

[649] See Acts viii. 16, xix. 5, with which compare Rom. vi. 1—11, Acts xxii. 16. *Didache*, 9.5; and *Apost. Const.* Bk. 11. 7, p. 20; cf. 148, 7, and elsewhere, in composite form. Against this Cyprian wrote, in *Ep.* 73, *ad Jubaianum*, 16—18; cf. Harnack, *Dogmeng.* 176.

The next element in the uncertainty which exists is as to how far the formula, either in the one case or the other, was conceived to involve the assent to any other propositions except those of the existence of the divine Persons or Person mentioned in the formula. Even this assent was implied rather than explicit. It is in the Apologists that the transition from the implicit was made. The teaching of Jesus Christ became to them important, especially in Justin Martyr.[650] The step by which it became explicit is of great importance, but we have no means of knowing when or how it was made.[651] It is conceivable that it was first made homiletically, in the course of exhortation to Christian duty.[652] When the intellectual contents of the formula did become explicit, the formula became a test. Concurrently with its use as a standard or test of belief, was probably the incorporation in it of so much of Christian teaching as referred to the facts of the life of Jesus Christ. But the facts were capable of different interpretations, and different propositions might be based upon them. In the first instance, speculation was free. Different facts had a different significance. The same facts of the life were interpreted in different ways. There was an agreement as to the main principle that the Christian societies were societies for the amendment of life. It is an almost ideal picture which the heathen Celsus draws of the Christians differing widely as to their speculations, and yet all agreeing to say, "The world is crucified to me, and I unto the

---

[650] Cf. von Engelhardt, *Das Christenthum Justins*, p. 107.

[651] Cf. Harnack, *Dogmeng.* p. 130 ff.

[652] Cf. Clement's account of Basilides' conception of faith in contrast to his own, *Strom.* 5.1.

world."[653] The influence of Greek thought, partly by the allegorizing of history, partly by the construction of great superstructures of speculation upon slender bases, made the original standard too elastic to serve as the basis and bond of Christian society. When theories were added to fact, different theories were added. It is at this point that the fact became of special importance that the Gospel had been preached by certain persons, and that its content was the content of that preaching. It was not a philosophy which successive generations might modify. It went back to the definite teaching of a historical person. It was of importance to be sure what that teaching was. It was agreed to recognize apostolic teaching as the authoritative vehicle and interpretation of Christ's. All parties appealed to it.[654] But there had been more than one apostle. The teaching was consequently that, not of one person, but of many.

Here was the main point of dispute. All parties within the Church agreed as to the need of a tribunal, but each party had its own. Each made its appeal to a different apostle. But since, though many in number, they were teachers, not of their own opinions, but of the doctrine which they had received from Jesus Christ, the more orthodox or Catholic tendency found it necessary to lay stress upon their unity. They were spoken of in the plural, *oi apostoloi*. While the Gnostics built upon one apostle or another,[655] the Catholics

---

[653] Orig. *c. Cels.* 5.65.

[654] Cf. *Ptolemaeus ad Floram*, c. 7, ed. Pet.

[655] Thus Basilides, ap. Hippol. 7.20, preferred to follow a tradition from Matthias, who was said to have been specially instructed by the Savior. The Naassenes, ib. 10.9, traced their

built upon an apostolic consensus. Their tradition was not that of Peter or of James, but of the twelve apostles. The *pistis* was *apostolika,* an attribute which implies a uniform tradition.[656]

It was at this point that organization and confederation became important: the bishops of the several churches were regarded as the conservators of the tradition:[657] while the bishops of the apostolic churches settled down to a general agreement as to the terms of the apostolic tradition.[658] In distinction from the Gnostic standards, there came to be a standard which the majority of the churches — the middle party in the Church — accepted. It is quite uncertain when the rule came to be generally accepted, or in what form it was accepted. But it is in the main preserved for us — with undoubtedly later accretions — in the Apostles' Creed.

---

doctrine to James, the Brother of the Lord. Valentinus, Clem. Alex. *Strom.* 7.17, was said to be a hearer of Theudas, who was a pupil of Paul. Hippol. 1, *proaem*, argued against all heretics that they had taken nothing from Holy Scripture, and had not preserved the *tinos agiou diadoxan.* Cf. Tert. *c. Marc.* 1.21. But see the very remarkable statement of Origen as to the cause of heresies, *c. Cels.* 3. 12; cf, Clem. Al. *Strom.* 7.17.

[656] Cf. Clem. Alex. *Strom.* 7.17, and the contention of Tert. *de praese. her.* 32; Harnack, pp. 133 ff, especially note 2, pp. 134—i36. Eusebius, *H. E.* 4. 7.

[657] Adamantius (Origen, ed. Delarue, i. 809).

[658] cf. Tert. *de presc. haer.* cc. 21. 36; Iren. 3. 1—3; Orig. *de princ; praef.* 2: Iren. 1.9.45; Tert. *adv. Mare.* 1. 21 (*regula sacramenti*); *de Virg. vel.* 1; *adv. Prax.* 2; *de prese. her.* cc. 3.12.42; *de monog.* 2. In general, see Weingarten, *Zeittafeln,* s.7.19.

Tertullian's contention is that this rule is not only apostolic and binding, but also adequate — a complete representation of apostolic teaching — that there were no necessary truths outside it.[659] The additions were made by the gradual working of the common sense, the common consciousness, of the Christian world. They were approved by the majority; they were accepted by the sees which claimed to have been founded by the apostles. The earliest form is that which may be gathered from several writers as having been generally accepted in Rome and the West: it is a bare statement. "I believe in God Almighty, and in Jesus Christ His Son our Lord, who was born of a virgin, crucified under Pontius Pilate, the third day rose again from the dead, sitteth on the right hand of the Father, from whence he is coming to judge the living and dead; and in the Holy Spirit." The term Son came to be qualified in very early times by "only begotten;" and after "the Holy Spirit," "the Holy Church, the remission of sins, and the resurrection of the flesh," were added.

2. Side by side with this question of the standard or authentic minimum of traditional teaching, and growing necessarily with it and out of it, was the question of the sources from which that teaching could be drawn, and of the materials by which the standard might be interpreted. The greater part of apostolic teaching had been oral. The tradition was mostly oral. But as the generations of men receded farther from the apostolic age, and as the oral tradition which was delivered came necessarily to vary, it became more and more uncertain what was the true form and content of the tradition. Written records came to be of

---

[659] *De praesc. her.* cc. 25.26.

more importance than oral tradition. They had at first only
the authority which attached to tradition. Their elevation to
an independent rank was due to the influence of the Old
Testament. There had been already a series of revelations of
God to men, which having once been oral had become
written. The revelation consisted of what was then known as
the Scriptures, and what we now know as the Old
Testament. The proofs of Christianity consisted to a large
extent in its consonance with those Scriptures. But the term
Holy Scriptures was less strictly used than is sometimes
supposed. The hedge round them had gaps, and there were
patches lying outside what has since come to be its line. It
was partly the indefiniteness of the Old Testament canon
which caused the term Scripture to be applied to some
writings of the apostolic age. But the question, Which
writings? was only answered gradually. The spirit of
prophecy had only gradually passed away. It was the
common ground for the reception of the Old Testament and
the New Testament; as the spirit of prophecy was common
to both, it was but natural that both should have the same
attributes. But prophecy was not in the first instance
conceived as having suddenly ceased in the Church. The
term Scripture is applied to the Shepherd of Hermas by
Irenaeus.[660] The delimitation of the body of writings that
could be so denoted was connected with the necessity of
being sure about the apostolical teaching — the *paradosis*.[661]
The term Scripture was applied to the recorded sayings of

---

[660] 4.20.

[661] See Overbeck, *die Anfange der patrist. Literatur, in the Hist.
Zeitschrift*, N.F. Bd. xii. 417—472.

Jesus Christ without demur.[662] It came to be applied also to
the records which the apostles had left of the facts of the life
of Christ. Then, finally, it tended more gradually to be
applied to the writings of the apostles and of apostolic men.

But questions arose in regard to all these classes, which
were not immediately answered. There were several
recensions current both of the sayings of Jesus Christ and of
the memoirs of the apostles. There were many writings
attributed to apostles and apostolic men which were of
doubtful authority. But the determination was slow, and the
date when a general settlement was made is uncertain.[663]
There is no distinction between canonical and uncanonical
books either in Justin Martyr or in Irenaeus. The first Biblical
critic was Marcion: the controversy with his followers, which
reaches its height in Tertullian, forced on the Church the
first serious consideration of the question, — Which
recensions of the words and memoirs of Christ, and which
of the letters and other writings of the apostles and apostolic
men, should be accepted? There came to be a recognized list

---

[662] Cf. Hegesippus, ap. Eus. *H.E.* 4.22.3; see Gebhardt and
Harnack on 2 Clement, p. 132, for examples; also Harnack,
Dogm. 131.

[663] Cf. Weingarten, *Zeittafeln*, p. 19, where he cites the
Muratorian fragment, Origen (ap. Eus. *H.E.* 6.25), and
Athanasius, in the last of whom he traces the first use of the term
"canon" in our sense. But we must carefully distinguish the *idea*
of a canon and the *contents* of the canon. It is uncertain whence
the idea of a canon of Scripture came, whether from the
ecclesiastical party or from the Gnostics; and if from the latter,
whether it was from Basilides, or Valentinus, or Marcion. Most
likely the last. Harnack, *Dogm.* 215 ff.; cf, 237— 240 for
Marcion as the first Biblical critic.

of the writings of the new revelations, as there came to be —
though it is doubtful whether there had yet come to be — a
list of the writings of the earlier revelations to the Jews.
Writings on the recognized list came in as the voices of the
Holy Ghost.[664] They were, as the writings of the prophets
had been, the revelation of the Father to His children. Hence
faith or belief came to take in the Christian world the sense
that it had in Philo — of assent not only to the great
conceptions which were contained in the notion of God, but
also to the divine revelation which was recorded in the two
Testaments.

3. It might have been well if the Christian Church had
been content to rest with this first stage in the
transformation of the idea of belief, and to take as its
intellectual basis only the simple statements of the primitive
creed interpreted by the New Testament. But the conflict of
speculations which had compelled the middle party in the
Christian churches to adopt a standard of belief and a
limitation of the sources from which the belief might be
interpreted, had also had the effect of bringing into the
Church the philosophical temper.[665] In the creed of the end
of the second century, the age of Tertullian, there are already
philosophical ideas — the creation of the world out of
nothing, the Word, the relation of the Creator to the world,
of the Word or Son to the Father, and of both to men. The
Creed, as given in the treatise against Praxeas, is equally

[664] Harnack, pp. 317 f.

[665] Tertullian, though in his treatise *de presc. her.* he abandons
argument with the Gnostics, yet in his *adv. Marc.* 1.22, relaxes
that line of argument, and enters into formal discussion.

elaborate.[666] With that Creed — traditional as he believed. it to be — Tertullian himself was satisfied. He deprecates the "curiositas" of the brethren no less than the "scrupulositas" of the heretics. He denies the applicability of the text, "Seek and ye shall find," to research into the content of Christian doctrine: it relates only to the traditional teaching: when a man has found that, he has all that he needs: further "seeking" is incompatible with having found. In other words, as among modem Ultramontanes, faith must rest not on search but on tradition (authority).[667] The absolute freedom of speculation was checked, but the tendency to speculate remained, and it had in the "rule of faith" a vantage-ground within the Church. There grew up within the lines that had been marked out a tendency which, accepting the rule of faith, and accepting also, with possibly slight variations, the canonical Scriptures, tried to build theories out of them: *gnosis* took its place side by side with *pistis*.[668] It grew up in several parts of Christendom. In Cappadocia, in Asia, in Edessa, in Palestine, in Alexandria, were different small groups of men who within the recognized lines were working out philosophical theories of Christianity.[669] "We know most about Alexandria. There was a recognized school — on the type of the existing philosophical schools — for the study of philosophical Christianity. Its first great teacher was Clement. He was the first to construct a large

---

[666] c. 2.

[667] Tert. *de praescr. her*. cc. 8, 18,

[668] Theories were framed as to the relation of *gnosis* and *pistis* ;e.g. the former was conceived to relate to the Spirit, the latter to the Son, which Clem. Alex. denies (*Strom*. 5.1).

[669] See Harnack, 549.

philosophy of Christian doctrine, with a recognition of the conventional limits, but by the help and in the domain of Greek thought. But he is of less importance than his great disciple Origen. In the *De Principiis* of the latter we have the first complete system of dogma; and I recommend the study of it, of its omissions as well as of its assertions, of the strange fact that the features of it which are in strongest contrast to later dogmatics are in fact its most archaic and conservative elements.

It is not to my present purpose to state the results of these speculations. The two points to which I wish to draw your attention in reference to this tendency to philosophize, are these:

(1) The distinction between what was either an original and ground belief or a historical fact of which a trustworthy tradition had come down, and speculations in regard to such primary beliefs and historical facts, tended to disappear in the strong philosophical current of the time. It did not disappear without a struggle. Tertullian, among others, gives indications of it. The doctrine of the Divine Word had begun in his time to make its way into the Creed: it was known as the "dispensation". "The simpler-minded men," he remarks, "not to say ignorant and uneducated, who always constitute the majority of believers — since the rule of faith itself transfers us from the belief in polytheism to the belief in one only true God — not understanding that though God be one, yet His oneness is to be understood as involving a dispensation, are frightened at this idea of dispensation."[670] But the ancient conservatism was crushed.

It came to be considered as important to have the right belief in the speculation as it confessedly was to have it in the fact.

(2) The result of the fading away of this distinction, and of the consequent growth in importance of the speculative element, was a tendency to check individual speculations, and to fuse all speculation in the average speculations of the majority. The battle of the second century had been a battle between those who asserted that there was a single and final tradition of truth, and those who claimed that the Holy Spirit spoke to them as truly as He had spoken to men in the days of the apostles. The victorious opinion had been that the revelation was final, and that what was contained in the records of the apostles was the sufficient sum of Christian teaching: hence the stress laid upon *apostolic* doctrine.

The battle of the third century was between those who claimed, as Marcion claimed, that inspired documents were to be taken in their literal sense, and those who claimed that they needed a philosophical interpretation,[671] — that while these monuments of the apostolic age required interpretation,[672] yet they were of no private interpretation,

---

[670] *Adv. Prax*, 3.

[671] Which had been the contention of the heretics whom Tertullian opposed: *de presc. her.* cc. 16, 17.

[672] Origen (*de princ., praef.* 3) follows in the line of those who rested upon apostolic teaching, but gives a foothold for philosophy by saying (1) that the Apostles left the grounds of their statements to be investigated; (2) that they affirmed the existence of many things without stating the manner and origin of their existence.

and that theories based upon them must be the theories of the apostolical churches. In other words, the contention that Christianity rested upon the basis of a traditional doctrine and a traditional standard, was necessarily supplemented by the contention that the doctrine and standard must have a traditional interpretation. A rule of faith and a canon were comparatively useless, and were felt to be so, without a traditionally authoritative interpretation. The Gnostics were prepared to accept all but this. They also appealed to tradition and to the Scriptures.[673] So far it was an even battle: each side in such a controversy might retort upon the other, and did so.[674] If it were allowed to each side to argue on the same bases and by the same methods, each side might claim a victory. A new principle had to be introduced — the denial of the right of private interpretation. In regard both to the primary articles of belief and to the majority of apostolic writings, no serious difference of opinion had existed among the apostolical churches. It was otherwise with the speculations that were based upon the rule of faith and the canon. They required discussion. The Christological ideas that were growing up on all sides had much in common with the Gnostic opinions. They needed a limitation and a check.

---

[673] Valentinus accepted the whole canon (integro instrumento), and the most important work of Basilides was a commentary on the Gospel: Tert. *de presc. her*. 38.

[674] Tert. *de presc. her*. 18. It is important to contrast the arguments of Tertullian with those of Clement of Alexandria, and of both with the practice which circumstances rendered necessary. In *Strom*. 7.16 and 17, Clement makes Scripture the criterion between the Church and the heretics, though he assumes that all orthodox teaching is apostolic and uniform.

The check was conterminous with the sources of the tradition itself; the meaning of the canon, as well as the canon itself, was deposited with the bishops of apostolical churches; and their method of enforcing the check was the holding of meetings and the framing of resolutions. Such meetings had long been held to ensure unity on points of discipline. They came now to be held to ensure unity on that which had come to be no less important — the interpretation of the recognized standard of belief. They were meetings of bishops. Bishops had added to their original functions the function of teachers and interpreters of the will of God.[675] Accordingly meetings of bishops were held, and through the operation of political rather than of religious causes their decisions were held to be final. Two important results followed.

(i.) The first result was the formulating of the speculations in definite propositions, and the insertion of such propositions in the Creed. The theory was that such insertions were of the nature of definitions and interpretations of the original belief. The mass of communities have never wandered from the belief that they rest upon an original revelation preserved by a continuous tradition. But a definition of what has hitherto been undefined is necessarily of the nature of an addition. Perhaps the earliest instance which has come down to us of such an expansion of the Creed, is in the letter sent by Hymenaeus, Bishop of Jerusalem, and his colleagues to Paul of Samosata.[676]

---

[675] The combination is first found in *Apost. Const.* Bk. ii. pp. 14, 10.16, 25.51.17, 20. 58, 22.

[676] Routh, *Rel. Sacr.* iii. p. 290; Harnack, p. 644.

The faith which had been handed down from the beginning is "that God is unbegotten, one, without beginning, unseen, unchangeable, whom no man hath seen nor can see, whose glory and greatness it is impossible for human nature to trace out adequately; but we must be content to have a moderate conception of Him: His Son reveals Him .... as he himself says, 'No man knoweth the Father save the Son, and he to whomsoever the Son revealeth Him.' We confess and proclaim His begotten Son, the only begotten, the image of the invisible God, the firstborn of every creature, the wisdom and word and power of God, being before the worlds, God not by foreknowledge but by essence and substance."

They had passed into the realm of metaphysics. The historical facts of the earlier creed were altogether obscured. Belief was belief in certain speculations. The conception of the nature of belief had travelled round a wide circuit. It will be noted that there had been a change in the meaning of the word which has lasted until our own day. The belief in the veracity of a witness, or in facts of which we are cognizant through our senses, or the primary convictions of our minds — in which I may include the belief in God — admit of a degree of certainty which cannot attach to the belief in deductions from metaphysical premises.[677] Belief came to mean, not the highest form of conviction, but something lower than conviction, and it tends to have that meaning still. But with this change in the nature of belief, there had been no change in the importance which was attached to it. The

---

[677] Cf. the definitions of faith in Clem. *Al. Strom*, 2, cc. 2 and 3.

acceptance of these philosophical speculations was as important as the belief in God and in Jesus Christ, the Son of God. The tendency developed, and we find it developing all through the fourth century. In the Nicene Council the tendency was politically more important, but it was not theologically different from what had gone before. The habit of defining and of making inferences from definitions, grew the more as the philosophers passed over into the Christian lines, and logicians and metaphysicians presided over Christian churches. The speculations which were then agreed upon became stamped as a body of truth, and with the still deeper speculations of the Councils of Constantinople and Chalcedon, the resolutions of the Nicene Fathers have come to be looked upon as almost a new revelation, and the rejection of them as a greater bar to Christian fellowship than the rejection of the New Testament itself.

(ii.) The second result was the creation of a distinction between what was accepted by the majority at a meeting and what was accepted only by a minority. The distinction had long been growing. There had been parties in the Christian communities from the first. And the existence of such parties was admissible.[678] They broke the concord of the brethren, but they did not break the unity of the faith. Now heretics and schismatics were identified; difference in speculative belief was followed by political penalty. The original contention, still preserved in Tertullian,[679] that every

---

[678] Clem. Al. *Strom.* 7.15, true system of Christian doctrine: Sext. Empir. (*Pyrrh.* p. 13, 16) only adherence to a system of dogmas (no standard implied).

[679] *Ad Scap.* 2.

man should worship God according to his own conviction, that one man's religion neither harms nor helps another man, was exchanged for the contention that the officers of Christian communities were the guardians of the faith. Controversy on these lines, and with these assumptions, soon began to breed its offspring of venom and abuse. But I will not pain your ears by quoting, though I have them at hand, the torrents of abuse which one saint poured upon another, because the one assented to the speculations of a majority, and the other had speculations of his own.[680]

It was by these stages, which passed one into the other by a slow evolution, that the idea of trust in God, which is the basis of all religion, changed into the idea of a creed, blending theory with fact, and metaphysical speculation with spiritual truth.

It began by being (1) a simple trust in God; then followed (2) a simple expansion of that trust into the assent to the proposition that God is good, and (3) a simple acceptance of the proposition that Jesus Christ was His Son; then (4) came in the definition of terms, and each definition of terms involved a new theory; finally, (5) the theories were gathered together into systems, and the martyrs and witnesses of Christ died for their faith, not outside but inside the Christian sphere; and instead of a world of religious belief, which resembled the world of actual fact in the sublime

---

[680] Philosophers had abused each other. Theologians followed in their track. The "cart-loads of abuse they emptied upon one another" (Lucian, *Eunuch*, 2) are paralleled in, e.g. Gregory of Nyssa.

unsymmetry of its foliage and the deep harmony of its discords, there prevailed the most fatal assumption of all, that the symmetry of a system is the test of its truth and a proof thereof.

I am far from saying that those theories are not true. The point to which I would draw attention is, first, that they are speculations; secondly, that their place in Christian thought arises from the fact that they are the speculations of a majority at certain meetings. The importance which attaches to the whole subject with which we are dealing, lies less in the history of the formation of a body of doctrine, than in the growth and permanence of the conceptions which underlie that formation.

(1) The first conception comes from the antecedent belief which was rooted in the Greek mind, that, given certain primary beliefs which are admitted on all sides to be necessary, it is requisite that a man should define those beliefs[681] — that it is as necessary that a man should be able to say -with minute exactness what he means by God, as that he should say, I believe in God. It is purely philosophical. A philosopher cannot be satisfied with unanalyzed ideas.

(2) The second conception comes rather from politics than from philosophy. It is the belief in a majority of a meeting. It is the conception that the definitions and interpretations of primary beliefs which are made by the majority of church officers assembled under certain conditions, are in all cases and so certainly true, that the duty of the individual is, not to endeavor, by whatever light of nature or whatever

[681] See Lecture V.

illumination of the Holy Spirit may be given to him, to understand them, but to acquiesce in the verdict of the majority. The theory assumes that God never speaks to men except through the voice of the majority. It is a large assumption. It is a transference to the transcendental sphere in which the highest conceptions of the Divine Nature move, of what is a convenient practical rule for conducting the business of human society: "Let the majority decide." I do not say that it is untrue, or that it has not some arguments in its favor; but I do venture to point out that the fact of its being an assumption must at least be recognized.

(3) The third conception is, that the definitions and interpretations of primary beliefs which were made by the majority, or even by the unanimous voice of a church assembly, in a particular age, and which were both relative to the dominant mental tendencies of that age and adequately expressed them, are not only true but final. It is a conceivable view that once, and once only, did God speak to men, and that the revelation of Himself in the Gospels is a unique fact in the history of the universe. It is also a conceivable view that God is continually speaking to men, and that now, no less than in the early ages of Christianity, there is a divine Voice that whispers in men's souls, and a divine interpretation of the meaning of the Gospel history. The difficulty is in the assumption which is sometimes made, that the interpretation of the divine Voice was developed gradually through three centuries, and that it was then suddenly arrested. The difficulty has sometimes been evaded by the further assumption that there was no development of the truth, and that the Nicene theology was part of the original revelation — a theology divinely communicated to

the apostles by Jesus Christ himself. The point of most importance in the line of study which we have been following together, is the demonstration which it affords that this latter assumption is wholly untenable. We have been able to see, not only that the several elements of what is distinctive in the Nicene theology were gradually formed, but also that the whole temper and frame of mind which led to the formation of those elements were extraneous to the first form of Christianity, and were added to it by the operation of causes which can be traced. If this be so, the assumption of the finality of the Nicene theology is the hypothesis of a development which went on for three centuries, and was then suddenly and forever arrested. Such a hypothesis, even if it be *a priori* conceivable, would require an overwhelming amount of positive testimony. Of such testimony there is absolutely none. But it may be that the time has come in which, instead of travelling once more along the beaten tracks of these ancient controversies as to particular speculations, we should rather consider the prior question of the place which speculation as such should occupy in the economy of religion and of the criterion by which speculations are to be judged. We have to learn also that although for the needs of this life, for the solace of its sorrow, for the development of its possibilities, we must combine into societies and frame our rules of [conduct, and possibly our articles of belief, by striking I an average, yet for the highest knowledge we must go alone upon the mountain-top; and that though the moral law is thundered forth so that even the deaf may hear, the deepest secrets of God's nature and of our own are whispered still in the silence of the night to the individual soul.

It may be that too much time has been spent upon speculations about Christianity, whether true or false, and that that which is essential consists not of speculations but of facts, and not in technical accuracy on questions of metaphysics, but in the attitude of mind in which we regard them. It would be a cold world in which no sun shone until the inhabitants thereof had arrived at a true chemical analysis of sunlight. And it may be that the knowledge and thought of our time, which is drawing us away from the speculative elements in religion to that conception of it which builds it upon the character and not only upon the intellect, is drawing us thereby to that conception of it which the life of Christ was intended to set forth, and which will yet regenerate the world.

The influence of Greek ideas and usages upon the Christian Church

Lecture XII. THE TRANSFORMATION OF THE BASIS OF CHRISTIAN UNION: DOCTRINE IN THE PLACE OF CONDUCT.

I spoke in the last Lecture of the gradual formation under Greek influence of a body of doctrine. I propose to speak in the present Lecture of that enormous change in the Christian communities by which an assent to that body of doctrine became the basis of union. I shall have to speak less of the direct influence of Greece than in previous Lectures: but it is necessary to show not only the separate causes and the separate effects, but also their general sum in the changed basis of Christian communion.

There is no adequate evidence that, in the first age of Christianity, association was other than voluntary. It was profoundly individual. It assumed for the first time in human history the infinite worth of the individual soul. The ground of that individual worth was a divine sonship. And the sons of God were brethren. They were drawn together by the constraining force of love. But the clustering together under that constraining force was not necessarily the formation of an association. There was not necessarily any organization.[682] The tendency to organization came partly from the tendency of the Jewish colonies in the great cities of the empire to combine, and to a far greater extent from the large tendency

---

[682] Socrates, *H. E.* p. 177.

of the Greek and Roman world to form societies for both religious and social purposes.

But though there is no evidence that associations were in the first instance universal, there is ample evidence that, when once they began to be formed, they were formed on a basis which was less intellectual than moral and spiritual. An intellectual element existed: but it existed as an element, not by itself but as an essential ingredient in the whole spiritual life. It was not separable from the spiritual element. Of the same spiritual element, "faith" and "works" were two sides. The associations, like the primitive clusters which were not yet crystallized into associations, were held together by faith and love and hope, and fused, as it were, by a common enthusiasm. They were baptized, not only into one body, but also by one spirit, by the common belief in Jesus Christ as their Savior, by the overpowering sense of brotherhood, by the common hope of immortality. Their individual members were the saints, that is, the holy ones. The collective unity which they formed — the Church of God — was holy. It was regarded as holy before it was regarded as catholic. The order of the attributes in the creed is historically correct — the holy Catholic Church. The pictures which remain of the earliest Christian communities show that there was a real effort to justify their name. The earliest complete picture of a Christian community is that of the "Two Ways." There are fragments elsewhere. From the Acts of the Apostles and the canonical Epistles, and the extra-canonical writings of the sub-apostolic age, it is possible to put together a mosaic.

But in the "Two Ways" we have a primitive manual of Christian teaching, and the teaching is wholly moral. It professes to be a short exposition of the two commandments of love to God and love to one's neighbor. The exposition is partly a quotation from and partly an expansion of the Sermon on the Mount. "Bless those that curse you, and pray for your enemies." "If any one give thee a blow on the one cheek, turn to him the other also." "Give to every one that asketh thee, and ask not back." "Thou shalt not be double-minded nor double-tongued." "Thou shalt not be covetous nor grasping." "Thou shalt not be angry nor envious." "Thou shalt not be lustful nor filthy-tongued." "But thou shalt be meek and long-suffering and quiet and guileless and considerate."[683] The ideal was not merely moral, but it was also that of an internal morality, of a new heart, of a change of character.

The book which is probably nearest in date, and which is certainly most alike in character to this simple manual, is the first book of the collection of documents known as the Apostolical Constitutions. It pictures the aim of the Christian life as being to please God by obeying His will and keeping His commandments. "Take heed, sons of God, to do everything in obedience to God, and to become well-pleasing in all things to the Lord our God."[684] "If thou wilt please God, abstain from all that He hates, and do none of those things that are displeasing to Him."[685] Individual Christians are spoken of as servants and sons of God, as fellow-heirs and fellow-partakers with His Son, as believers, i.e., as the phrase is expanded, "those who have believed on

---

[683] *Didache*, cc. 1-8.

[684] *Apost. Const.* p. 1.15—17.

[685] *Ib.* 5.20—22.

His unerring religion."[686] The rule of life is the Ten Commandments, expanded as Christ expanded them, so as to comprehend sins of thought as well as of deed. It was a fellowship of a common ideal and a common enthusiasm of goodness, of neighborliness and of mutual service, of abstinence from all that would rouse the evil passions of human nature, of the effort to crush the lower part of us in the endeavor to reach after God.[687]

It is even possible that the baptismal formula may have consisted, not in an assertion of belief, but in a promise of amendment; for a conservative sect made the candidate promise — "I call these seven witnesses to witness that I will sin no more, I will commit adultery no more, I will not steal, I will not act unjustly, I will not covet, I will not hate, I will not despise, nor will I have pleasure in any evil."[688]

The Christian communities were based not only on the fellowship of a common ideal, but also on the fellowship of a common hope. In baptism they were born again, and born to immortality. There was the sublime conception that the ideal society which they were endeavoring to realize would be actually realized on earth. The Son of Man would come again, and the regenerated would die no more. The kingdoms of this world would become the kingdom of the Messiah. The lust and hate, the strife and conflict, the

---

[686] *Ib*. 1.6.

[687] "We Christians are remarkable," says Tertullian (*Ad Scap*. 2), "only for the reformation of our former vices." The plea of the Apologists was based on the fact that the Christians led blameless lives, Tert. *Apol*. c 4.

[688] The Elchasaites, ap. *Hipp*. 9.15.

iniquity and vice, which dominated in current society, would be cast out for ever; and over the new earth there would be the arching spheres of a new heaven, into which the saints, like the angels, might ascend. But as the generations passed, and all things continued as they had been, and the sign of the Son of Man sent no premonitory ray from the far-off heaven, this hope of a new earth, without changing its force, began to change its form. It was no longer conceived as sudden, but as gradual. The nations of the world were to be brought one by one into the vast communion. There grew up the magnificent conception of a universal assembly.[689] There would be a universal religion and a universal society, and not until then would the end come: it would be a transformed and holy world.

The first point which I will ask you to note is, that this very transformation of the idea of a particular religion into that of a universal religion — this conception of an all-embracing human society, naturally, if unconsciously, carried with it a relaxation of the bonds of discipline. The very earnestness which led men to preach the Gospel and to hasten the Kingdom, led them also to gather into the net fish of every kind. There was always a test, but the rigor of the test was softened. The old Adam asserted itself. There were social influences, and weakness of character in the officers, and a condonation by the community. It became less and less practicable to eject every offender against the Christian code. It was against this whole tendency that Montanism was a rebellion — not only against the officialism of Christianity,

---

[689] Weingarten, *Zeittafeln*, p.12, See also Lightfoot, *Ignatius*, vol, ii. pp: 310—312.

but also against its worldliness.[690] The earlier conception of
that code, in which it embraced sins of thought, came to be
narrowed. The first narrowing was the limitation to open
sins. The Christian societies fell under the common law
which governs all human organizations, that no cognizance
can be taken of the secret thoughts of the heart. The second
limitation was, that even when a man had committed an
open sin, and had been therefore excluded from the
community, he might be re-admitted. The limitation was not
accepted without a controversy which lasted over a great
part of two centuries, and which at one time threatened to
rend the whole Christian communities into fragments. The
Church was gradually transformed from being a community
of saints — of men who were bound together by the bond
of a holy life, separated from the mass of society, and in
antagonism to it — to a community of men whose moral
ideal and moral practice differed in but few respects from
those of their Gentile neighbors. The Church of Christ,
which floated upon the waves of this troublesome world was
a Noah's ark, in which there were unclean as well as clean.

Side by side with this diminution in the strictness of the
moral tests of admission and of continued membership, was
a growth in the importance of the intellectual elements, of
which I spoke in a previous Lecture. The idea of holiness
and purity came to include in early times the idea of sound
doctrine. Hegesippus,[691] in speaking of a church as a virgin,
gives as his reason, not its moral purity, but the fact that it
was not corrupted by foolish doctrines. The growth, both

---

[690] Weingarten, p. 17.

[691] Eusebius, *H. E.* 4.22, 4.

within the Church and on its outskirts, of opinions which were not the opinions of the majority — the tendency of all majorities to assert their power — the flocking into the Christian fold of the educated Greeks and Romans, who brought with them the intellectual habits of mind which dominated in the age — gave to the intellectual element an importance which it had not previously possessed. Knowledge, which had always been in some sort an element in Christianity, though not as a basis of association, came to assert its place side by side with love. Agreement in opinion, which had been the basis of union in the Greek philosophical schools, and later in the Gnostic societies, now came to form a new element in the bond of union within and between the Churches.[692] But the practical necessity, when once an intellectual element was admitted, of giving some limitations to that element by establishing a rule of faith and a standard list of apostolic documents, caused stress to be laid at once upon the intellect and the region within which it moved. It was, that is to say, necessary to

---

[692] The very terms heresy and heterodox bear witness to the action of the Greek philosophical schools on the Christian Church: *Heresy* is used in Sext. Empir. *Pyrrh.* p. 13, of any system of dogmas, or the principle which is distinctive of a philosophical school: cf. Diels, *Doxogr. Gr.* pp. 276, 573, 388. In Clem. Alex. *Strom.* 7. 15, it is used to denote the orthodox system. *Heterodox* used of the dogmatics from point of view of a sceptic: Sext. Empir. *adv. Math.* p. 771, 40. Josephus uses it of the men of the other schools or parties as distinguished from the Essenes, *de Bell. Jud.* 2.8.5. For the place of opinion in Gnostic societies, with its curious counterpart in laxity of discipline, see Tert. *de presc.* 42—44. Cf. Valentinians, *adv. Val.* Cf. Harnack, 190 ff., also 211. The very cultivation of the Gnosis means the supremacy of the intellect.

ensure that the intellectual element was of the right kind, and this of itself gave emphasis to the new temper and tendency. The profession of belief in Christ which had been in the first instance subordinate to love and hope, and which had consisted in a simple recognition of him as the Son of God, became enucleated and elaborated into an explicit creed; and assent to that creed became the condition, or, so to speak, the contract of membership. The profession of faith must be in the words of the Christian rule.[693] The teaching of the catechumens was no longer that which we find in the "Two Ways" — the inculcation of the higher morality; it was the *traditio symboli*, the teaching of the pass-word and of its meaning. The creed and teaching were the creed and teaching of the average members of the communities. In religion, as in society, it is the average that rules. The law of life is compromise.

There were two collateral causes which contributed to the change and gave emphasis to it.

(1) The one arose from the importance which was attached to baptism. There is no doubt that baptism was conceived to have in itself an efficacy which in later times has been rarely attached to it. The expressions which the more literary ages have tended to construe metaphorically were taken literally. It was a real washing away of sins; it was a real birth into a new life; it was a real adoption into a divine sonship. The

---

[693] Tertullian, *de Spectaculis*, c. 4. If *gnosis* was important as an element in salvation side by side with *pistis* – or if *pistis* included *gnosis* —then also the rejection of the right faith was a bar to salvation: hence heresy was regarded as involving eternal death: Tert. *de presc.* 2.

renunciatio diaboli — the abjuring of false gods and their wicked worship — was also an important element.[694] These elements were indeed even more strongly emphasized by certain Gnostic societies than by the more orthodox writers; but they directly suggested a question which soon became vital, viz. whether all baptism had this efficacy. Was the mere act or ceremonial enough, or did it depend on the place where, the person by whom, and the ritual with which it was administered? In particular, the question of the minister of baptism became important. It came to be doubted whether baptism had its awful efficacy, if the baptizer were cut off from the general society of Christians on the ground of either his teaching or his practice. It became important to ensure that those who baptized held the right faith, lest the baptism they administered should be invalid, and should carry with it all the evil consequences of a vitiated baptism. The rules which were laid down were minute. There were grave controversies as to the precise amount of difference of opinion which vitiated baptism, and the very fact of the controversies about opinion accentuated the stress which was laid upon such opinion. It drew away attention from a man's character to his mental attitude towards the general average of beliefs.

(2) There was another feature of early Christian life which probably contributed more than anything else to strengthen this tendency. It was the habit of intercourse and intercommunion. Christians, like Jews, travelled widely — more for trade and commerce than for pleasure. The new

---

[694] Tert. *de Spect.* c. 4.

brotherhood of Christians, like the ancient brotherhood of the Jews, gave to all the travelling brethren a welcome and hospitality. A test had been necessary in the earliest times in regard to the prophets and teachers. It is mentioned in the Teaching of the Apostles. But the test was of moral rather than of intellectual teaching. "Whoever comes to you and teaches you all these things" (i.e. the moral precepts of the "Two Ways"), receive him. But in case he who teaches, himself turns and teaches you another teaching[695] so as to destroy (this teaching), listen not to him: but if he teaches you so as to add to your righteousness and knowledge of the Lord, receive him as the Lord."[696] So of the prophets: "Not every one who speaks in the spirit is a prophet, but only he who has the moral ways of the Lord: by these ways shall be known the false prophet and the true prophet Every prophet who teaches the truth, if he does not what he teaches, is a false prophet."[697] So also of the travelling brethren: "Let everyone who comes in the name of the Lord be received; afterwards ye shall test him and find out ... If he wish to settle among you and is a craftsman, let him work and so eat. If he be not a craftsman, provide some way of his living among you as a Christian, but not being idle. If he be unwilling so to do, he is *chrisemporos*— making a gain of godliness."[698]

The test here also is a test of character and not of belief. But when the intellectual elements had asserted a

---

[695] here expressly used of the moral precepts in c 2.1.

[696] c. 11.1, 2.

[697] C. 11.8, 10; cf. Herm. *Mand.* 11.7 and 16.

[698] c. 12. 1, 3-5.

prominence in Christianity, and when the acceptance of the baptismal formula had been made a test of admission to a Christian community, it gradually became a custom to make the acceptance of that formula also a condition of admission to hospitality.[699] It was, so to speak, a *tessera* or pass-word. By being a pass-word to hospitality, it became also a form which a man might easily strain his conscience to accept, and in religion no less than in politics there are no such strenuous upholders of current opinion as those who are hypocrites. The importance of the formula as a passport attached not only to individuals, but also to whole communities.[700] The fact that the Teaching of the Apostles makes the test personal and individual, shows that in the country and at the time when that book was written the later system had not yet begun to prevail. This later system was for a community to furnish its travelling members with a circular letter of recommendation. Such a letter served as a passport. The travelling Christian who brought it received an immediate and ungrudging hospitality. But when churches had wide points of difference, they would not receive each other's letters. The points of difference which thus led to the renunciation of fellowship, related in the first instance to discipline or practice. They came to relate to belief. Points of doctrine, no less than points of discipline, came to be discussed at the meetings of the representatives of the churches in a district, concerning which I spoke in the last Lecture. Doctrine came to be thus coordinate with character as the basis on which the churches joined together in local or

[699] Tert. *de praesc*. 20.

[700] Tert. *ibid*. 21.

general confederations, and accepted each other's certificates. The hierarchical tendency grew with it and out of it. The position of the bishops, which had grown out of the assumed desirability of guarding the tradition of truth, tended to emphasize that tradition. It gave to tradition not only a new importance, but also a new sanction. It rested belief upon living authority. Men were no longer free to interpret for themselves.

This elevation of doctrine to a coordinate position with life in the Christian communities was the effect of causes internal to those communities. Those causes were in themselves the effects of other causes, the influence of which I have traced in previous Lectures: but in their direct operation within the churches they were altogether internal. But that which gave importance to their operation was not internal, but external. It was the interposition of the State. The first instance of that interposition was in the days of Aurelian, in the case of Paul of Samosata. The principle which was then established has been of enormous importance to the Christian communities ever since. It is clear that confederation of churches was so far established in Syria in the middle of the third century, that the bishops of a district claimed a right to interfere in the affairs of a neighboring church. There was not yet the complete confederation, on the basis of the organization of the Empire, which we find after the Nicene Council; it was a question only of neighborhood. The Bishop of Antioch, Paul of Samosata, who was a statesman as well as a theologian, had a difference of opinion with the leading bishops of Syria on one of the new questions of the metaphysical theology, which was forcing its way into the Christian churches. Meetings were held, at the first of which there appears to have been a compromise. At the second, Paul was condemned. He was formally deposed from his see. He refused to recognize the authority of the meeting, and probably with the support of his people, remained in possession of the church-buildings. An appeal as of "civil right" was made by his opponents to the Emperor. The answer of the Emperor determined the principle already referred to. The tenant of the buildings held them on condition of being a Christian. The Emperor did not determine what Christianity was. But he determined that whatever was taught by the bishops of Italy might be properly taken as the standard. This determined Roman policy, and it went far to determine Christian doctrine for the future.

When Christianity came to be recognized by the State, Constantine adopted the plan of assembling the bishops on his own authority, and of giving whatever sanction the State could give to their resolutions. He said in effect, "I, as Emperor, cannot determine what Christian doctrine is, but I will take the opinion of the majority, and I will so far recognize that opinion that no one shall have the privileges of Christians, a right to hold property and an exemption from civil burdens, who does not assent to that opinion." The succeeding Christian Emperors followed in his track. The test of being a Christian was conformity to the resolutions of the Councils. One who accepted them received immunity and privileges. One who did not was liable to confiscation, to banishment, to death. I need hardly draw out for you, who know what human nature is, the importance which those resolutions of the Councils assumed.

Against this whole transformation of the basis of union there were two great lines of reaction.

1. The one was the reaction of the Puritan party in the Church — the conservative party, which was always smoldering, and sometimes burst forth into flame. The most important of such reactionary outbursts were those of the Novatians in the third century, and of the Donatists in the fourth. I will speak now only of the former. Its first cause was the action of the Roman bishop, Callistus, who allowed the return to the Church of those who had been excluded on account of sins of the flesh, and of return to idolatry. The policy was continued. In 250, a determined stand was made against it. The election of a bishop who belonged to the lax party forced on a schism. The schism was strong. It had sympathizers all over the Christian world — in Egypt, in Armenia, in Asia Minor, in Italy and Spain. It involved the whole theory of the Church — the power of the Keys. It lasted long. It was so strong that the State had to recognize it. It did not die out until at least five centuries after its birth. It lingered on in detached communities, but it ceased to be a power. The majority, with the support not only of the State, but also of human nature, dominated the Christian world.

2. The other reaction was stronger and even more permanent. It consisted of the formation within the Christian community of an inner class, who framed for themselves and endeavored to realize a higher than the common ideal. They stood to the rest of the community as the community itself stood to the rest of the world. The tendency itself came, as I have tried to point out in a previous Lecture,[701] mainly from the Greek philosophical

schools, and was fostered to a large extent by the influence on the main body of Christians of the philosophic parties upon its borders. But it asserted its place as a permanent element in the Christian world mainly as a reaction against the change of the basis of the Christian communities, and the lowering of the current standard of their morality. Henceforward there was, side by side with the *tagma tov klarikon* and the *tagma tov laikon* a third rank, *tagma tov askaton.* The ideal has been obscured by its history: but that ideal was sublime. It was impracticable and undesirable; and yet sometimes in human life room must be found for impossible ideals. And the blurred and blotted picture of it which has survived to our own times, cannot take the place of the historical fact that it began as a, reaction against Christianity as it was and as it is — an effort to regenerate human society. But Monachism, by the very fact of its separation, did not leaven the Church and raise the current morality. The Church became, not an assembly of devout men, grimly earnest about living a holy life — its bishops were statesmen; its officers were men of the world; its members were of the world, basing their conduct on the current maxims of society, held together by the loose bond of a common name, and of a creed which they did not understand. In such a society, an intellectual basis is the only possible basis. In such a society also, in which officialism must necessarily have an important place, the insistence on that intellectual basis comes from the instinct of self-preservation. But it checked the progress of Christianity. Christianity has won no great victories since its basis was changed. The victories that it has

---

[701] Lect. vi.

won, it has won by preaching, not Greek metaphysics, but the love of God and the love of man. Its darkest pages are those which record the story of its endeavoring to force its transformed Greek metaphysics upon men or upon races to whom they were alien. The only ground of despair in those who accept Christianity now, is the fear — which I for one cannot entertain — that the dominance of the metaphysical element in it will be perpetual.

I have now brought these Lectures to a close. The net result is the introduction into Christianity of the three chief products of the Greek mind — Rhetoric, Logic, and Metaphysics. I venture to claim to have shown that a large part of what are sometimes called Christian doctrines, and many usages which have prevailed and continue to prevail in the Christian Church, are in reality Greek theories and Greek usages changed in form and color by the influence of primitive Christianity, but in their essence Greek still. Greece lives; not only its dying life in the lecture rooms of Universities, but also with a more vigorous growth in the Christian Churches. It lives there, not by virtue of the survival within them of this or that fragment of ancient teaching, and this or that fragment of an ancient usage, but by the continuance in them of great modes and phases of thought, of great drifts and tendencies, of large assumptions. Its ethics of right and duty, rather than of love and self-sacrifice; its theology, whose God is more metaphysical than spiritual — whose essence it is important to define; its creation of a class of men whose main duty in life is that of moral exhortation, and whose utterances are not the spontaneous outflow of a prophet's soul, but the artistic periods of a rhetorician; its religious ceremonial, with the darkness and the light, the initiation and the solemn enactment of a symbolic drama; its conception of intellectual assent rather than of moral earnestness as the basis of religious society — in all these, and the ideas that underlie them, Greece lives.

It is an argument for the divine life of Christianity that it has been able to assimilate so much that was at first alien to it. It is an argument for the truth of much of that which has been assimilated, that it has been strong enough to oust many of the earlier elements. But the question which forces itself upon our attention as the phenomena pass before us in review, is the question of the relation of these Greek elements in Christianity to the nature of Christianity itself. The question is vital. Its importance can hardly be over-estimated. It claims a foremost place in the consideration of earnest men. The theories which rise out of it are two in number. It is possible to urge, on the one hand, that Christianity, which began without them — which grew on a soil whereon metaphysics never throve — which won its first victories over the world by the simple moral force of the Sermon on the Mount, and by the sublime influence of the life and death of Jesus Christ, may throw off Hellenism and be none the loser, but rather stand out again before the world in the uncolored majesty of the Gospels. It is possible to urge that what was absent from the early form cannot be essential, and that the Sermon on the Mount is not an outlying part of the Gospel, but its sum. It is possible to urge, on the other hand, that the tree of life, which was planted by the hand of God Himself in the soil of human society, was intended from the first to grow by assimilating to itself whatever elements it found there. It is possible to maintain that Christianity was intended to be a development, and that its successive growths are for the time at which they exist integral and essential. It is possible to hold that it is the duty of each succeeding age at once to accept the developments of the past, and to do its part in bringing on the developments of the future.

Between these two main views it does not seem possible to find a logical basis for a third. The one or the other must be accepted, with the consequences which it involves. But whether we accept the one or the other, it seems clear that much of the Greek element may be abandoned. On the former hypothesis, it is not essential; on the latter, it is an incomplete development and has no claim to permanence. I believe the consideration of this question, and practical action on the determination of it, to be the work that lies before the theologians of our generation. I claim for the subject which we have been considering an exceptional importance, because it will enable us, if on the one hand we accept the theory that the primitive should be permanent, to disentangle the primitive from the later elements, and to trace the assumptions on which these later elements are based; and if on the other hand we adopt the theory of development, it will enable us, by tracing the lines of development, to weld the new thoughts of our time with the old by that historical continuity which in human societies is the condition of permanence. I am not unaware that there are many who deprecate the analysis of Christian history, and are content to accept the deposit. There has been a similar timidity in regard to the Bible. It seemed a generation ago as though the whole fabric of belief depended on the acceptance of the belief that Genesis is the work of a single author. The timidity has virtually ceased. The recognition of the fact that the Book of Genesis was not made, but grew, so far from having been a danger to religion, has become a new support of the faith. So it will be with the analysis of Christian doctrine and of Christian history; and therefore I am earnest in urging its study. For though the Lectures are ended, the study of the subject has only begun. I have ventured as a pioneer into comparatively unexplored ground: I feel that I shall no doubt be found to have made the mistakes of a pioneer; but I feel also the certainty of a pioneer — who after wandering by devious paths through the forest and the morass, looks out from the height which he has reached upon the fair landscape — and speaking as one who has so stood and so looked, I am sure that you will find the country to be in the main what I have described it to be, and that you will find also that it is but the entrance to a still fairer landscape beyond. For though you may believe that I am but a dreamer of dreams, I seem to see, though it be on the far horizon — the horizon beyond the fields which either we or our children will tread — a Christianity which is not new but old, which is not old but new, a Christianity in which the moral and spiritual elements will again hold their place, in which men will be bound together by the bond of mutual service, which is the bond of the sons of God, a Christianity which will actually realize the brotherhood of men, the ideal of its first communities.

Printed in Great Britain
by Amazon

53733768R00205